THE LOGICAL TRADER

THE LOGICAL TRADER

Applying a Method to the Madness

Mark Fisher

John Wiley & Sons, Inc.

Published by John Wiley & Sons, Inc., Hoboken, New Jersey.
Published simultaneously in Canada.

This publication is designed to provide accurate and authoritative
information in regard to the subject matter covered. It is sold with
the understanding that the publisher is not engaged in rendering
professional services. If professional advice or other expert assistance
is required, the services of a competent professional person should
be sought.

Wiley also publishes its books in a variety of electronic formats.
Some content that appears in print may not be available in electronic
books. For more information about Wiley products visit our Web site
at www.wiley.com.

Library of Congress Cataloging-in-Publication Data

Fisher, Mark, 1960-
   The logical trader : applying a method to the madness / Mark Fisher ;
foreword by Paul Tudor Jones.
       p. cm.—(Wiley trading)
   ISBN 0-471-21551-1 (CLOTH : alk. paper)
   1.   Stocks. 2.   Speculation.   I. Title. II. Series.
   HG4661 .F49 2002
   332.63'22—dc21

                                                          2002007074

Printed in the United States of America.

10 9 8 7 6 5 4 3 2

Dedicated to Grandpa Sam,
who taught me that it is more important
to invest in people than in ideas.

TABLE OF CONTENTS

Foreword by Paul Tudor Jones   ix

Introduction   1

Chapter 1   Know Your ACDs   9

Chapter 2   The Pivot Concept   35

Chapter 3   Putting It Together: ACD and Pivot Ranges   55

Chapter 4   Macro ACD   83

Logical Trader: Midterm   109

Chapter 5   Pivot Moving Averages   113

Chapter 6   The Advanced Trader   133

Chapter 7   The ACD Version of
"Ripley's Believe It or Not!"   163

Chapter 8   Trader Interviews   191

Appendix   205

Glossary   239

Index   251

FOREWORD

My first face-to-face encounter with Mark Fisher occurred in the silver pit in the early 1980s on the COMEX in New York where he often resided. An occasional visitor to that club of gentlemanly behavior, I was given an order to buy 200 contracts of silver on the close by one of my upstairs friends. The treatment I received was something akin to that of a piece of red meat thrown into a cage of half-starved lions. I remember being pounced upon by four or five "locals," not the least of which was this short blur of energy shouting, cajoling, and talking to me so fast that I could only recognize the badge *FSH* (or Fish as he was known to thousands on the trading floor). As he always does, he somehow innately knew exactly how many I had to buy and waited until I had bought all but 20 or 30 contracts before selling me the top tick of the close. There was no one better and there never will be anyone as good as Mark Fisher when it comes to smelling an order that a pit broker has in his hand.

It will not take you long in reading this book to realize that Mark Fisher is being powered by some type of energy source that is not endemic to the normal human condition. And to say that he is a control freak is an understatement. But to anyone who wants to learn how to trade and takes the time to read this book, there is zero doubt that Fish's messianic willingness to share with the public the successful system he has developed is an opportunity to be exploited. He details in very methodical and systematic fashion a unique way of approaching markets and creating fantastic reward/risk opportunities over virtually any time frame, from day trading to long-term positioning. Creating these favorable reward/risk trades is the genesis of all profitable trading and his plan is one that has been successfully implemented by hundreds. I know this first hand as many of the traders who worked for me when I had a floor operation used his system successfully to trade profitably.

For anyone starting out in the trading business, Mark's trading experiences and ACD system provide an invaluable blueprint for trading success. Central to his trading methodology is his incredible discipline, which has been his hallmark as a trader over the years. As he stresses throughout the book, the most important factor for traders to identify is the point at which to get out if they are wrong. If traders learn nothing else from this book, the lesson of knowing where to get out is one that will spare them much physical, emotional, and financial pain.

While presenting a logical method to approach the market, Mark also shares with the reader colorful and entertaining stories of the breakdowns and breakthroughs of several traders who he has worked with over the years. In addition, Chapter 7 entitled "The ACD Version of 'Ripley's Believe It or Not!'" presents incredible, real stories from the trading pit. Experienced traders will see themselves and their flaws in these stories, while novices can learn from these professional traders' mistakes.

When I meet someone who is interested in learning the trading business, I always refer them to what I consider to be the four Bibles of the business: *Reminiscences of a Stock Operator* by Edwin Lefevre, the fictionalized biography of the fabled Jesse Livermore; *Technical Analysis of Stock Trends* by McGee and Edwards, which was written in the first half of the twentieth century and whose tenets still hold today; *The Elliott Wave Theorist* by Robert Prechter and A. J. Frost, a classic; and finally *Market Wizards* by Jack Schwager, which is a compilation of interviews with great traders. *Reminiscences* is a wonderfully entertaining read that mostly illuminates the emotional highs and lows that go with trading and tape reading. *Technical Analysis of Stock Trends* and *The Elliott Wave Theorist* both give very specific and systematic ways to approach developing great reward/risk ratios for entering into a business contract with the marketplace, which is what every trade should be if properly and thoughtfully executed. Finally, *Market Wizards* is a great read if but to learn one lesson over and over again from virtually every single trader who tells his tale in the book—that is, to make great sums of money you first have to learn how to lose much smaller sums of it when you're wrong.

I mention the other four books because, after having read *The Logical Trader*, I am going to add Fish's book to my list of must reads for the beginning trader. Having seen hundreds of traders matriculate through the doors here at the Tudor Group, I am consistently amazed that virtually all of them have different ways of approaching and reaping profits from the marketplace. There really are dozens if not hundreds of ways of making money. But ultimately, though all of them may have different techniques, they share the common trait of somehow creating very favorable reward/risk ratios for trading despite their myriad approaches. That is also what *The Logical Trader* accomplishes in a straightforward fashion. It gives you a well-developed, systematic way to competently apply leverage in the marketplace and garner great performance from it. How could we not pay close attention with great gratitude to the vision that one of the most successful floor traders of all time has decided to share with us? Over the past 20 years that I have known him, Fish has been a giving and generous person in every aspect of his life. This is but another in a long line of incredibly valuable gifts he has given to people that he both knows and doesn't know. Thank you, Mark.

PAUL TUDOR JONES
CHAIRMAN AND CEO OF TUDOR INVESTMENT CORP.

ACKNOWLEDGMENTS

When I first decided to write this book, I thought it was going to be a breeze. No problem, I told myself. In two months' time I'd be able to spit it out. Little did I know what I was getting myself into.

Without the help of Joe Terranova there is no way this book would ever have become a reality. The two of us spent countless hours writing, dissecting, rewriting, and otherwise trying to make this book as appealing as possible to a broad trading audience. I would also like to thank Seth Cohen, my all-time favorite intern for his help in customizing the charts in this book. I'm not sure I should thank or strangle my friend, Mike Wallach, for suggesting that I take on this project in the first place.

Finally, a special thanks to Patricia Crisafulli. I warned Tricia when we first started this book that even though she was accustomed to dealing with traders from the Chicago Mercantile Exchange and the Chicago Board of Trade, working with a bunch of "psychos" from New York was a whole different ballgame! Her perseverance and her patience are present in each and every page of this book.

INTRODUCTION

A Trader's Plan

In trading, as in life, you need a plan. This plan includes not only the *micro*—a strategy for each and every trade you make—but also the *macro*—meaning why you trade, how you intend to reach that goal (your means to the desired end), and what you'll do as an alternative if that doesn't work out. In my 20 years of trading, and nearly as many years teaching other people to trade, I've observed that very few people operate according to a plan. In the micro sense, too many traders are undisciplined in their trading. They try to pick tops only to have the market keep rallying, or they buy what they think is a dip, only to have the market fall some more. They cannot manage their risk, their capital, or themselves. This need to have a trading plan is as important for the novice trader as it is for the experienced professional, and vice versa.

In the macro sense, too few people have any real clue about what they want to do in life. I've seen this repeatedly in the summer internship program at my firm, which is open to high school and college students and aspiring traders from all backgrounds. The 25 to 30 summer interns that I teach every year include some who graduated from Harvard, Wharton, and other Ivy League schools. Others didn't even finish high school. I always try to include some kids who come from poor or working-class neighborhoods, because I think it's important to have people with a variety of backgrounds. The reasons I have the summer internship program are both altruistic and self-serving. On the one hand, I want to give back since someone, a long time ago, gave me a break. On the other hand, I am motivated by the hope of finding and recruiting talented traders to work for me. These are also my reasons for writing this book.

Based on what I've seen from the summer internship program, I have to tell you that one's educational background really doesn't matter much when it comes to a successful trading career. And, I say that despite the fact that I graduated summa cum laude with an MBA from the Wharton School/University of Pennsylvania. Rather, what matters most is a plan—your plan—to get you where you want to go, with a back-up in case that doesn't work out.

There are other attributes to good traders, including an athlete's ability to see the whole playing field, which we'll discuss later in this Introduction. But for now, let's focus on the plan—the subject of this book.

The Logical Trader: Applying a Method to the Madness is based, literally, on my own experience as a trader and the plan that I've used over the years to trade successfully. Moreover, I've taught this methodology over the years to an estimated 4,000 people. That includes about 300 of the 500-or-so traders on the floor of the New York Mercantile Exchange (Nymex) where I trade and where my clearing firm, MBF Clearing Corp., operates. (MBF is the largest clearing firm at the Nymex, clearing one out of every five crude oil contracts traded in the world, and one out of every four natural gas futures contracts in the world. See our website at *www.mbfcc.com.*) Plus, our 50-plus proprietary traders have been taught this method to trade both on the floor and in our upstairs offices where we trade energy, individual stocks, and other commodities, using this system. In other words, this method has been extensively tested, adapted, and utilized.

When I built my clearing firm, I needed customers. An obvious statement. But instead of trying to lure them and keep them with clearing rates that were cheaper than the next guy's and then cheaper than the one after that, I knew that the real advantage for traders would be to learn how to trade—just like I learned over the years, starting with my own apprenticeship as a kid. You know the old saying, "teach someone to fish and you can feed him for a lifetime?" Well, I like to think of this as "teach someone to trade and you'll have a loyal customer for a lifetime." Thus *The Logical Trader: Applying a Method to the Madness* was born. This book encapsulates the methodology that I use and teach, as well as the lessons that it encompasses.

Of the 4,000 people I attempted to teach, we'll say half of them fell asleep in class or in general had no serious interest. That leaves about 2,000 who paid attention long enough to learn something. Of this group, we'll say 1,000 probably implemented what they learned. Now, don't think this is discouraging to me, the teacher, because it's not. Why? Because of those 1,000 who have used this methodology, about 100 of them now make in excess of $750,000 a year trading. And for a clearing firm, that's a nice customer base to have!

But for you, the reader, these statistics are also very meaningful. They should tell you that this system has not only worked for me, but that it has been adopted and adapted by others who have also made it work. Most importantly, it can work equally well if you're trading on the floor or off, commodities or individual stocks. You can use this system if you trade at home, in a day-trading room, or on the floor. If there is sufficient *volatility* and *liquidity* in a market, this system can be used. And, based upon the results that I've seen over the 15 or so years that I've been teaching this method, I can tell you that it can help you vastly improve your chances of success. For example, I estimate that, just going into trading, you have about a 10 to 15 percent chance of being successful to some degree at this. But the traders whom I have taught have had a 40 to 50 percent success rate. That's basically triple the odds of success.

But don't take my word for it. This book includes stories, examples, and anecdotes from other traders who use this methodology to trade. If you're still skeptical, consider that over the years, I'm the one who taught the original floor brokers who worked for Paul Tudor Jones, the legendary hedge-fund manager.

My trading methodology, which I call ACD, is not magic, and it won't require you to buy costly software in order to implement this system. This is a logical system that, if you'll excuse me, I've tried to make moron-proof over the years. This system will give you reference points against which to trade—the A and C points for entry, the B and D as stops. Using the ACD methodology, you'll be able to calculate the prices above which you'd want to be long and the prices below which you'd want to be short. Then, using other indicators and measures, which are layered on top of the ACD base, you'll be able to construct a trading plan based upon the prevailing prices and the market activity.

(For commentary and daily ACD values, see our website at *www.thelogicaltrader.net.*)

Moreover, you will be able to incorporate ACD into your trading discipline and risk management. In fact, the system works best with a very disciplined approach to controlling risk and preserving your capital. I'm no fan of trading systems that have huge swings and drawdowns, which are (hopefully) offset to the plus side by one or two big trades. I believe in getting out of losing trades quickly—a concept I call *Next!*—and having a plan and a target to let your profits run. Or, you may use the ACD system to help confirm your signals, so you know when the odds of a profitable trade are heavily in your favor, with a minimum of downside risk. I like to call that knowing when to step on the gas pedal. If the systems all line up and it looks like a go, then step on the gas. If you (like all of us traders, from time to time) go against the plan and take the trade anyway, then maybe this will help you to keep off the gas and to step on the brake instead. In other words, if you're going to make a dumb trade, then at least keep it small.

If this sounds simple and logical, then congratulate yourself for discovering the elegance of this system. It's not e = mc^2. It's not quantum physics. It's not even algebra. It's simple, like arithmetic. That's the beauty of it.

Think of the ACD system as an inverted triangle. The point, which is at the bottom, is actually the fulcrum upon which the whole thing balances. That point is the ACD system. Without it, the whole structure would come tumbling down. Other indicators and methods are layered upon the ACD, but none can be used without this foundation.

Along the way, I'll discuss some very important psychological lessons that combined with ACD can be adapted to any trading style or methodology. These include:

- Having a Point of Reference
- Gambling Theory
- No Ego
- The Concept of Next!
- Why No Pain, No Gain Is No Good!
- Maximum Size, Minimize Risk
- Good News, Bad Action
- Why the Hardest Trades to Make Are the Best Ones

Before we launch into this methodology, let me explain to you its origins. The ACD system was part of my research at Wharton School/University of Pennsylvania. I was a full-time trader while I was in college, juggling two very demanding endeavors. Since I couldn't be in two places at the same time, I hired a proxy: a fellow student whom I paid to take notes for me in the classes that I couldn't attend. The deal was, if I graduated summa cum laude, I'd bring her to the floor of the Commodity Exchange, give her a trading internship, and lease a trading seat for her. In the meantime, I led a dual professional life: I'd trade until 2 P.M. or so, take the Amtrak train from New York to Philadelphia in the afternoon, and then attend classes at Wharton in the evening. I'd return to New York that night or the next morning, and the cycle would begin again.

For me, that was my plan. Sure, I could have just gone to the trading pit and stayed there. I had been working in the commodities markets, literally, since I was an underaged, 13-year-old runner for a brokerage firm. (More on that later. . . .) But I knew that my life plan needed a back-up, something I could do if trading for some reason didn't work out for me. That's why I went to the Wharton School, working on an MBA in an accelerated program. With that credential, I knew I could get a job in investment banking or even upstairs in a brokerage firm. Trading, I believed, was my vocation, but I couldn't have blinders on either. I could only commit myself to trading if I knew that I had some other professional credential to fall back on—if I needed it.

While at Wharton, I studied the random walk, market efficiency, and all the other theories that say you can't beat the market. With all due respect to my former professors at my alma mater (where I have since been a guest lecturer on many occasions), I must confess that as a 20-year-old trader, I wanted to test those theories and, if possible, prove them wrong. After all, I had grown up in the markets and had been trading on a regular basis since I was 18 (using an account in my grandfather's name). I believed that the markets weren't random, even though they might appear to be. I believed there was a discernible pattern to the market activity, which could be plotted, analyzed, and then used as a guide.

Since the age of 12—when I cajoled my neighbor into giving me a job as a runner at the Commodity Exchange—I had been immersed in the markets. For years, I had studied the daily market statistics in the Wall Street Journal, which showed the open, high, low, close for various commodities. Day in and day out, I saw something in these numbers that fascinated me, which seemed to refute the idea that the markets behaved randomly. To prove my observation, I went to one of my finance professors and told him that I wanted to do a research paper based on a market-timing model. My premise was to devise a method to make money in short-term trading in commodities. For the purpose of the paper, I studied soybeans, silver (after all, I had once been apprenticed to the largest silver broker on the Commodity Exchange, who handled the Hunt brothers' business), and U.S. Treasury Bills.

We gathered statistics and crunched numbers, and the result was the basis of the trading model—ACD—that I still use today and that I will teach to you in this book. If at any point you can't grasp one of the concepts, then just go back and start again. The book is constructed like the system—starting with ACD and then adding concepts or layers as we go along.

But the system, alone, won't improve your results as a trader. You have to have the discipline and the resolve to follow it, to take the signals that it generates, to get out quickly if you're wrong, and then move on. That requires you to check your ego at the door. I don't care how smart you are, or all the fascinating things you know about the financial markets. When you study ACD, I want you to put that all aside. Because, based on the summer interns that I've trained over the years, I can tell you that lofty educational degrees mean virtually nothing in the market. What counts the most are certain inherent abilities. Most of all you must be able to:

- Collect information
- Analyze information
- Make a decision
- Implement your decision

As far as I know, there is no graduate school that can teach you that. Either you have these abilities, or you're willing to develop them, or you don't. And the faster you are at putting these steps together, and still have discipline, the better your chances of success as a trader.

It also helps if you are quick with numbers, a skill I call *cashier math*. You know when you go to the convenience store or the deli on the corner and you buy a sandwich, a soft drink, and a cookie. The cashier just looks at what you bought and says, "$4.26, please." As a trader, it helps to be able to do math like this.

Consider the story of a guy we'll call Rob. He used to be an ice cream vendor. So picture him at the service window of the ice cream truck, with "Turkey in the Straw," or some other annoying song playing over and over again, while 40 kids are screaming out orders to him and their mothers are digging through their purses to get the money. Rob could take this all in and say, "Three cones—that's $3.75. Two Popsicles—$1.50. Two cones and two ice cream bars—$5.00." He could do this all day and never miss an order, never short change a kid, and never over (or under) charge a customer.

Now, would it be much of a stretch of your imagination to picture Rob in the trading pit, with a bunch of traders screaming out bids and offers in a fast-moving market? Suppose I told you that Rob's innate ability to assimilate this information and do the math in his head helped him become a very successful futures traders? It's a true story!

When you trade—on the floor or off—there is a flow of information hitting you from different sources. You need to be able to observe and assimilate information from all these sources. One prerequisite for doing this is to be able to juggle 10 different things at once. If you have tunnel vision and you can only focus on one thing at a time, you'll be missing the whole picture of the market.

Why do you think athletes tend to do well in the markets? It's not only because they're competitive by nature. Rather, most athletes—regardless of the sport they play—have the ability to see the whole field. So when they try trading, many of them can adapt this skill to seeing the whole marketplace. Their field of vision is broad. If you're going to trade, you need to have—or develop—this ability.

Let me share with you one of my favorite stories about two people whom I trained at the same time. One was a Harvard Law School graduate, top five in his class. He had an impressive background, and I hired him. At the same time, I brought on a guy who sold hardware—nuts and bolts—door to door. He told me his wife was expecting a baby and that he needed to have a better job beyond door-to-door hardware sales. "I have no ego about this," he assured me. "I know I don't know anything. But I'm willing to work my butt off."

So, I hired them both and I began training them at the same time. What do you think happened to these two guys? Let's just say that the guy from Harvard is back practicing law, probably billing his clients $500 an hour. Sure he's doing very well, but he's not trading. And as for the hardware salesman, he did indeed bust his butt to learn trading. He worked nights and weekends selling hardware and traded during the day. Today, he's a floor trader who makes a seven-figure annual income.

Why? The Harvard Law graduate thought he knew everything, so it was very difficult for him to learn anything. The hardware salesman was an average guy who had a great work ethic and a great motivation. He wanted to succeed so much that he was able to swallow his pride and become like a sponge, learning everything he could. In the end, he had the last laugh.

These are the lessons that you must keep in mind as you study this trading system. Understanding and applying the ACD methodology is vital to your success in using it. But so is understanding yourself and your willingness to put aside for the moment everything that you know. Approach this, like everything else you learn, with an open mind and no ego. Make this part of your plan as you study ACD and begin trading, or apply it to your trading. Know what you want to accomplish, how you intend to get there, and what you will do if it does—or does not—work out. Have a plan, and stick with it. That works in trading, as well as in life.

Chapter 1

KNOW YOUR ACDs

When you go in for your annual physical, the doctor takes your blood pressure, listens to your heart and lungs, draws some blood, etc. Based on all these indicators, the doctor makes a determination about how healthy you are. Now, assume that the patient drops dead right there on the examination table. The patient has no pulse! Then it doesn't matter what the cholesterol level was, right? No pulse . . . no life.

I use this analogy to explain the *ACD methodology.* In trading, you'll be looking at a variety of factors, including pivots, moving averages, and so forth. But there will always be one underlying factor—like the patient's pulse—without which everything else becomes meaningless. That pulse is the ACD factor. It doesn't matter whether 64 out of 65 indicators are a go for a trade. If the ACD is the one missing indicator, then there is no trade.

So what is this ACD and what's it all about? ACD is the name I've given to my trading methodology, which can be applied to virtually any commodity, stock, or currency as long as there is sufficient volatility and liquidity. The basic premise of ACD is to plot particular price points, which we'll discuss in depth, in relation to the opening range. As I mentioned in the Introduction, I have traded using ACD for nearly 20 years and I still use it today. I've taught it to thousands of other people over the past 15 years who in turn have adapted it to suit their own trading styles and parameters. My point is that ACD has a proven track record, not only for me, but also for numerous other professional traders. Therefore, it can be incorporated into your

9

trading system to help you plot out and execute your trading strategy.

But before we go any further, I must state that trading is an inherently risky endeavor and therefore not suitable for everyone. Any investment in derivatives or stocks may put you at risk of losing an amount even greater than your original investment. (See the full Disclaimer in the front of this book.)

My purpose in this book is not to sell you on trading, but to show you the methodology that I, as well as others whom I have trained, have used. As you go through this book, keep a pen and a pad of paper handy so you can follow along with the trading examples. Whether you're a novice trader or you've been at this for a while, I believe you'll find that the ACD system has something for you and your style of trading.

The Opening Range

ACD starts with the concept of the opening range. The opening range is the initial time frame of trading for a stock, commodity, currency, bond, or other financial derivatives at the start of each new trading session. For stocks, the opening range time frame is generally the first 20 minutes of the day, meaning if Stock X trades from 30.00 to 30.75 in the first 20 minutes of the day, that is the opening range to be used in the ACD system for that particular day. However, if a stock has a delayed opening, you must take the first 20 minutes of active trading.

In commodities, the length of time used for the opening range varies from 5 minutes to 30 minutes, depending upon an individual trader's time horizon. Some commodity futures contracts open using a monthly rotation at the start of the trading day. When this occurs, I use that initial trading period—from the time the contract for a particular month is opened and then closed temporarily while the next month opens—as the opening range. Alternatively, if you're a short-term day-trader in a particular commodity, you may decide that the opening range you'll use is five minutes—particularly if you trade on the floor. Or if you day-trade upstairs, you might choose a 10- to 15-minute opening range, or a longer time frame—such as 20 to 30 minutes—if you typically take a position in a market that has a longer trade duration. (See our current list of opening range time frames in the Appendix.) The key is to define the time period for the opening range and then be consistent when you trade using that time period.

There is one other important consideration about the opening range, and that is making sure it's based on its domicile market. What do I mean by that? If you're trading natural gas futures, then you know the domicile market is the New York Mercantile Exchange. That's where the opening is established. But if you were trading, say, Japanese yen, then the opening of the U.S. currency markets wouldn't apply. Rather, you'd have to look to the opening of the Japanese markets. The same applies with a foreign-domiciled commodity such as North Sea Brent crude oil. In stocks, for example, the opening range for UK-based Vodaphone (VOD) is in London, which would be approximately 3:00 A.M. to 3:20 A.M. New York time, even though the stock also trades in the United States. The same thing occurs with American Depository Receipts (ADRs) representing foreign stocks that trade on U.S. exchanges. The true opening range is established in the domicile market.

I discovered this years ago the proverbial hard way when I tried to apply the ACD system to some foreign currencies and bonds. I couldn't figure out why the system wasn't working at first and then I realized that the United States wasn't the primary market for these instruments. Therefore, I had to look to the opening in the market where these commodities, currencies, and bonds are based.

Once you have identified the opening range, this price range is an important reference point for your trading strategy. Here's why.

If you subscribe to the *random walk theory*, which states that the market's movements are random and totally unpredictable, then the opening range would not be any more important than any other price level during the trading day. Right? For example, crude oil trades from 9:45 A.M. Eastern time until 3:10 P.M. Eastern Time. If you divided that day into 10-minute intervals, you'd have 32 parcels of time (and 5 minutes left over). So, each 10-minute time interval would account for roughly 1/32 of the market activity.

Using random walk theory, you'd expect that the opening range (established in the first 10 minutes of trading) would be the high 1/32 of the time, or it would be the low 1/32 of the time. Therefore, random walk theory would dictate that 1/16 of the time the opening range would be either the high or the low.

Now, what if I told you that in volatile markets—not static, and not necessarily trending markets—the opening range tends to be the high or the low 17 to 23 percent of the time? Would that get your attention? Yes. Because this observation would tell you that the opening range being at the high or the low of the day roughly one-fifth of the time is what we call *statistically significant*. In complete layman's terms, this means the opening range is not just another 10-minute interval out of 32 of them in the trading day. It has more weight than any other time interval.

Let's take another example. Let's say that you divide the trading day up into roughly 64 five-minute intervals. Random walk theory would state that the opening, five-minute range would be the high 1/64 of the time or the low 1/64 of the time. So it would be either of those extremes 1/32 of the time. However, in volatile markets, that five-minute opening range is actually the high or the low of the day about 15 to 18 percent of the time. So instead of about 3 percent of the time, as random walk theory would predict, the first five minutes of the trading day turns out to be the high or the low 15 to 18 percent of the time. Again, this is statistically significant. And, from a trader's perspective, if you knew that something was going to market the high or the low 15 percent of the time, you'd want to know that. Right?

Further, if you take a look at the other 5- or 10-minute intervals in the trading day, the opening range price extremes are repeated a miniscule percentage of the time. That means once the opening range is put in, the market returns to that price range only on rare occasions—far less than the random walk theory would predict. Thus, here's the first concept of the ACD methodology:

The opening range is the statistically significant part of the trading day, marking the high or low for the day (in volatile markets) about 20 percent of the time.

So what do you do with that information? As a trader and a student of the market, I believe the opening range to be statistically significant. Thus, I constructed a trading model based on breakouts of the opening range on the premise that once this occurs, the market is likely to continue in that direction. These breakouts are determined using a time and price filter that is applied to the opening range. As you'll learn in this chapter, once you have defined the opening range, you can determine your A points at which to establish a short or long position, as well as the B, C, and D points. First, let's take a look at the starting point—Point A.

Point A

For the purpose of this exercise, let's say you are day trading crude oil, of the U.S. variety, with its primary market for futures at the New York Mercantile Exchange (Nymex). As a pit trader, you decide that your opening range is the first five minutes of trading. On this particular day, the opening range for crude oil is 25.60 to 25.70. Thus, the opening range has been established. Let's mark it down in a graph (see Figure 1.1).

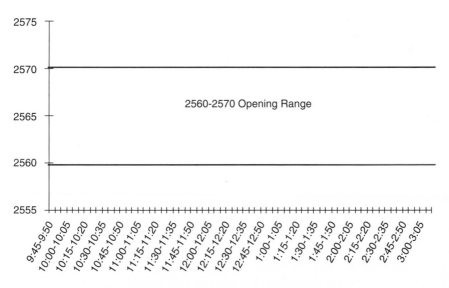

Figure 1.1 Crude oil opening range.

Based on this opening range, the A point to enter a long or short position is plotted above or below the opening range, based on set variables. These variables are based on our own proprietary research, the process of which I won't share with you except to say that the ACD values are based on the volatility measurements of a particular stock, commodity, or financial derivative. (Please see the table in the Appendix that gives the current A values for several commodities and stocks, along with current opening range time frames.)

Using our example of crude oil, the A points are plotted 7 to 8 ticks above or below the market. Figure 1.2 shows how it would look.

If the market were to immediately trade above the opening range and reach the price level of 25.77 to 25.78—and trade there for a period of time equivalent to half the opening range time frame—then the market has established an *A up*. Thus, if the market traded up to 25.77 to 25.78 and stayed there for 2½ minutes (half the five-minute time frame for the opening range), you would establish a long position/bias above 25.77 to 25.78.

Conversely, if the market immediately traded below the opening range to 25.53 to 25.52 and traded there for 2½ minutes,

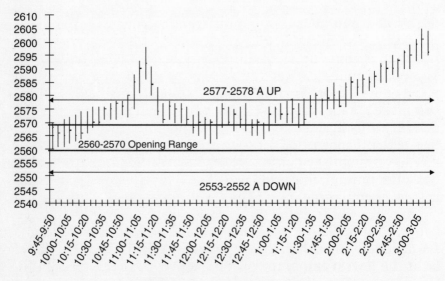

Figure 1.2   Plotting the A points.

the market would have established an *A down*. At this point, you would establish a short position/bias below 25.53 to 25.52.

A points—up or down—are based upon a certain number of ticks above or below the opening range, if trading is sustained at these levels for a period of time equivalent to half the duration of the opening range that you have chosen.

Remember, on any given day you can have either an A up or an A down. The A level is determined when (and if) the market trades above or below the opening range. If the market goes up to 25.77 to make an A up, then there is no A down, even if the market turns around and trades below the opening range.

There is only one A per day. That means, once an A up is established, there can be no A down for that trading day. Or, if an A down is established, there can be no A up for that trading day.

As you plot the various price reference points, you must ask yourself at all times where you'd get out if you were wrong. After all, if you were to go into business, wouldn't you want to know how much capital you needed to invest and how much you'd be at risk for? Trading must be treated the same way. When you make a trade, you must know where your exit point is if the market turns against you, and how much you would stand to lose if that happened. That's where the B level comes in. Once you have established an A—up or down—your stop for getting out of an unprofitable trade is B. The B level, where you would be bias neutral, is delineated by the opening range.

In other words, using the example above, if you established a long position above 25.77 to 25.78 and then the market broke immediately and traded lower, your stop to exit the trade would be at the lowest end of the opening range, or in this case 25.60. Conversely, if you went short below 25.53 to 25.52, your stop to exit the trade would be the highest end of the opening range, or 25.70.

Keep in mind when exiting any trade that the price at which you want to get out may not be where you will be filled. *Slippage*—the difference between your target price and the price at which your order is filled—is a reality in the market. Slippage can be small or significant depending largely upon market conditions.

As you follow the ACD system, remember that it is symmetrical. The strategy for the upside (a long position) is the mirror opposite of the strategy for the downside (a short position).

Let's assume that the market did reach the A target on the upside, which I call *making an A up.* In the example we just used, the market traded up to 25.77 to 25.78, stayed above this level for more than 2½ minutes, and you went long at, say, 25.79. You stayed long all the way to 26.10, at which you exited the trade profitably. Now, the market trades lower and falls below the opening-range low of 25.60. What do you do? The answer is you do nothing.

In this case, the market has made an A up and now is trading below the opening range, which is Point B, at which your bias is neutral. The next step is to wait for the next ACD signal for a new bias, in this case for the market to trade to Point C.

Point C

Once an A has been made, the next probable entry point in the ACD system is *Point C.* Point Cs are calculated (just like As) based upon a certain number of ticks above or below the opening range. In the example of crude oil, As are 7 to 8 ticks above or below the market. Point Cs in crude oil are 11 to 13 ticks above or below the market. (A reference list of our current values to calculate Point Cs on various stocks and commodities also can be found in the Appendix.) As you'll see, for commodities the price differential to calculate a Point A is different than that to calculate a Point C. For a stock, however, the differential to calculate a Point A or a Point C is the same. Now take a look at our trade graph in Figure 1.3.

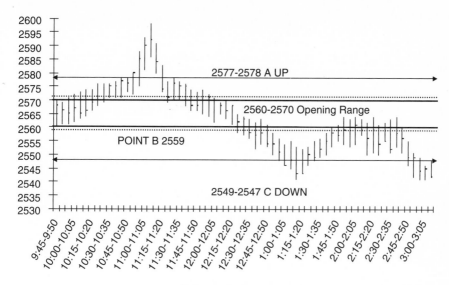

Figure 1.3   Point C.

Using this example, what would happen if the market traded all the way to the C down point? Point C is the *crossover point* at which your bias shifts from bullish to bearish, or vice versa. Here, if the market traded down to 25.49 to 25.47 and traded at or below that level for 2½ minutes (half the length of time of the opening range) you would establish a short position/bias.

Point C is the crossover point at which your bias shifts from bullish to bearish, or vice versa.

If you establish a short position below Point C, what's the first thing you must ask yourself: Where will you get out if you are wrong? Just as with Point A, the stop for Point C coincides with the opening range. If you have a C down, the stop—known as Point D—would be 1 tick above the top of the opening range (see Figure 1.4.)

Since this system is symmetrical, Figure 1.5 shows what it would look like in the case of an A down and a C up. (If you have a C up, the Point D stop would be 1 tick below the bottom of the opening range.)

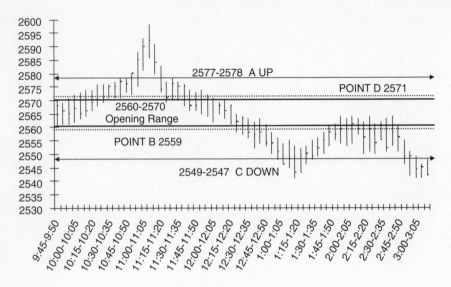

Figure 1.4   Point D.

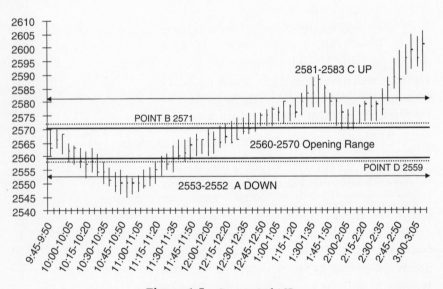

Figure 1.5   Symmetrical ACD.

The Time Factor

As you plot your trades based on Point A up/down and Point C up/down, there is another concept that you must keep in mind: *time*. Too many traders focus only on price, and not enough on time. In other words, when plotting out your trade, it is not only if a price level is reached but how long the market spends there. The vast majority of traders I know trade on price, but not on time. How many people have you heard say that if you take a position and it doesn't go anywhere in 20 or 30 minutes, then you should get out? Very few, if any. I'm here to state that time is the most important factor in trading. If the scenario you've envisioned doesn't materialize within a certain time frame, then just move on and look for the next trade.

In trading, time is actually more important than price.

How do you factor time into your trades? Simple. You set the time parameters for a certain scenario to occur. As a *minimum*, the market must trade at a certain level for a time period equivalent to half the opening range. As a *maximum*, if the market has not acted the way you expected within a time frame equivalent to the opening range, then get out. We'll discuss the maximum time frame shortly. For now, let's take a look at what happens when the market touches a certain price point, but fails to spend enough time there.

If you have an A up plotted at, say, 62.125 and the market goes up to that price, touches it and immediately sells off, was your target reached? No. The market must spend time equivalent to half the length of your opening range at a price target in order to be valid. Here's what I mean. If you're day-trading and you have an opening range of 5 minutes, then the market must spend at least 2½ minutes at your price targets to trigger them. So in the example above, if the market didn't spend 2½ minutes at 62.125—but rather, just touched it and immediately went down—then you didn't have an A up.

Now, a question to see if you've been paying attention: If you didn't have an A up, what happens to the A down target?

Answer: It's still in the running. The market has not made A up—yet—although it might later on. Or, it could continue to sell off and make an A down. At this point, you could conceivably have an A on the upside or the downside. Once again, you must wait to see what the setup is before taking action.

Now, let's say you're a short-term trader, holding positions for a day or sometimes a couple of days. The opening range you like to use is 20 minutes. The market trades below the opening range and touches the A down target. How long would it have to trade there in order to be a valid A down? Did you remember? Of course, it's 10 minutes.

Suppose the market then rallies sharply, trading through the opening range and hits your Point C. (Remember, Point C is always in the opposite direction of Point A. If you have an A up, Point C is on the downside. If you have an A down, then Point C is on the upside.)

Continuing with the example given above, how long would the market have to stay at or above Point C to be valid? Exactly 10 minutes.

Before we go further, let's take a look at some specific trading strategies to illustrate the Point A and Point C principles that we've discussed thus far. Here's an example from June 12, 2001, the July natural gas futures market. As you can see in Figure 1.6,

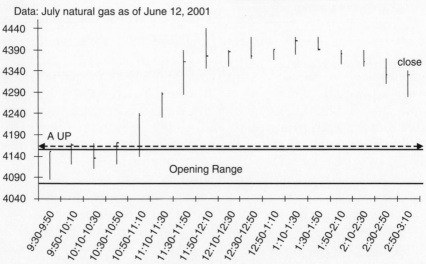

Figure 1.6   Good A up.

the opening range was set at 4.085 to 4.150 during the first 20 minutes of the day. The A value for natural gas futures is 15 ticks. Thus, the A up is 4.165. Looking at the 20-minute bar chart above, you can see that the market made an A up on the fourth 20-minute bar of the day. In fact, from that moment on, the market never traded below the opening range. It closed well above the opening range that day at 4.330.

Remember, this system is symmetrical. What works on the upside also works on the downside.

The example in Figure 1.7 is from June 27, 2001, in the July unleaded gasoline contract. The opening range from the first 20 minutes of trading was .7440 to .7580. The A value is 25 ticks. As you can see in Figure 1.7, the market quickly traded lower and made the A down on the second 20-minute bar. From that point

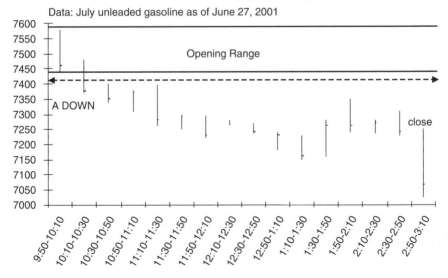

Figure 1.7 Good A down.

until the close of trading, the market never traded in or above the opening range. The market closed sharply lower at .7065.

In the previous examples, we looked at an A up and an A down in markets that move basically in one direction for the day. Now, let's take a look at trades that take into account both a Point A and a Point C. To review, once an A is made (up or down) if the market then reverses, the target becomes Point C, at which the bias crosses over from bullish to bearish, or vice versa.

The example shown in Figure 1.8 is from unleaded gasoline futures for May 29, 2001. The opening range on that day was .9700 to .9780. The A value is 25 ticks. As the market moved higher from the opening, an A up was made at .9805 on the second 20-minute bar of the trading day. The market continued to trade higher, topping out on the fifth bar. The market then sells off and trades into and ultimately below the opening range. Remember, once an A up is made, when the market trades back below the opening range, you are not looking to establish a short

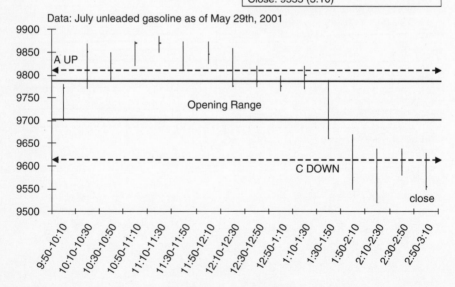

Figure 1.8 Good C down.

position. Rather, your bias is neutral until you reach the downside target to enter the market, which would be Point C.

The Point C value for this market is 85 ticks below the lower end of the opening range. Thus, a Point C down was established at .9615. Once the market traded at that level for 10 minutes (equivalent to half of the length of time for the opening range), you could have established a short position. The market then traded lower—approaching .9500—before recovering somewhat. At the close, however, it remained below the Point C at .9555.

In the next example, we look at the opposite, but symmetrical, scenario of a market that established an A down and then rallied to make a C up. Figure 1.9 shows Broadcom Corp. (BRCM) on March 1, 2001. (As I mentioned before, the ACD System works equally well with stocks and commodities, as long as the market has sufficient volatility and liquidity.)

In this stock, as in any stock, the price differentials for Point A and Point C are the same. In the case of Broadcom, the

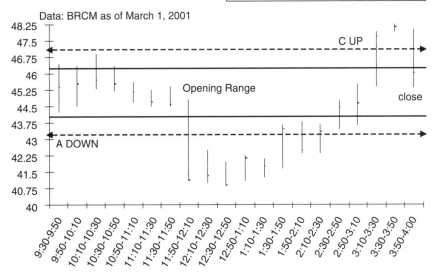

Figure 1.9 Good C up.

differential is 76 cents. The opening range for BRCM was 44.25 to 46.44. The stock traded mostly within the opening range for the first seven 20-minute bars. Then it traded below the range and established an A down at 43.49 on the next bar. The stock continued to break, putting in a low for the day around 40.76. The market then traded steadily higher, continuing through the opening range (at which you would have had a neutral bias) to make a C up at 76 cents above the high of the opening range at 47.20. This occurred late in the session and the stock traded as high as 48, before settling within the opening range at 46.00.

In each of the previous examples, Point As and Point Cs were established because the market not only traded to these levels, but traded there for a time period equivalent to half the opening range. What happens, however, when the market touches a certain level—such as an A up target—but does not stay there? Rather than sustaining trade at that level, it seems to snap back. This is what I call a *rubber band trade*.

Find a rubber band somewhere. Hold the rubber band between your thumb and index finger of your left hand and your right hand. Move your hands apart until the rubber band is stretched to the limit. What happens when you let go of the rubber band? It snaps back.

When the market seems to stretch in the same way but can't go any further, it tends to snap back quickly in the other direction. Keeping the rubber band visual in your mind, imagine that Point A (up or down) is the limit. So if the market has to stretch to get at or near that point, you'd expect a quick reversal.

Here's an example of what I mean: Crude oil futures establish an opening range for the first five minutes of the day at 20.60 to 20.70. The A up target would be 20.78. The market struggles to the upside and just touches 20.77—1 tick away from the A up target—and starts to move down quickly. An A up was not established. The market nearly touched the target, but like a rubber band that is stretched to the limit, it couldn't go any further and starts to snap back the other way (see Figure 1.10).

Now, if you determine the market is accelerating to the downside, on this rubber band trade you do not have to wait until the A down to get short. Once the market snaps back at or near the A up target you can opt to go short below the snap back point since you had a failed A up (see Figure 1.11).

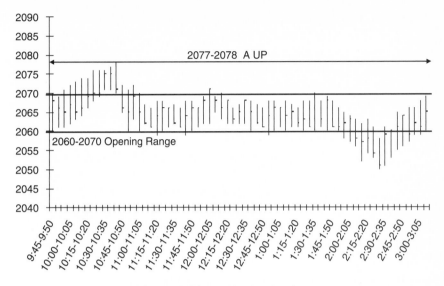

Figure 1.10 Rubber band trading.

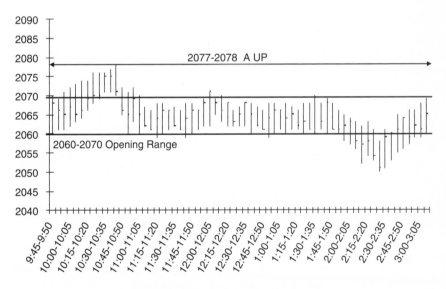

Figure 1.11 Rubber band trading.

At this point, take a look at what you're risking. Remember, the question you must always ask yourself is, where do I get out if I'm wrong? In this case the A up target is still a valid one—since you're above the opening range. But it is only 5 ticks above your entry level. Thus, if the market goes back up to the A target at

20.78, you're stopped out and you lose 5 ticks. And, if the market doesn't start to accelerate to the downside within the next 10 minutes (remember, time is more important than price), you exit.

Let's say the market does accelerate, going through the opening range and trades below 20.60. At this point, you can choose a profitable exit point for your short position. Chances are, however, if the market trades from here back into the opening range, you'd exit the short position. Again, the risk was only 5 ticks to the upside, for a possible long ride down. Remember, nobody gets blown out of trading for risking 5 ticks when they stand to make 20!

Let's take a look at the concept of a *failed Point A* from the opposite perspective (see Figure 1.12). In this scenario, the market trades lower after the opening and approaches the A down target at 20.52. But with an opening range of 5 minutes, the market must spend at least 2½ minutes at 20.52 to establish an A down. Instead, the market trades down to 20.53, then like a rubber band stretched to its limit, seems to snap back to a higher level. At this point, with a failed A down, your risk of establishing a long position after the snap back is small, as long as you know where you'd get out if you're wrong—the A down target.

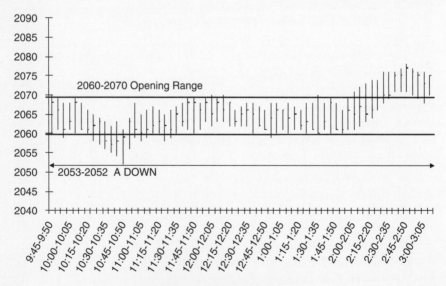

Figure 1.12   Failed point A.

> **Establishing a short position on a failed A up or a long position on a failed A down provides the potential to make a profit that far outweighs the risk.**

Remember, this concept of the rubber band trading only works if you have a failed A or a failed A down. Once an A has been established, you must retain a bullish bias above the opening range and a bearish one below.

Of course, traders sometimes violate the rules of even the best system. Consider it a part of human nature, or an exercise of free will. Who knows! It might even work out for you on occasion. But what I hope will happen when you make these no-rhyme-or-reason trades is you do so with small positions. By that I mean you know that the ACD System is not dictating this trade you're about to take. In fact, you may take a trade because you're annoyed with yourself for missing a trade that the system was dictating. An A up was established, you missed the opportunity to get long, and now the market is back below the A up point. You should be waiting for a point of reference to initiate a long position. But instead, you decide to get short below Point A just because you feel like it. And if this rationale is going on inside your head, no one (except you) can talk you out of it.

These are not good reasons to trade. But traders are humans, and often highly emotional creatures at that. Thus, they do not follow logic like little robots. Believe me, after trading for 20 years and teaching literally thousands of traders I know this.

So what do you do—in the real world? If the ACD system is not aligned with what you're bound and determined to do, then don't step on the gas. Don't load up on this trade. Rather, if you're going to make this trade anyway, then do so with a small scaled-down position. Ride the brake a little. If you make this dumb trade (any trade for which you do not have a good reason is a dumb trade, even if it is profitable), then at least your risk exposure won't be too great.

Believe me, I could preach discipline and the need to take only those trades that are dictated by the system until the next millennium, and there would be times when traders—including

myself and those who work for me—will disregard the system
and trade their own insane ways. When this happens to you,
you'll have your own emotional, irrational reasons. Maybe
the night before, your significant other sent a dish flying like a
Frisbee at you in the middle of a "discussion." The next morning you're mad as hell and you're going to buy this market. Or,
your mother-in-law decides to visit . . . for the next six weeks.
In a moment of blind rage, you decide you're selling this market
because it's the end of the world . . . as you know it.

I can't stop you from doing these trades. You can't even stop
yourself! But if you can retain one shred of discipline, you won't
load up on these trades. You'll risk 10 contracts—and not 100.

Now back to our example. Let's say that you are following
the ACD system. Commodity Z has an opening range of 14.10 to
14.40. The A value is 10 ticks. The market struggles above the
opening range and then creeps higher, touching 14.49, before
selling off sharply. What could you do?

If you recognized this as a potential rubber band trade, then
you'd establish a short position at, say, 14.46 after the market
touches 14.49 and snaps back. Your buy stop to exit the trade
would be at 14.50—the A up point. Your risk, you know, is
4 points to the upside. Now, let's say the market sells off sharply,
trades through the opening range, and goes as low at 13.20. And
let's say that you decide to get out right there and, because this
is your lucky day, that turns out to be the low of the day. You
made 126 ticks and risked 4!

A rubber band trade is made when the market approaches
or just touches a target and snaps back. In that instance,
you would go short just below the A up or go long just
above the A down. Your stop on the trade would be the
A up/down price point. Or, you'd exit the trade if the market didn't move in the direction you anticipated within
your time frame.

At this point, we've really only begun to discuss the ACD
methodology. But already, what's important to note is that this

system is comprised of price reference points. In other words, you have prices to lean against as you make your trades, enabling you to maximize your size and minimize your risk. The A points in the ACD system should be leaned upon the same way you'd use some information in the market. For example, what would be the risk to sell 1,000 share of Microsoft short at $95^3/_4$ if you see there is an order to sell 1 million shares short at 96! You'd have all the confidence in the world, right? Use the Point A targets in the same way.

Points of reference in ACD give you something to lean against as you make your trades. At all times, you know where you're getting out if you're wrong. The result is confidence to trade.

Using the rationale that you always know where to get out if you're wrong, you can use the ACD system to do other types of trades such as buying dips and selling rallies, with ACD points as references (see Figure 1.13.)

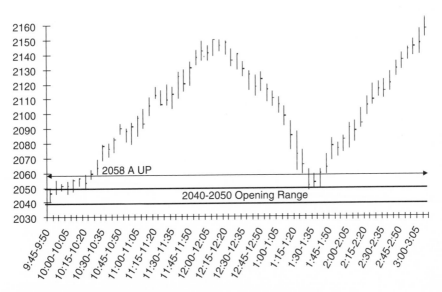

Figure 1.13 ACD point of reference trading.

According to the ACD system, once an A is established, your bias has to reflect the market's relation to the opening range—long above it and short below it. So, let's say the market makes an A up at 20.85 and you hold that long position to exit profitably at 21.50. Now, the market trades lower and goes below the Point A—but it's still above the bottom of the opening range. You believe that the market still has some upside potential. Thus, you decide to buy this dip.

What's crucial, however, is that you buy the bounce. Never try to pick the top or the bottom. Let the market discover a price low and begin to move higher. Then, you'd have a point of reference—in this case the low of that move—against which to establish a long position.

Once again, the question at all times is where will you get out if you're wrong? In the scenario just described of getting long below the A up, your stop point—where your bias turns from bullish to neutral—would be the bottom of the opening range.

Let's take the opposite scenario. Assume the opening range is 20.50 to 20.40, and the market makes an A down at 20.33, where it trades for 2½ minutes. You establish a short position, and exit profitably when the market moves down to 19.85. Now, the market starts to rally a bit but is still below the opening range. At 20.38, the market stalls and then begins to trade lower. You go short at 20.37 with a stop at the top of the opening range.

These buy the dip, sell the rally variations on the ACD strategy do not violate any of the basic rules. Once the A up or the A down is established, you retain a bullish bias above the opening range and a bearish one below. The decision to fade is based upon what you observe in the market. At all times, however, you know where your stop is.

If you trade with this kind of discipline, you can take the little hits that are inevitable—when you buy the dip, for example, but the market ends up breaking. No one is right in this market 100 percent of the time. But you need to think of yourself like a boxer. If you protect yourself (using stops), you can take the little jabs. But you'll avoid the knock-out punch. Those who can will become the veterans in this market, the survivors. Using the reference points of the system, you'll be able to draft your strategy—always knowing where you'll get out if you're wrong.

The following five ACD rules should greatly improve your trading.

1. Plot Point As and Cs as points of reference.
2. Lean against these reference points as you execute your trades.
3. Maximize your size when the trading scenario is favorable. At all times, minimize your risk.
4. Know where you are getting out if you're wrong.
5. If you can answer 4, you will trade with confidence.

Let's examine another strategy based on the A and C reference points—in this case, fading Point Cs. First let's review. Once an A has been established—to the upside or the downside—a C comes into play when the market moves in the opposite direction to sufficient magnitude.

For example, in crude oil, the A value is 7 to 8 ticks. The C value is 11 to 13 ticks. Thus, if the opening range is 20.50 to 20.60, the A up would be made at 20.67 to 20.68. The C down would be 20.39 to 20.37.

Now, let's say that crude oil does make an A up and trades higher, then starts to sell off. It accelerates to the downside, trading through the opening range (at which your bias is neutral) and then approaches your C down price level at 20.39 to 20.37. But instead of trading at that price and then going lower, it touches 20.38—and like the rubber band in previous examples—it snaps back and trades higher.

That is a classic failed C down. The market touched the Point C level, but it did not trade there for a period of time equivalent to half the opening range. After the market bounces from the failed C down, you could decide to fade that moving, taking a long position just above it. Your stop would be Point C, at which you'd have to abandon your upward bias. Now, your profit potential is extended all the way from the entry point, through the opening range, while your risk potential is comparatively smaller.

Here's another real-world example of this kind of trade, which we call *Good A Up, Failed C Down* (or, the opposite, *Good A Down, Failed C Up*). Figure 1.14 shows the March contract for S&P futures (based on the Standard & Poor's 500 Stock Index) on

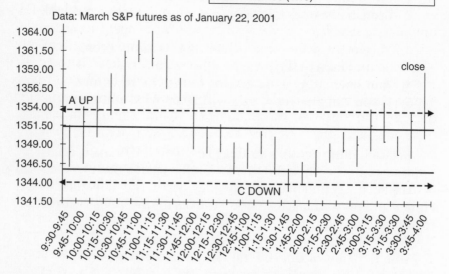

A Value: 2.00
C Value: 1.50
A Up: 1353.50 (10:07) C Down: 1344.50 (1:42)
Opening Range: 1346.00- 1351.50 (9:30-9:50)
Close: 1351.30 (4:15)

Data: March S&P futures as of January 22, 2001

Figure 1.14   Good A up, failed C down.

January 22, 2001. An A Up at 1353.50 is confirmed on the third 15-minute bar of the day. Then, later in the day, the market breaks down and touches the C down level at 1344.50, but it fails to stay there for the time limit of at least 7½ minutes. Rather, the market trades higher from there and closes well above the opening range.

The importance of time cannot be stressed enough, particularly in these opening pages. As you saw in the preceding example, while the market did touch the Point C level, it did not trade for a sufficient length of time there. That failure to trade at or below Point C for 7½ minutes (half the time span of the opening range) is what made it a failed Point C down.

But what about the other extreme of time—too much time? As I mentioned earlier in the chapter, the time factor includes a minimum of time that the market must trade at a certain level, and a maximum amount of time in which something must happen. In other words, if the market hasn't made the move you expected within a reasonable amount of time (as it relates to your trading time frame), then exit the trade.

Let's say you have a 15-minute time frame for a day trade and you decide, as in the previous example, to go long S&P futures above the failed Point C. But let's say that, instead of trading steadily higher, the market just sits there and doesn't go anywhere for 15 minutes. In that scenario, you'd exit the trade and look for the next setup. Why? Because the more time spent at a certain price level allows too many traders to do the same thing. Remember, the masses are usually wrong, and when the trade is too easy to make, it generally doesn't result in a profit. Therefore, if you hang on too long waiting for the desired outcome to materialize, then you run the risk of becoming what I call the *retail bus people.*

If you live in the New York area as I do, you're familiar with the busses that take people down to the casinos in Atlantic City. Maybe the bus ride is even free and they get $10 in chips once they get there. By the time they leave Atlantic City, however, the money is definitely in the pockets of the casinos and not the bus patrons. The trading universe also has its bus people: the amateurs, the uninformed, or the uninitiated. Now, I've probably offended somebody with this description, but for the moment, just suspend your judgment. The point is this group of individuals, when it comes to investing, is almost always 100 percent wrong. So as a trader, you don't want to do what the retail bus people are doing. Thus, if you put on a trade and the market just sits there, you run the risk of more people acting the same way that you have—buying where you bought or selling where you sold. And if this is the case, the result is inevitably a trade that goes against you.

When you trade, pick your time frame and stick with it. Don't become one of the bus people by hanging onto a position too long. Remember, the bus people are almost always wrong.

Of course, there are times when the market really fakes you out. It trades lower, makes an A down, then quickly reverses and stops you out at the opening range, then it rallies to make a C up, at which you get long, and then reverses again and settles right in the middle of the opening range—down, up, and then nowhere. This is an F—you trade, when the market essentially gives you the proverbial finger. Even though you followed the ACD system to the letter, literally, you didn't make any headway—in fact you've got two losing trades for the day.

Luckily, those days are usually in the minority, as long as your market meets the basic criteria:

- *Sufficient liquidity.* You want to make sure there's enough volume of trades that you can enter and exit at or near your price targets.
- *Intraday volatility.* A market like the Eurodollars has great volume, but it doesn't move intraday. With no volatility, there is no opportunity to trade the ACD system. The volatility has to be there.

At all times, know where to get out if it all goes against you. If you don't, you could end up like a trader, whom we'll call HUBB. HUBB traded heating oil futures for my firm at the Nymex. One day, he found himself in the unfortunate position of being the only bidder. Everybody else was selling, but ol' HUBB was buying—from everybody. And, of course, the market was moving lower (which was why everybody else wanted to be a seller).

Who knows why—perhaps HUBB was fishing for the bottom and the eventual turnaround. Or maybe he just forgot to say "Sell 'em" instead of "Buy 'em." Whatever the reason, HUBB kept buying. In the final moments, HUBB suddenly stormed the podium in the trading pit. Now mind you, the podium is where the exchange officials stand to monitor the prices and make any price-related announcements. HUBB commandeered the podium mike and announced he was "60 bid, for whatever you want." He told the astonished crowd that he was leaving his trading cards at the podium and anyone who wanted to sell to him could just write down their names. As the story goes, some 25 brokers ran up and wrote down their names to sell to HUBB at 60.

Needless to say we gave HUBB a little rest after that. Once he got control of himself again, he eventually returned to trading—but this time with a better sense of discipline.

Now, what was the rule that HUBB forgot? He didn't know where (or in his case how) he was getting out when he was obviously wrong.

Chapter 2

THE PIVOT CONCEPT

As a trader, you look to identify key areas at which the market is likely to find support or meet resistance. You know that if the market finds support at a level, it's likely to bounce and trade higher, or if it meets resistance at another level it will reverse and trade lower. You could also surmise that, if the market had enough "force" to break through that support level or penetrate that resistance, it would likely make a significant move in that direction.

You now understand the importance of our next concept in the ACD system: the *pivot range*. Pivot ranges pinpoint these key areas of support/resistance, to act as a guide for your trading strategy. Just as the Point As and Point Cs outlined in Chapter 1 helped you to determine where you'd have a long or short bias/position, the pivot range will also help you to identify key value areas.

What Is a Pivot Range?

The pivot range identifies an area that I like to call the meat of the market. Focusing on this range, which is calculated based on the high, low, and close of a trading period, will help you to see where the market is likely to find support, encounter resistance, and where—if it breaks through—a significant move should follow.

The pivot range also seeks to identify areas in which the buyers are likely to step up (support) or sellers should dominate (resistance). The difference with some other systems, however, is that the pivot range is easily calculated (as explained later in

35

this chapter), using the high, low, and close of a trading period. In other words, you can identify the pivot range yourself just as easily as you could find the Points A and C in Chapter 1.

Just as the opening range is significant in relation to daily highs and lows and in identifying breakout points at which to establish positions, the daily pivot range will help you see where something has to happen. The pivot range is just that; it's pivotal in terms of the market's direction. If the market is below the pivot range and makes a move upward, it will meet resistance at that level. If the market does manage to break through the pivot range, it should have enough force behind it to make a significant upward move. Conversely, if the market is above the pivot range and makes a move downward, it will find support at that level. If the market does breach that support, it should have enough force behind it to make a significant downward move.

The pivot range is where the market is likely to find support or meet resistance. If it manages to break through the pivot range, the market would likely make a significant move in that direction.

Here's an image that might help explain the concept of the pivot range. Picture a chubby man standing in profile. The space between his stomach and his backbone is the pivot range. Now, imagine the market is a sword. If the man is wearing a suit of armor, that sword isn't going to penetrate that man's stomach. It's going to bounce off it. But what happens if the suit of armor is weak? It's rusty and has a hole in it. In that case the sword of the market will break through the armor and penetrate the man's stomach. It may take some effort to break through, but once the blade of the sword hits his soft belly, it won't take much force to get through the other side. Then the man (the pivot range) is going to have a sword (the market) sticking out of its back!

Now that you get the idea of what the pivot range is, let's take a look at how you calculate it. The pivot range is calculated based upon the high, low, and close of a specific trading period. If you're a day-trader, you will use the high, low, and close of the previous trading day. If you are a longer-term player, as we'll discuss later in this chapter, you will use the high, low, and close of a longer time period. But for now, let's look at how a day-trader would calculate the daily pivot range.

The daily pivot range is calculated based upon the high, low, and close of the previous trading period.

Computing the Daily Pivot Range

To calculate the daily pivot range, you begin by calculating the daily pivot price. First, add the high, low, and close of the previous trading day and divide by three. Let's say that Commodity X had a high of 21.00, a low of 20.00, and closed at 20.75. Those three numbers added together and divided by three would be 20.58 (rounded to the nearest cent). That is the *daily pivot number.*

Now, add the high and the low and divide the sum by 2. In this example, adding the high of 21.00 and the low of 20.00, then dividing by 2 would give you 20.50. Then, figure the difference between 20.58 (the daily pivot number) and the second number you calculated (20.50). The result—8 ticks—is the *daily pivot differential.*

The *daily pivot range* is equal to the pivot number plus or minus the pivot differential. In this case, the pivot number would be 20.58 plus 8 and 20.58 minus 8, or 20.50 to 20.66.

The daily pivot range is based upon the daily pivot number, plus or minus the daily pivot differential.

Calculate the daily pivot and daily pivot range using the following formula.

$$\frac{High + Low + Close}{3} = \text{Daily Pivot Price}$$

$$\frac{High + Low}{2} = \text{Second Number}$$

Difference between Daily Pivot Price and Second Number
= Daily Pivot Differential

Daily Pivot Price Plus or Minus Pivot Differential
= Daily Pivot Range

Example: Commodity Y has a high of 24.50, low of 22.50, and close of 23.25

$$\frac{24.50 + 22.50 + 23.25}{3} = 23.42 \text{ (rounded)(Daily Pivot Price)}$$

$$\frac{24.50 + 22.50}{2} = 23.50$$

23.50 − 23.42 = 0.08 (Daily Pivot Differential)
23.42 + 0.08 to 23.42 − 0.08 = 23.50 to 23.34
= Daily Pivot Range

Using the Daily Pivot Range

Now that you have calculated the daily pivot range, what does it tell you? First, the underlying tone or sentiment of the market is revealed when you look at the close of the previous trading day compared with today's pivot range. If the previous close was above today's daily pivot range, that would be considered *bullish* for today's trade. If it closed below the daily pivot range, it would be considered *bearish*.

Remember, today's high, low, and close establishes the daily pivot and daily pivot range for tomorrow.

For example, if the market closed yesterday at 20.75 and the pivot range were 20.45 to 20.60, it would set a bullish tone. Conversely, if the market had closed yesterday at 20.30 and the pivot range were 20.45 to 20.60, it would indicate a bearish tone.

The next step is to factor the daily pivot range into your trading strategy for today. Depending upon where the market settled the previous day, the daily pivot range would either be support (below the close) or resistance (above the close). If the market settled within the daily pivot range, it would be neutral.

Now, based upon what the market does today, the pivot range would either validate or dismiss the previous day's action. For example, let's say that on a Monday, the market rallied intraday and settled strongly above the daily pivot range. That obviously sets a bullish tone for the market going into Tuesday. For this bullish sentiment to be validated, the market would have to find support at the daily pivot range and not trade below it. But what if the opposite happened, and the market on Tuesday broke through the daily pivot range and traded lower? Then Monday's bullish indication would be invalid.

But that action—breaking through the daily pivot range to the downside—would indicate something else. Since, in this instance, the daily pivot range delineates support, breaking through that zone would indicate a strong downward move would likely follow. (Remember the sword going easily through the guy's stomach?) If you had identified the daily pivot range as support and saw the market going easily through it, you mostly likely surmise that this would be a good place to get short. Why? Because the market broke through the daily pivot range so easily that it was likely headed much lower.

In a nutshell, that's how the daily pivot range—by itself—can help you to plot out your trades. Before we look at specific examples, let's summarize what we've covered thus far about pivot ranges:

- A pivot range is based upon the high, low, and close of a specific trading period. (For day traders, this would be the previous trading day.)
- Where the market closes in relation to the pivot range gives an indication of sentiment (i.e., above the pivot range is bullish and below it is bearish).
- A pivot range above the market is resistance and below it is support.
- If the market breaks through the pivot range (support/resistance), you could expect a significant move in that direction.

Pivot Range Strategies

Let's take a look at some specific strategies using only the pivot range. As you can see in Figure 2.1, Stock X has a daily pivot range of 35.00 to 35.20, and closes at 35.40, setting a bullish tone. The next day, the stock opens at 35.35. The pivot range at 35.00 to 35.20 is support. The stock trades lower, approaching 35.20, but does not go below 35.22. At that point, the price bounces and trades immediately higher to 35.25. What does that tell you?

In this instance, the market has snapped back near the pivot area, similar to what we discussed in the rubber band trade outlined in Chapter 1. The market stretched just so far but did not reach the pivot range. Rather, as it got close to the pivot range, it reversed quickly, which I call snapping back. In this instance, you would use the strategy of the rubber band trade, going long after the market bounces off the 35.22 low.

Let's take a look at the rationale. The pivot range identified support. The market traded to near that support level, but it couldn't go further. As it snapped back, the likelihood was for an upward move.

As in every trade, the question you must always ask yourself is where do I get out if I'm wrong? Just as the opening range and

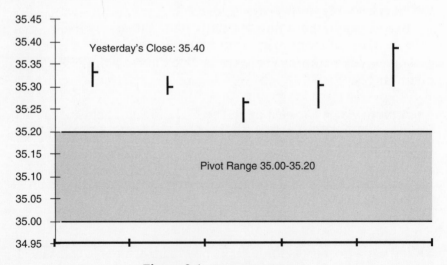

Figure 2.1   Pivot range support.

Points A and C in Chapter 1 helped you to determine stop placement, so does the pivot range. In this example with a long position/
bias initiated above the pivot range, your stop would be the
other side of the pivot range, at which your bias would shift to
neutral.

Now, let's change the scenario. In Figure 2.2, you can see that
Stock X has a daily pivot range of 35.00 to 35.20, and as in the previous example it closed at 35.40. It opens the next day at 35.35 and
it trades lower. In this scenario, however, let's assume that as the
market approaches the pivot range, the selling intensity increases.
The stock trades 35.25, 35.20, and then 35.15, as the market slices
easily through that pivot range (remember the sword?) and trades
down to 35.10. At this point, you are watching to see if the stock
does indeed trade below the pivot range. If it trades below 35.00,
you would initiate a short position. Once again, where is your
stop? It is the top of the pivot range, above 35.20.

As with all scenarios in the ACD system, everything is symmetrical. What works when the market is above the pivot range
also is applicable when it is below the pivot range. For example,
in Figure 2.3, Stock XYZ has a pivot range of 44.72 to 44.80 and
closes at 44.65. The next day it opens at 44.68.

The market stalls around the opening range, and then trades
slowly up to 44.70, 44.71, and then 44.72. At that point the market reverses and trades 44.71, 44.70, and 44.69. What would you
do? Of course, this is a classic rubber band scenario, and once the

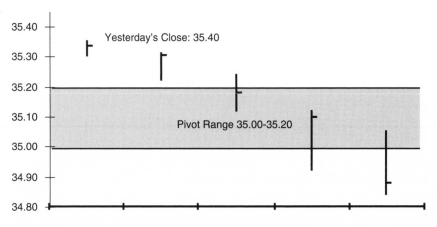

Figure 2.2   Broken pivot range support.

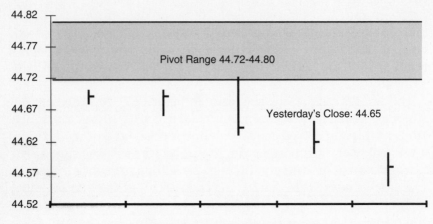

Figure 2.3   Pivot range resistance.

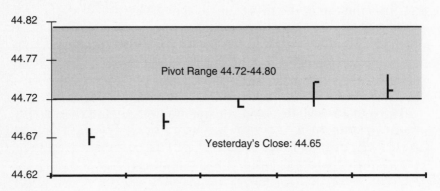

Figure 2.4   Trading in the pivot range.

market snapped back at 44.72, it was an opportunity to get short. Why? The market touched the edge of the pivot range, but it could not penetrate the resistance zone. The likelihood was then a move downward. Your risk to the upside would be the other side of the pivot range.

Another scenario, again using our example of Stock XYZ: In Figure 2.4, you can see the pivot range is 44.72 to 44.80 with a close at 44.65. This time, we'll say that the market opens at 44.68 and trades steadily higher to 44.70, 44.72, and 44.75—right in the middle of the pivot range. What would you do then? You would wait. Trading in the pivot range is like trading in the

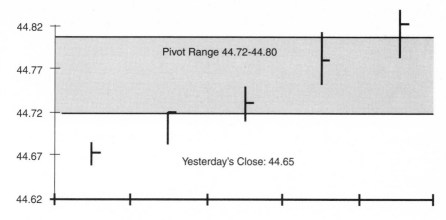

Figure 2.5 Getting long above the pivot range.

opening range. This is a neutral area until the market gets through one side or the other.

Under yet another scenario, Stock XYZ has a pivot range, once again, of 44.72 to 44.80 (see Figure 2.5). But this time, the market trades steadily higher from the opening, to 44.78, 44.79, 44.80, and 44.81.

As you can see, the market was able to slice through this resistance zone easily and out the other side. What would you do now? The answer is obvious. With the pivot range (resistance) broken through to the upside, your strategy would be to get long. Your stop is, of course, the bottom of the pivot range below 44.72.

To recap, we used the activity of the market around the pivot range to determine our strategy. If the market bounced off the pivot range, it indicated an opportunity to fade the move. Believing that the market had gone as far as it could—either down to a support pivot range or up to a resistance pivot range—we initiated an opposite position. We sold after the market couldn't trade any higher and reversed, and bought after the market couldn't trade any lower and bounced. Conversely, if the market did manage to break through the pivot range, we established a short or long position/bias depending upon the market direction. If it broke through a support pivot range, we became sellers; if it penetrated a resistance support pivot, we were buyers.

Trading with Pivot Ranges

Moving away from our hypothetical examples, let's take a look at how pivot ranges can be applied to real markets in real time. Figure 2.6 shows natural gas futures as of August 7, 2001.

As you can see, the daily pivot range is established between 3.025 and 2.997. In the first 20-minute bar on the chart, the market trades as high as 3.100, then trades lower in subsequent bars, approaching the daily pivot range. The market stays above the daily pivot range, however, until the 1:50 to 2:10 P.M. bar, at which it trades below the daily pivot range. In the next bar, it trades steadily below the daily pivot range and then settles the day well below it. As you can clearly see, once the market broke through the daily pivot range (support) it had enough downward momentum to trade to the other side and ultimately to settle well below the daily pivot range.

Small Pivot Ranges and Pivot on Gap Days

Examining pivot ranges in relation to daily price ranges, another observation becomes apparent: Trading days that have a normal

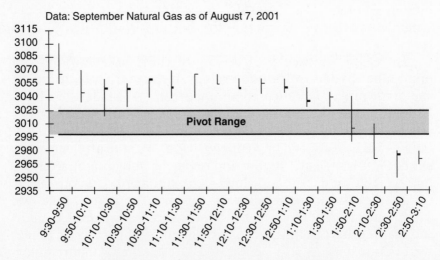

Figure 2.6 Getting short below the pivot range.

trading range but produce a very narrow daily pivot range for the following day usually indicate a larger price range the following day. To illustrate, examine Figure 2.7 of September crude oil futures for four consecutive trading days from June 25, 2001 through June 28, 2001.

On June 25, the market has a daily pivot range of 26.72 to 26.78 (6 cents) and a trading range for the day of 42 cents. On June 26, the daily pivot range is from 27.04 to 27.13 (9 cents) and the range for the day is 36 cents. Now, on June 27, the market has a daily pivot range of only 2 cents. Remember, this pivot range is based on the activity for the previous day—a day in which the market had a normal range of 36 cents. What would this setup indicate? It indicates a larger than normal price range, just as you can see in the chart of the activity for June 27.

On June 27, the market gapped strongly lower (creating a pivot on gap day at 26.97 to 26.99) and had a much larger than normal trading range of 1.12. Keep in mind that a pivot on a gap day lower remains as important resistance going forward for

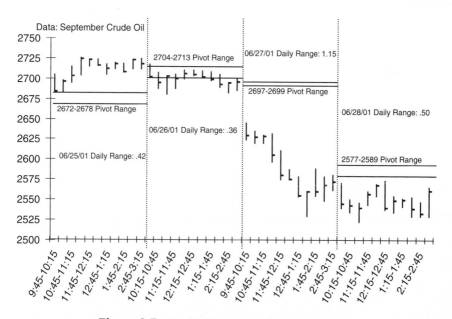

Figure 2.7 Small pivot ranges and pivot on gap days.

future trading. Thus, in subsequent days or weeks should the market approach at 26.97 to 26.99 pivot area, you would expect significant resistance at this level. Conversely, had the market gapped higher and traded above the daily pivot range, in the following days and weeks you would expect the pivot on gap day to be significant support for the market.

Significant Time Frames

As you have learned thus far, much of the ACD system is based upon the premise that certain time frames—whether it's an opening range or a pivot range—are significant in helping you to establish a bullish or bearish position/bias. There are other significant time frames, particularly for a longer-term perspective

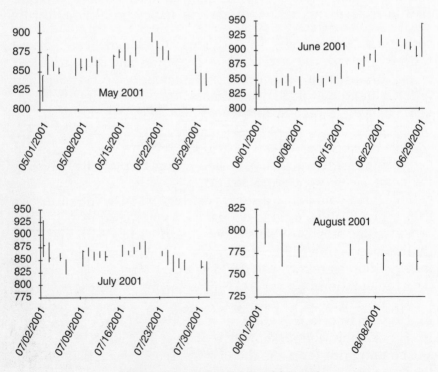

Figure 2.8   First trading day of the month.

that can be used to gauge your bias. Among them is the first trading day of the month, which is more frequently the high or the low for the month than you'd otherwise suspect. In other words, the first trading day of the month is statistically significant to the rest of the month, just as the opening range (as discussed in Chapter 1) was statistically significant for the rest of that trading day.

To illustrate this point, look at Figure 2.8 of sugar futures for four consecutive months in 2001. Take notice of how the first trading day for May, June, July, and August is either the high or low trading day for the month.

Three-Day Rolling Pivot

Another pivot concept that can be employed is the *three-day rolling pivot*, which may be used by those who take intermediate-term positions, spanning several days or even, with profitable trades, weeks. As the name suggests, this pivot is based up three consecutive trading days. To calculate it, use the highest high and the lowest low of the three-day trading period, and the settlement of the third trading day. These three reference numbers are then plugged into the Pivot Range Formula (see "Computing the Daily Pivot Range," earlier in this chapter) to calculate the three-day rolling pivot range.

The three-day pivot can be utilized in many ways, such as to determine an entry point for a trade, using the three-day pivot as the point above which you'd establish a long position/bias and below which you'd have a short position/bias. Or, the three-day rolling pivot can be used to determine a trailing stop.

A trailing stop is like a safety net that travels with you. The trailing stop is moved in the direction of the trade—upward for a long position and downward for a short position—to protect you over the duration of a trade. Using a three-day rolling pivot, in which the earliest day is eliminated as a new day is added, the trailing stop can be calculated and moved along with your position.

For example, let's assume that you establish a short position at a certain price level. As the market trades lower, you can use the three-day rolling pivot to determine your stop. (With a short position, a stop is placed just above the top end of the pivot range. With a long position, a stop is placed just below the bottom of the pivot range.) Using the trailing stop, you can manage your position until you exit profitably or until the market penetrates the pivot range, at which point your bias would shift to neutral. However, because this is a trailing stop, which moves in the direction of the trade, your profits are locked in until the stop is triggered.

One key consideration in using a rolling pivot to determine your trailing stop is consistency. You must use the same time frame to calculate the pivot each time. If you start out with a three-day rolling pivot, you must use a three-day time frame for the duration of the trade. You can't switch, for example, to a two-day or a three-day pivot in the middle of the trade.

Using this longer time horizon for a pivot can help you manage a position despite a sudden increase in volatility on one particular day due to an outside event. For example, if you are trading a short-term system, it is virtually impossible to carry a position into a potentially market-moving report, such as GDP or the Employment Report. The reason is that with a short-term system, the breakout points are fairly close to the market. However, if you use a longer-term pivot, then that helps to smooth out the market's one-day reaction to a particular economic report. With a broader time frame over which to spread the market activity, a fake-out—a spike up that goes nowhere, or a spike down that doesn't continue—won't affect your trading position.

The rolling pivot is another extension of the pivot range concept. Whether you're looking at one trading day or three (or a longer time frame as we'll discuss later in this chapter), the concept is the same. The high, low, and settlement of a particular trading period yields a pivot range that helps you to plot your entry points and determine your protective stops.

In Figure 2.9 of June unleaded gasoline futures, a three-day rolling pivot on May 11 delineates support just below 1.070. When the market breaks through that pivot level, it reaches the A down target at 1.051, at which a short position was established. Looking at the chart, notice now the market continued to trade below the three-day rolling pivot, reaching a low of nearly 0.95 on May 16. Then, on May 17, the market broke through the

Data: June Unleaded Gasoline as of 2001 (60 minute chart)

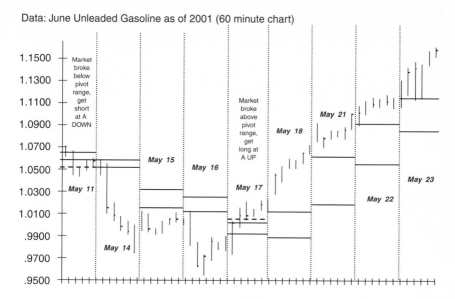

Figure 2.9   Three-day rolling pivot range.

three-day rolling pivot to the upside (which was far below where the three-day rolling pivot had been on May 11) and made an A up at 1.0010 on May 17. Again, looking at the figure, see how the market traded above the three-day rolling pivot for the next four trading days.

Plus and Minus Days

Another concept that is derived from the pivot range is what I call the *plus* and *minus* days. This is a simple scoring that is based on how the market performed on a particular day in relation to the pivot range. I call this *assigning a value to the pivot.*

• If the market opens below the pivot but closes above it, it's a plus day. Put another way, if the opening is less than the pivot and the pivot is less than the close, it's a plus day.

Opening Range < Pivot Range < Close = Plus Day

- If the market opens above the pivot, but closes below it, it's a minus day. (Or, if the open is greater than the pivot and the pivot is greater than the close, it's a minus day.)

Opening Range > Pivot Range > Close = Minus Day

- Everything else is a zero day (or has a neutral rating).

Just as the pivot is based on previous activity, but is applied to future activity, so this scoring is also used going forward—on a 30-day trading cycle. Over the years, what I have found is that if 30 trading days ago it was a plus day (opening below the pivot but closing above it) and a volatile session, then there is a statistically significant chance that the current trading day will also be a plus day and also experience another volatile session. Conversely, if 30 trading days ago was a minus day (opening above the pivot but closing below it) and a volatile session, then there is a good chance that the current trading day will be a minus day and also experience another volatile session.

How can you use this information? Let's assume that 30 trading days ago was a plus day. (Remember, that means the market opened below the pivot and closed above it.) Now, for the current trading day, the pivot range is 75 to 85. The market is opening below this pivot range, with an opening range of 60 to 70. Since the previous trading day was a plus, what is the likely scenario for this trading day? If the 30-day trading cycle did indeed repeat itself, you would expect the market—which is opening below the pivot range—to trade above it and to settle above it.

There are two key considerations to keep in mind here. The first is to be aware of whether there was a plus or a minus day 30 trading days ago. Second, for history to repeat itself on the current day, the scenario must line up from the opening. For example, if 30 trading days ago was a plus day (opening below the pivot but closing above it), then you could assume that there was a good chance that today would follow that pattern. But today, if the market opens above the pivot, then it is not lining up to be a plus day. Even if the market eventually closes above the pivot, it's still not a plus day because the first factor was missing—it did not open below the pivot. Thus when you apply the 30 trading day plus/minus day indicator, make sure that the scenario is lining up before you make any assumptions about how the market would likely close on a particular day (see Figures 2.10 and 2.11).

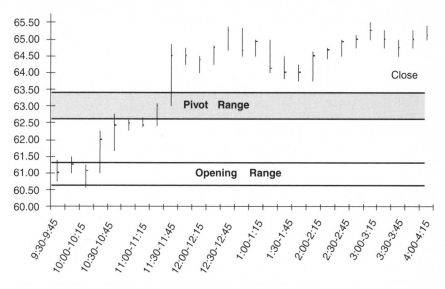

Figure 2.10   Plus day.

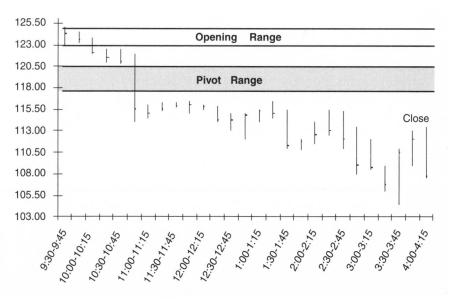

Figure 2.11   Minus day.

Longer-Term Pivots

Finally, there is one other important concept: applying a pivot range to a longer period of time whether it be weeks or even months. As I explained earlier in this chapter, the concept remains the same: you calculate the pivot range using the highest high and the lowest low of the time frame, and the settlement on that time frame. For example, if you were looking at a two-week trading period, you would determine the highest price for that period, the lowest price for that period, and then the settlement on the last trading day of that period. Now, using those three numbers, you would calculate the pivot range, using the same formula as you did for the daily pivot.

Further, when it comes to long-term pivot ranges, we have found that certain time frames are statistically significant. In particular, the pivot range calculated on the first two weeks of the year is statistically significant for the first half of the year. The pivot range calculated on the first two weeks after mid-year (meaning the first two weeks of July) is statistically significant for the second half of the year. In other words, the pivot range that is calculated on the first two weeks of the year delineates important support/resistance for the market for the first half of the year. The market then resets at mid-year, and the pivot range based on the first two weeks of July defines support/resistance for the second half of the year.

Once you have calculated the pivot range for this extended period of time, such as for the first two weeks of the year, you would determine the price targets at which you would have a long bias or a short bias. These targets are known as the A up and the A down. But unlike the Point As used in daily strategies against the opening range in Chapter 1, these A up and A down targets take into account a longer-term view.

Let's take a look at an example. Figure 2.12 is a weekly chart for natural gas futures January through mid-year 2001. The pivot range based upon the first two weeks of the year is 9.005 to 8.650. (The pivot range was calculated with a high of 9.870 from January 9, a low of 8.140 on January 3, and the close of January 12 of 8.472.)

Based upon this pivot range, the A up and A down targets are calculated. Since this is a long-term perspective, instead of a daily one, we use a larger A value, in this case 200 ticks. (By

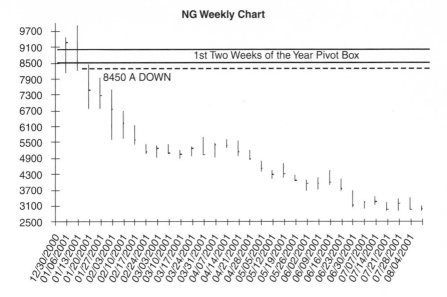

Figure 2.12 Longer-term pivots

comparison, for a daily Point A based up on the opening range, you would use only 15 to 20 ticks.) That would make the A up target based on this two-week pivot range 9.205 (9.005 plus 200 ticks), and the A down target 8.450 (8.650 minus 200 ticks).

Now, look at what happens on the third weekly bar of the chart. The market trades below the A down of 8.450, at which point you would have a short bias/position. The market trades steady lower and, despite a slight up-tick in April, continues to trade lower until mid-year. In fact, when the mid-year cycle ends on the last day of June, natural gas futures were trading at 3.200. That is a significant drop from the A down price of 8.450!

Interestingly, you'll note on the first bars after June 30, the market does not make any significant moves. Rather, it appears to be moving sideways in a small range. That's because the market is resetting for the second half. Remember, for the second half of the year, you would calculate a pivot range based upon the first two weeks of July. That pivot range would then apply to the market activity from July through December, at which point the market would reset again.

While this chart shows a dramatic example of how a pivot range can determine a long-term profitable position, the question arises, where would you cover your long-term position once it was established? The answer is when your time frame ends, which in this example is the last day of June. Otherwise, you would cover and exit the trade when it traded back above pivot range, your point of reference. Short term or long term, the key consideration is where to cover a position, your point of reference, if you are wrong. Once again, the pivot range is the key. For a short position, if the market traded above the top of the pivot range, you would exit. For a long position, if the market traded below the bottom of the pivot range you would exit.

The concept of the pivot range is a fairly straightforward one. Identifying the pivot range helps you to gauge the sentiment of the market and to plot the points at which you'd expect support and resistance. In this chapter, we've looked at using pivot ranges only. But as you know from the Introduction, the ACD system is cumulative, with one layer of indicators added to another. In Chapter 3, we'll take a look at using pivot range in conjunction with Points A and C to determine your trading strategy.

Chapter 3

PUTTING IT TOGETHER: ACD AND PIVOT RANGES

At this point, you've learned the basics of the ACD system, using Point As and Cs as reference points for a short or long position/bias. In Chapter 2, you reviewed how pivot ranges define key support and resistance levels and also can be used for trade entry points. Now, we're going to put the two strategies together, using both the ACD reference points and pivot range to fine-tune your trade entry points and stop placement. By combining the two strategies, you will have a higher probability of success by virtue of the fact that you are using two indicators. This will allow you to maximize position size, while minimizing your risk.

Keep in mind that while we are using two indicators together, the more important one is the ACD. And remember, this system is symmetrical. Whatever works on the upside, also works on the downside.

Point As and Pivot Ranges

The first combo strategy I will discuss is a Point A through the pivot. To recap, a Point A is made when the market trades to a specific level above the opening range (Point A up) or below the opening range (Point A down). But what happens if that Point A target is near or within the pivot range? With two indicators coinciding at a particular price level, it emphasizes the importance of this reference level. And, when the market trades at and

55

through that reference area, the signal is twice as strong. That is what we call a *good A through the pivot.*

To illustrate, let's take a hypothetical example. Assume that Commodity X has a daily pivot range—based on the previous day's activity—at 27.90 to 27.95, and it settled to 27.85. At first glance, you know that sets up a bearish tone for the next day since the settlement was below the pivot range. Now, today Commodity X's opening range, established in the first 10 minutes of trading, is 27.80 to 27.85. Assuming the A value for Commodity X is 10 ticks, that would make an A up at 27.95 and an A down at 27.70.

Let's assume that the market does trade higher, easily penetrating the lower end of the pivot range at 27.90 and trades all the way to the other side of the pivot range at 27.95, which is where it makes an A up. At this point, the market has both made an A up (the first indicator) and has traded through the pivot (the second indicator). With these two signals acting in concert, you would establish a long position/bias above 27.95 based on a good A up through the pivot (see Figure 3.1).

With these two indicators working in concert, you might also want to not only go long at 27.95 but also increase your size. Why? With two signals on this trade, you have increased your confidence in this trade position. (Remember, maximizing

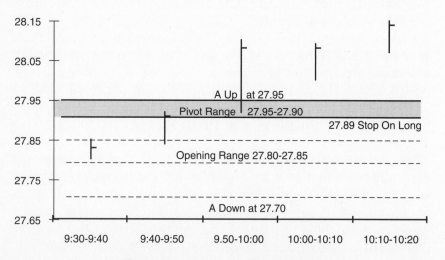

Figure 3.1   Good A up through the pivot.

size.) At the same time, using ACD and the pivot range together, you would use a narrower stop than with the ACD alone. As mentioned in Chapter 1, the stop for an A up is Point B, which is just below the bottom of the opening range. In this example, that would be below 27.80, which is 15 ticks below your entry point. However, going long with an A up through the pivot, your stop would be just below the bottom of the pivot range, or in this case 27.90, only 5 ticks below your entry point (again, minimizing risk.)

Going long at a Point A up after the market trades through the pivot increases your confidence to make the trade. Putting your stop just below the bottom of the pivot range minimizes the risk.

Let's look at an example of a good A up through the pivot from our trade archives, this time looking at S&P futures from July 17, 2001. In Figure 3.2, the opening range established in the first 15 minutes of the day was between 1203.50 and 1208.80. With an A value of 2.00, it would make the A up target 1210.80, and an A down at 1201.50. The daily pivot range, based upon the previous day's activity, was 1212.14 to 1215.40. The pivot range is above the A up target at 1210.80.

As shown in Figure 3.2, the market traded higher and made an A up on the 10:30 bar of the day. But at this point, the market did not penetrate the pivot range. So instead of taking a long position/bias at the A up, given the fact that the pivot range is just above it, you would opt to wait to see what the market does. In other words, if the pivot is sitting above an A up (or below an A down) you might as well wait for the market to take out the pivot and confirm that the A is really valid. If it penetrates the pivot range above the A up, you'd be long; otherwise, you're on the sidelines.

After trading lower, the market by midday trades higher, crossing the A up and this time continuing higher through the pivot range. At this point, the market clearly demonstrated its upside momentum, which increases your confidence for the

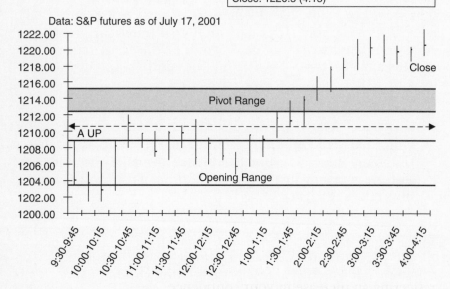

A Value: 2.00
A Up: 1210.8 (10:41)
Pivot Range: 1212.14-1215.4
Opening Range: 1203.5-1208.8 (9:30-9:45)
Close: 1220.5 (4:15)

Figure 3.2   S&P futures, July 17, 2001.

upside. The market, in fact, traded steadily higher and closed near the highs of the day at 1220.50.

A Down Through the Pivot

Now, let's take a look at this strategy from the opposite side, specially the case of a good A down through the pivot. As you can see in Figure 3.3, Commodity B has a daily pivot range, based on the previous day's activity, of 39.80 to 39.70. Today, the opening range set in the first 20 minutes of trading is 40.10 to 39.90. With a 20-point A value, an A down target would be made at 39.70 and an A up would be made at 40.30.

Let's assume that the market trades lower, through the pivot range to make the A down at 39.70, where it trades for the minimum of 10 minutes (half the duration of the opening range). At this point, you have two reasons to establish a short

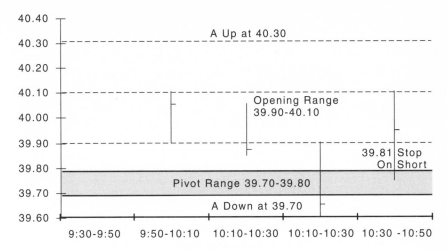

Figure 3.3   Using the pivot range to minimize risk.

position/bias: an A down has been made and the market has moved easily through the pivot range. With two indicators in concert, you have the potential to maximize your trade size, reflecting an increase in your confidence.

As for the risk—remember, always know where you'd get out if you're wrong—the pivot range becomes your reference point. When you trade using only a good A down, your stop—Point B—is just above the top of the opening range. In this case that would be just above 40.10, which is 40 ticks above your A down of 39.70. Using the pivot range as your reference, however, your stop would be just above the top of the pivot range—or 39.80, which is 10 ticks above the A down entry point. That's far less risk than using the typical Point B stop.

Going short after the market makes an A down through the pivot increases your confidence in the trade. Minimize the risk by putting your stop just above the top of the pivot range.

The concept of maximizing size while minimizing risk is vital for the individual trades that you make and your trading career. Nobody ever went broke risking 5 or 10 ticks! At the same time, if you can risk only 5 or 10 ticks but make 10 or 20 with increased trade size, then the rewards are more than commensurate with the risk.

Here's what I mean: Let's say you were going to buy 10 crude oil futures contracts after the market made a good A up. Your risk, however, was Point B, just below the bottom of the opening range. But that was 25 ticks away. At the current crude oil price, those 25 ticks on 10 contracts would be a total risk exposure of $2,500.

On the other hand, if the A up was made through a daily pivot, your conviction to make that trade would be much greater. Hence you could increase your trade size, say to 25 contracts instead of just 10. And, because you are using the pivot range as a reference point, your risk would be lower because your stop would be just below the bottom of the pivot range, which we'll say is only 10 points away from your entry point. Therefore, your total risk exposure—for 25 contracts instead of only 10—is $2,500 because your stop placement is tighter. Put another way, you could trade with conviction and a valid reference point with a position that is two-and-a-half larger while not increasing your overall risk.

Each time you add another indicator, it is like seeking another opinion on the market. The greater the consensus, the more confidence you have in the trade that you're making. For example, suppose the market makes an A up through the pivot. With those two signals of a long position/bias, you'd have confidence to increase your trade size. Now, suppose that you add in the 30-day trading cycle. As you recall from Chapter 2, trading days are valued a plus or a minus based upon how they open and close versus the pivot range. (If a market opens below the pivot, but closes above it, it is a plus day. If a market opens above the pivot, but closes below it, it is a minus day.) And, we have found that the market tends to move in 30-trading-day cycles. Thus, if 30 trading days ago was a plus day and the market lines up for this scenario again today, there is a good chance that today will be a plus day.

So, if it was a plus day 30 trading days ago and the market lines up for it again today, there would be a good chance that today will be a plus day. That means the market would open

Putting It Together: ACD and Pivot Ranges   **61**

below the pivot and then close above it. Already, the market has opened below the pivot but traded higher to make an A up and trade through the pivot. Now, we're adding a third, positive consideration: There is a good chance that the market will close above the pivot as well. What's the likelihood that if you go long at an A up through the pivot that you'll have a profitable trade? A very strong likelihood. The market has already cleared two hurdles—making an A up and trading through the pivot. With the odds strongly in favor of a close above the pivot as well (for a plus day), your confidence increases even more. Now, perhaps instead of trading your usual 10 contracts, you might risk 20 or 30 contracts. Why? When the signals line up, it's time to maximize the trade size, because you are already minimizing the risk.

Each indicator you use is like adding a layer of confidence. For example, if the market makes an A up through a pivot and 30 trading days ago was a plus day, the likelihood of an upward move is very strong.

The other side of this, however, is when your confidence in something occurring erodes. That's where the time factor comes in. As you'll recall from Chapter 1, if the market doesn't move the way that you anticipate within a reasonable amount of time, you must exit the trade and move on. The longer the market just sits there, the greater the chance that the trade will go against you. (That's when all the retail bus people have a chance to pile onto the same trade that you're making, and they are almost always wrong.) This same time concept applies to trading with pivot range. If the market starts to trade in the pivot range—whether it's to the upside or the downside—but instead of making it to the other side, it just sits there, then get out. If the market stays within the pivot range for longer than three times the duration of the opening range (meaning 30 minutes if the opening range is 10 minutes), then that pivot is a meaningless concept for that day. Exit the trade and move onto something else. You want to see something happen when the market reaches these reference areas. If not, get out of the trade.

> If the market stays too long in the pivot range, that concept is invalidated for the day. When the market reaches a key price reference area, it must move—or else the price level is meaningless for that day.

Failed A Against the Pivot

But what happens if the market does not spend enough time at the A up or down targets? Or, what happens if the market goes through the pivot but can't get all the way to the A up or down? Suppose the pivot range did, indeed, prove to be strong enough support or good enough resistance to stop a move, so that the market ran out of momentum before it reached the Point A? What would the scenario be? The answer is, a failed A against the pivot.

Since each of the concepts builds upon the other, first we'll review. As described in Chapter 1, a failed A occurs when the market touches or approaches an A up or an A down, but doesn't spend enough time there (half the duration of the opening range) to validate that point. Or, it approaches an A up or an A down, but snaps back, which we called a rubber band trade. Now, if those same situations occur with a failed A in the pivot range—meaning the market just barely makes it into the pivot range but snaps back at or before the Point A—your conviction to trade that signal increases.

Let's take an example. In Figure 3.4, you can see the pivot range for Commodity C is 20.15 to 20.25. The opening range for the following day is 20.08 to 20.13. Using a Point A differential of 7 ticks, a Point A up would be made at 20.20, which would be right in the middle of the pivot range.

Now, let's assume that the pivot range was, indeed, significant resistance. The market struggled through the first part of the pivot range but never quite made it to the Point A up. At 20.19, the market snapped back, resulting in a classic failed A up in the pivot. Thus, the failure at 20.19 is even more significant in this resistance zone. As a trader, you would most likely put those two facts together and come up with one conclusion: The risk of getting short at 20.19 is minimal. The failed A coupled

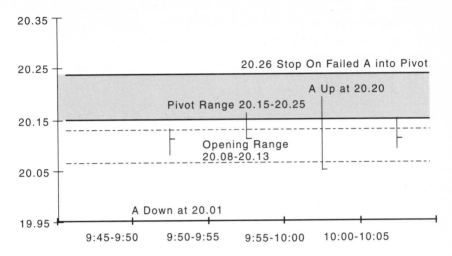

Figure 3.4 Failed A up against the pivot.

with a failure within the pivot range increase the likelihood of the market reversing to the downside. The possibility appears very slim that the market would turn around at this point and make it through the pivot range. Just in case, however, you'd have a stop at 20.26, one tick above the pivot range.

A failed A up just above or within the pivot range confirms resistance in that area, and it increases the likelihood of success for a short position at that price level.

Let's look at the opposite scenario with a failed A down in the pivot. In Figure 3.5, the pivot range for Commodity D is 20.40 to 20.50, and the opening range is 20.55 to 20.60. An A down in this scenario would be made at 20.47 (8 ticks below the bottom of the opening range).

Now, let's assume the market traded lower, through the edge of the pivot range at 20.50 and then 20.49, but didn't make the A down at 20.47. Instead, it reversed quickly and traded to 20.50 and then 20.51. In this case, the market has had a failed A down, which coincided with the pivot range. This failure to trade any lower confirms support at this level and increases the probability that the

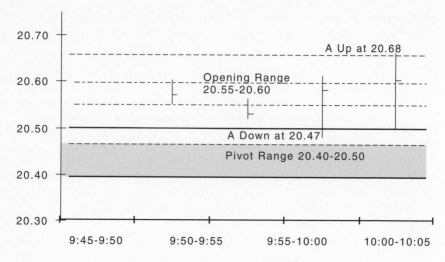

Figure 3.5   Failed A down into the pivot.

market will trade higher. Thus, going long at the snap back point on this rubber band trade carries a minimal risk that is greatly outweighed by the potential reward. But as always, you must know where you would get out if you were wrong, and in this case it would be just below the bottom of the pivot range.

A failed A down just below or within the pivot confirms support at that level, and it increases the likelihood of a profitable long position made at that price level.

The concept of a failed A against the pivot is an important consideration when this occurs early in the trading day, particularly in a trending market. Let's say the market has been trending higher overall. But on one particular day, the market trades below the opening range, displaying weakness early. However, the early weakness dissipates and the market has a failed A down as it bounces off that level and trades higher. At this point, this failed A down in the pivot identifies a very low risk point of entry. You have two signals to indicate getting long: the pivot range proved to be support and the market snapped back from the A down level. Plus, the market had already been trending in the direction of this daily reversal to the upside. Your risk is minimal: a few ticks to the failed A down. But your potential can be considerable.

Now, add yet another consideration. (The ACD system adds indicators like layers, each building upon the last one.) Let's say the market has been in an uptrend. Today, it has a failed A down and the pivot is above the opening range. In addition, let's assume that 30 trading days ago was a plus day (opening below the pivot but closing above it.) That's a reason to get long after the failed A down, because if history repeats itself, there is an even greater likelihood that the market will also settle above the pivot range.

Before we move on, here's a list of possible scenarios discussed thus far for using Point As and pivot ranges.

- *Good A up through the pivot range.* Buy at the A up through the pivot and consider increasing your trade size. Minimize risk by putting your stop just below the bottom of the pivot range or use a time stop (meaning if the market doesn't move the way you anticipate in a certain time frame, then exit the trade).
- *Good A down through the pivot range.* Sell at the A down through the pivot and consider increasing your trade size. Minimize risk by putting your stop just above the top of the pivot range, or use a time stop.
- *Failed A down against the pivot.* Buy after the failed A down through or against the pivot, as the market snaps back. Put your stop just below the bottom of the pivot range, or use a time stop.
- *Failed A up against the pivot.* Sell after the failed A up through or against the pivot, as the market snaps back. Put your stop just above the top of the pivot range, or use a time stop.

Point C Pivots

Thus far, I've explained the use of pivots with Point As. Now, let's look at how you can use pivots against the other entry point in the ACD system—Point C. As you recall, Point C is the price level at which your bias/sentiment changes. If the market makes an A up and then reverses, your bias shifts from bullish (at the A up) to neutral (through the opening range) to bearish at Point C. And since this system is symmetrical, if the market makes an A down and then rallies, your bias shifts from bearish (at the A down) to neutral (through the opening range) to bullish at Point C.

Analyzing this action against the pivot range gives you a potentially powerful reversal strategy that I call the *Point C pivot trade*. This is not the kind of trade you're likely to see occur frequently. But when it does, it is a scenario that often yields a significant move to capitalize upon.

First, certain factors must line up in order for there to be a Point C pivot:

- The opening range must be above the pivot range.
- The market must make a Point A up.
- The market must then break below the opening range and trade lower going through the Point C pivot range.

or

- The opening range must be below the pivot range.
- The market must make a Point A down.
- The market must then rally through the opening range and trade higher going through the Point C pivot range.

When these kinds of dramatic reversals occur, the result is usually a significant move. Again, these aren't the kind of trades that occur frequently. In fact, I call them the once-in-a-blue-moon kind of a trade, meaning they are a rare occurrence. But as you examine your markets in light of the ACD system, you will look for certain setups to occur. And when you see a Point C pivot trade develop, you'll know what to do.

The beauty of the Point C pivot trade is that, because of the market factor involved, it helps you identify areas and situations in which you can really maximize your trade size, while minimizing the risk. In other words, in a classic Point C pivot trade scenario it's the perfect time to step on the gas. The road is clear with no obstacles to a profitable trade ahead.

First, let's review what happens with a normal Point C. If a Point A up is made earlier in the day, you have a long bias. Now, should the market later reverse, trading down through the opening range all the way to the Point C, you would shift to a short bias. Taking a short position at Point C, your stop, if the market reversed, would be Point D—right above the top of the opening range.

Conversely, if the market makes an A down earlier in the day, you have a short bias. Should the market then reverse and trade higher, through the opening range all the way to Point C on the upside, your bias would shift to long. If you went long at Point C, your stop would be Point D, in this case below the bottom of the opening range.

Now let's add in the pivot range. If the market, for example, makes an A down early in the day, then rallies strongly later on—through the opening range and through the pivot range to make a Point C on the upside—you have double the reason to go long at this point. Not only did you make a Point C, but you made a *Point C through the pivot.* This convergence of bullish indicators dramatically increases your confidence and your trade size potential. Further, you minimize the risk by placing your stop just below the bottom of the pivot range, instead of the usual Point D below the bottom of the opening range.

Here's a hypothetical example. In Figure 3.6, Stock XYZ has an opening range of 55.00 to 55.30 and a daily pivot range, based

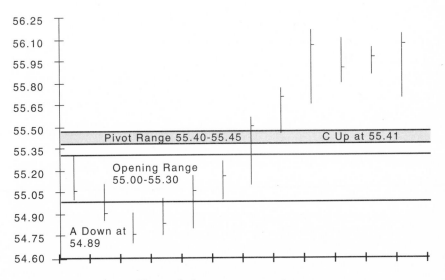

Figure 3.6   Point C pivot trade up.

on the prior day's activity, of 55.40 to 55.45. Early in the day, the market trades lower, making an A down (11 cents below the bottom of the opening range) of 54.88. Now, the market rallies strongly, it trades back through the opening range at 55.00 to 55.30—at which your bias shifts from bearish to neutral—and trades high enough to make a Point C on the upside (11 cents above the top of the opening range) at 55.41. At this point, your bias shifts to bullish.

More importantly, Point C is right in the middle of the pivot range, which extends up to 55.45. As the market moves steadily higher and trades above the upper end of the pivot range, your bullish sentiment becomes stronger. You establish a long position at or above 55.45 based on two concurrent indicators: the Point C and the pivot range resistance that was easily breached. This is a scenario in which to increase your trade size. At the same time, your stop on this trade would be below the bottom of the pivot range—or in this case 55.40—instead of the usual Point D below the bottom of the opening range of 55.00.

A Point C through the pivot on the upside increases your conviction for a long position, with a protective stop to minimize your risk at the bottom of the pivot range.

Looking at the opposite scenario, in Figure 3.7, Stock XYZ has an opening range of 55.00 to 55.30 and a daily pivot range of 54.80 to 54.85. The market trades steadily higher and makes an A up at 55.41 (11 cents above the top of the opening range), at which point your bias is bullish.

Later in the day, however, the market begins to sell off steadily. The selling pressure intensifies, the market then trades through the opening range, at which point your bias shifts to neutral, to make a Point C down at 54.89 (11 cents below the bottom of the opening range). At that point your bias is bearish, and your sights are on the pivot range just below at 54.80 to 54.85. As the market continues to trade lower, this pivot range support level is easily broken. Your conviction to take a short position at this price level is increased, along with your trade size. Your risk is minimized by putting your protective stop

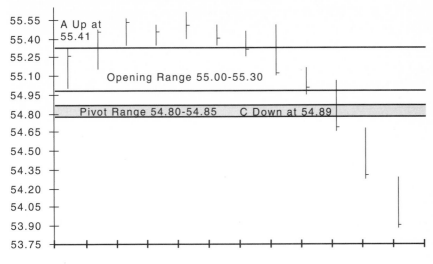

Figure 3.7   Point C pivot trade down.

above the top of the pivot range, in this case 54.85, instead of at the usual Point D, which would be above the top of the opening range at 55.30.

A Point C through the pivot on the downside increases your conviction for a short position, with a protective stop to minimize your risk just above the top of the pivot range.

Late-Day Point C Pivot

There is a variation on this scenario that, when it occurs, not only increases your conviction and your trade size, it gives you the confidence to carry your position overnight for what is likely to be a very profitable trade. This is called the *late-day Point C pivot trade.*

In this scenario, the market behaves just as it did with a regular Point C pivot trade. An A up or down is made earlier, and then a reversal to a Point C that is within or near the pivot range. Once the Point C is made and the market trades through the pivot range, you have a profitable scenario for this reversal trade.

Now, what if the Point C pivot occurs late in the trading day? First of all, a reversal of this magnitude—enough to move the market not only to Point C but through the pivot range as well—usually means one thing. The general sentiment of the market was wrong. The vast majority of traders and speculators were short early in the day. When the rally ensued, they were trapped and panicked out of short positions by buying at whatever price they could get. That buying action propelled the market higher all the way through the Point C and the pivot.

When you have a late-day Point C pivot, what is occurring is the majority of players are caught on the wrong side of the market—they're short when the market rallies or long when it breaks. Because it's late in the day, there is a limited time frame in which to exit the market. For example, let's say a broker in a trading pit is given an order at 11 A.M. to buy 5,000 futures contracts. He has the rest of the session—three or four hours—to execute them at what he sees as the best prices. But what happens if he's given that order to buy 5,000 contracts and it's three minutes before the close? He's going to be frantic as he tries to fill that order. Given the short time frame, he's going to be far less efficient in filling that order than he normally would be. Thus, it's not humanly possible in most instances to execute 5,000 contracts in the three minutes remaining in a session—particularly if the market is rallying or breaking sharply. I like to compare this to the disaster scenario of somebody yelling "Fire!" in a crowded movie theater and 200 patrons trying to rush out the door at once.

In trading, this kind of panic to cover positions results in some leftover orders that still need to be filled the next day. For one thing, there are the orders that couldn't be filled in the last minutes of the session. Then there are the undisciplined traders who need the overnight period to assess how wrong they really are. They're still short in a market that rallied to the close. But the next morning, they're going to have to bite the bullet to get out, buying at the opening. Put that together, and you can assume that, after a late-day Point C pivot trade, there is going to be a gap open in the direction of the trade (the rally or the break) the next morning.

Remember, Point C pivot scenarios develop when people are wrong and caught on the wrong side of the market. But the Point C pivot allows you to identify that they are wrong before they know what's happening. It's an early warning signal that there is going to be a strong reversal—in one direction or the other—as people bail out of their position. Only you're there ahead of them. You've already established a long position before they bail out of their shorts, bidding the market up strongly. Or, you're already short before they dump their long positions, selling aggressively.

That is why, when this kind of panicky, late-day Point C trade scenario develops, you have a low-risk high-probability trade to carry overnight. Your setup occurs as the Point C through the pivot is made late in the day. Your position—short or long—is carried overnight with the anticipation of a strong gap opening in the direction of the trade. Thus, if you're short, you'd expect a gap opening lower as aggressive selling to exit long positions pressured the market. If you're long, you'd expect a gap opening higher as aggressive buying to exit short positions bolstered the market.

In the late-day Point C pivot trade scenario, you only go home with a position if the market closes above the pivot and above the Point C.

Pivot First Hour High/Low

The last pivot we're going to discuss in this chapter is a short-term trading concept called the *pivot first hour highs and lows.* When it comes to trading, the one thing that everybody wants to know is when there is going to be a trend day, steadily in one direction or the other. For short-term trading only, the first hour highs and lows give you an early indication of trending days.

For this to happen, several criteria must be met, regarding the Point As and the daily pivot range, which of course is established based upon the previous day's trading activity.

- The daily pivot range must engulf the high or the low made in the first hour.
- At the end of the first hour, the market must have made an A up or an A down.

- Further, at the end of the first hour, the market must be within 15 percent of one of the price extremes (the high or the low) set thus far for the trading day.
- If these criteria are met, it's a probable sign of a trending day.

Here's an example of a setup for a first hour pivot high or low. Let's say the first hour's range for crude oil futures is 25.10 to 25.60. The daily pivot range, based on the previous day, is 25.05 to 25.15—engulfing the first hour low of 25.10. With an opening range of 25.15 to 25.30, the market makes an A up within the first hour at 25.38.

Now, at the close of the first hour, the market is at 25.56. That price is within 15 percent of the extremes of the first hour. In other words, it's trading near the edge of the high at 25.60.

In this scenario, with the market making an A up at 25.38, you would have a long position/bias. But now, with a pivot first hour low, you would increase your long position at 25.56 in anticipation of an upward trending day. Your stop would be placed at 25.38, the A up. Or, use a time stop equivalent to twice the opening range duration. In other words, if the market doesn't go in the direction you anticipate in that time frame, exit the trade.

With a pivot first hour high/low, look for an A up or an A down to be made in the first hour, and for the market to close the first hour within 15 percent of the extremes of the day thus far.

As always, everything is symmetrical. Looking at the opposite scenario, let's say the first hour's range for crude oil futures is 25.00 to 25.35. The pivot range is 25.30 to 25.40, which engulfs the high of the first hour. Based on an opening range of 25.15 to 25.25, the market makes an A down (assuming an 8 tick A down value) within the first hour of 25.07. At the end of the first hour, the market is at 25.03. This is a pivot first hour high and a sure sign of a trend lower. If you went short at the A down, you would increase your short position at the end of the first hour since the price was within 15 percent of the low. To review, let's take a look at some possible scenarios to see if you can pick out those that represent a pivot first hour high/low.

Scenario 1

- Natural gas futures have a first-hour range with a 4.00 low and a 4.06 high.
- The opening range is 4.015 to 4.03.
- Assuming an A up value of 0.02 ticks, the market makes an A up within the first hour at 4.05.
- The pivot range is 4.01 to 4.015.
- At the end of the first hour, the market is trading at 4.055.

Is this a pivot first hour low? Let's take a look at the criteria. The market did make an A up in the first hour and it did end the first hour within the 15 percent of the extremes, in this case just 1 tick below the high. But what about the pivot range? The pivot range was 4.01 to 4.015. The low, however, was below that pivot range at 4.00. Since the low was not made within the pivot range, this is not a pivot first hour low.

Scenario 2

- Crude oil futures has a first-hour range of 24.50 to 25.10.
- The opening range is 24.95 to 25.05. Assuming an 8-tick A down value, the market makes an A down at 24.87.
- The daily pivot range is 24.90 to 25.20.
- The market closes the first hour at 24.55

Given this scenario, was a pivot first hour high made?
    Let's look at the setup. An A down was made in the first hour. The high of the first hour (25.10) is encompassed within the pivot range (24.90 to 25.20). The market closed at 24.55, within 15 percent of the low for the day. Thus, this is a pivot first hour high and an indication of a trending day.

Scenario 3

- Crude oil futures have a first-hour range of 27.10 to 28.20.
- The opening range is 27.16 to 27.22. Assuming an 8-tick A value, it makes an A up at 27.30.
- The pivot range is 27.09 to 27.11.
- At the end of the first hour, it is trading at 28.00.

Given this setup was a pivot first hour low made?

Once again, let's examine each of the criteria. An A up was made in the first hour. The low of the first hour (27.10) is encompassed in the pivot range of 27.09 to 27.11. The market closed the first hour at 28.00, within 15 percent of the high at 28.20. This is a pivot first low and an indication of a trending day. Also notice that the first-hour range is relatively large. Going back to the theory discussed in Chapter 2 of an unusually small pivot range (a very narrow 27.09 to 27.11), this would be the setup for a day with a wide trading range.

The Treacherous Trade

As we discuss pivot concepts, there is one potentially treacherous trade that I'll discuss here, but with a caveat of caution. This is the failed C against the pivot. This occurs if the market has been exceptionally volatile, with wide swings between the Point A and the Point C. It's a very difficult trade to make, because you know the market is volatile and can easily move against you. Here's the setup.

Let's say the market makes a good A up and with this strong move upward everybody gets long. Now, later in the day, the market really crashes. The market goes through the opening range, past the Point B where you would become neutral, all the way toward Point C. This Point C target is also where the daily pivot is. But instead of making a good Point C through the pivot, the market just touches that area or snaps back a few ticks away. Now you have a failed Point C against the pivot.

There is a chance to fade this move, getting long as the market bounces off the Point C against the pivot. But if you do, this is an instant gratification scenario. In other words, take your profit quickly, because the market could very easily reverse and go the other way.

System-Failure Trade

This brings us to the next trading topic, the *system-failure trade*. This trade should be made when markets are nonvolatile and choppy. For example, trading stocks from January 2001 through July 2001 provided an excellent opportunity to employ this strategy. What you'll observe happening in these choppy market conditions is that, while the good Point As and Point Cs are being made, the market then reverses and you're stopped out of these trades. Thus, when the market is choppy—meaning erratic with no clear direction—you do not want to make a trade based on, for example, a good A up through the pivot. Why? Because in a choppy market you know there is probably not enough momentum in the direction of that ACD trade. Rather, the market is likely to reverse and go the other way.

So what do you do? In this scenario, you would wait until the market fails above the A up and then trades back below the pivot. At this point you would want to get short just below the bottom of the pivot range. What you are doing, in effect, is getting short at the same point where you would have been stopped out had you taken the good A up through the pivot trade. Conversely, if the market fails below an A down through the pivot, you would get long when the market traded back through the pivot range to the upside. Your entry point would then be just above the top of the pivot range, the point at which you would have been stopped out on the A down through the pivot trade.

A word of caution: These are risky trades because you do not have a defined point of reference for your stop. Therefore, you need to be very cautious in your execution. Look for immediate gratification and take your profits quickly.

Putting It Together

As you can see, once you understand the premise behind each of the indicators in the ACD system—the Points A and C, the pivot ranges, the pivot first hour high/low, and so forth—you can check the market's activity against this criteria. The market either matches up with the scenarios, or it doesn't. If certain events occur—for example, if the market makes an A up through the pivot or if it meets the criteria for a pivot first hour high/low—then you can draw certain conclusions and trade accordingly. If the market activity does not pan out, then there is no trade for that day. The beauty of the overall ACD system is its simplicity; one layer added upon another. In other words, it follows a logical progression.

To conclude this chapter, I want to share with you some notable trades that clearly show the principles that I've discussed thus far. I assure you that these trade scenarios are real.

The first is, in my mind, an example of the all-time late-day Point C pivot trade. Remember, in this scenario a dramatic market reversal up to a Point C occurs late in the day. When this happens, you go home with a position—long or short—in anticipation of a gap open the next day in the direction of your trade.

There was a certain crude oil broker in the trading pit at the New York Mercantile Exchange, who was (and still is) a friend of mine. We'll call him Grease. He was a major crude oil broker for the world's largest oil-trading firm, and he dealt in some major volume.

On this particular Wednesday, August 1, 1990, the crude oil futures opening range was 20.95 to 21.05. The daily pivot, based on the previous day's action, was 21.20 to 21.26. Soon after the opening, the market went straight down to 20.78, and in the process made an A down at 20.87.

At this point—just based on the A down and the scenario thus far—you'd think that my bias would have been bearish. But there were two factors that I knew: 30 trading days before had been a plus day. What does that mean? The market on that day opened below the pivot range but closed above it. On this particular day the market had already opened below the pivot range. So I knew there was a good chance of a late-day rally that would push this market upward through the pivot range with a settlement above it. And also, the 30-day cumulative number line (which we will discuss in depth in Chapter 4) was losing a bearish value, and any kind of bullish value for this particular day was going to suggest a bullish bias going forward.

On Wednesday afternoon, about one hour before the close, the market started to rally, higher and higher. I could feel what was going on. It was going to be a plus day with a trade through the pivot and a settlement above it. Anticipating that, after inhaling my nutritional lunch of two Pepsis and four Yodels, I went into the pit and put on a large long position at 21.15 to 21.25. My broker-friend Grease, I knew, was short from 21.10. In the trading pit, you can observe other people's trading activity as they make their bids and offers in open outcry, which is literally an open auction forum. Based on this, I knew the price level from which Grease was short. And I also knew that a strong rally had not only taken place—it was going to steamroll ahead!

Five minutes later, this market was through the pivot range at 21.20 to 21.26, and above it 21.30. Now, going back to the basics of ACD, with an A down already made and an opening range of 20.95 to 21.05, where would the C up be made? In those days, C values were about 16 to 18 ticks, so using 17 that would make Point C for a reversal in sentiment at 21.22—right within the pivot range.

Here was the once-in-a-blue-moon late-day Point C pivot trade setup. I had already anticipated that this would happen, which is why I went long near the top of the opening range. Now, with Point C made through the pivot, I knew we were going significantly higher!

Point C pivot scenarios occur when the marketplace is wrong, and traders have to bail out at any price. The panicky short-covering pushed this market from 21.30 directly to 21.60 in the last 10 to 15 minutes of the day. The market settled at 21.55.

Now, to be truthful, the long position that I was carrying at this point was huge. I was really carrying far more contracts than I should. In the emotion of the day and knowing that it was a late-day Point C pivot, I got a little carried away. To put it in perspective, I probably bought a total of 500 to 600 contracts, and maybe sold about 200 along the way.

Looking at my position after the close, I decided I had better liquidate some of these. So I turned to my friend, Grease, whom I knew from his trading actions was massively short, and said to him, "I'm selling 50 contracts. Do you want them?" Let's just say that my friend told me in no uncertain terms that he didn't want them.

Okay, fine, I said to myself. He had his chance. I'll carry the entire position into the next day. So at the end of that trading day, and going into Thursday morning, I was carrying a long position of some 400 contracts for what I anticipate to be a huge gap open higher. (After all, it was a late-day Point C pivot trade.)

Then, at 2 A.M. Thursday morning, the phone rang. It sounded like Grease on the line.

"Do you still want to sell me those 50 lots?" I heard Grease's voice saying to me.

Too groggy from sleep to really comprehend this, I hung up the phone.

A little later, I was awake enough to wonder, did Grease really call me? Was I dreaming—or maybe it was a nightmare? But it was 3 A.M. in the morning by this time. I couldn't call him and say, so, do you want to buy 50 contracts?

Fully awake at this point, I went downstairs for a snack in the kitchen. I sat at the table and turned on the television set in the kitchen. Iraq had just invaded Kuwait! Crude oil prices on the overseas market were already $2.00 higher!

When I established my long position in crude oil from 21.15–21.25, I didn't know anything about Iraq and Kuwait. I had traded solely on the basis of the ACD system. We made an A down, but the market was starting to rally. I knew that 30 trading days before had been a plus day, meaning a close above the pivot. Based on those factors, I knew the risk was small and the reward was potentially big to get long. Then when the market made a late-day Point C pivot, I knew that a long position held until the next trading day (in this case Thursday morning) was highly likely to be profitable.

Needless to say, come Thursday morning, crude oil prices were significantly higher, and there I was, long from 21.15 to 21.25. As for Grease, well, being short from 21.10 wasn't such a good position. But I had offered to sell him 50 at the close on Wednesday of 21.55!

That, to me, was the ultimate Point C pivot trade. Remember, it's like the fire in the movie theater scenario. Everybody has to rush out through one door. There is going to be panic. In market terms, that panic is going to translate into a strong move in one direction—whether it is upward as short positions are covered or downward as buyers bail out of their long positions.

And when that panic happens late in the day, you know there are still going to be traders, like my friend Grease, who are trapped and need to get out of the market at the opening of the next session.

Here's another example of a Point C trade. In this case in the heating oil futures market on December 29, 1989, it was the last trading day of the year and the market was closing early at 1 P.M. Eastern time. On that day, the January heating oil futures contract was expiring. Because of those factors—the last day of the year and a shortened session at that, and contract expiration—many traders were cautious about actively trading this market. This was largely due to delivery concerns. Remember, with a contract such as heating oil, if you aren't flat—meaning neither short nor long—at expiration, you are in a position to either take delivery of heating oil or to make delivery of heating oil. In either case, as a speculative trader, it is not a position that you want to be in.

The opening range for January heating oil was 0.9700 to 0.9750. Now, keep in mind that heating oil was trading in 25-point increments in those days, and every penny in the price of one heating oil contract was worth a total of $420. It was also important to note that, at this time, the highest that heating oil futures had ever traded up to was about 1.02. And to further embellish the story, because this was the last trading day of the year, and we are talking about heating oil—a commodity that impacts both industries and consumers—there were about 10 people from the Commodity Futures Trading Commission (CFTC), the U.S. regulatory body for futures trading, and from the exchange's compliance department standing around the pit. They were watching the trading activity just to make sure everything was orderly.

After the market opened, it dropped to 0.9350 and made an A down in the process. But later in the day—and remember December 29 has an early close—heating oil started to rally. It went through the opening range of 0.9700 to 0.9750 and kept on going. It rallied all the way to 0.9875, approaching the Point C at 0.9950. Then sold off, which initially looked like an opportunity to fade a Point C up. But then the market began to rally again.

I bought 27 January heating oil futures contracts at 0.9950 to establish a long position. Then came the final half-hour of trading.

This is when a broker in the heating oil pit started asking, "Where's January heating oil?" We'll call him OHNO. (That is not his real badge name, but for this story "Oh, no" is definitely appropriate.)

Heating oil was bid at 0.9950, then 1.00, and then Phibro, a major commodity trading brokerage house, bid 1.02—the all-time contract high price. The market kept going to 1.03 and then 1.04. OHNO began bidding, trying to buy 200 contracts.

The minute I saw his eyes, I could see the panic. He had to buy and this was a market that was roaring higher. The price rose to 1.06 and then at 1.10 OHNO was filled on only three contracts—but he had something like 197 more to buy!

OHNO was bidding strongly at 1.15, and then 1.20, at which he was filled on another five lots. The ring reporter, who worked for the exchange recording price transactions in the pit, was nearly out of his mind, trying to keep track of this frantic activity. The Nymex price podium posted 1.02 as the price, even though OHNO was already bidding 1.20 and getting filled at that price.

OHNO bid 1.30, and then higher still. At 1.50 I sold him my 27 contracts—a 51 percent gain from my entry price of 0.9950. In 10 minutes, with the market completely in my favor based on the Point C pivot trade, I was up about $570,000.

You can't imagine the pandemonium in the trading pit! The CFTC was there. The president of the exchange, Pat Thompson, was there. The head of surveillance was there. It was a mad scene. Meanwhile, the price reporting at the exchange was lagging the activity, and I was trying to make sure that my trade to sell 27 contracts to OHNO at 1.50 was good.

In the end, the exchange made an executive decision. Even though there were trades reportedly made as high as 1.60, the exchange deemed that the highest price was 1.10. I couldn't believe it. I had legitimately sold to OHNO at 40 cents higher than that at 1.50.

"Pat," I told the president of the exchange, "this decision is really costing me. You're taking money out of my pocket!"

"That's the decision of the exchange," Pat told me.

I decided that I wasn't going to adjust my price on the trade with OHNO to 1.10 from 1.50. Rather, I decided to stay long the 27 heating oil contracts, taking them to delivery if necessary.

Then, the market was closed—not only for the day but for the year. Still angry, I went back to my office, upstairs at the exchange. A little while later, Pat Thompson and other top officials from the exchange, including the head of compliance and the head of operations, paid me a visit. "We need to talk with you," they told me.

To make a long story short, the exchange urged me to sell OHNO the 27 contracts at 1.10. "This is for the betterment of the exchange," they told me. "We need you to sell him the 27 contracts." (I soon learned that the exchange could not find another seller to fill OHNO's order.)

Altruism aside, doing that for the betterment of the exchange was going to reduce my profit by about $450,000!

"Let me be clear on this," I told them finally. "I'm taking the exchange out of a $450,000 error."

An investigation ensued into the heating oil trade activity on that day. In my interview with the exchange's compliance department, I was asked pointedly about my decision, as a major local or independent trader, to be active in the pit on the last trading day of the year—when so many others were cautious about being aggressive. And yet there I was, buying at 0.9950 and hanging on through an aggressive round of bidding in the final minutes, not only of the trading day but the final day of the year!

Why, they wanted to know. Why did I make that trade?

Easy. It was a good Point C pivot trade!

Now, in all fairness, I have to finish the story. At the start of the New Year, January heating oil was off the board, expired. February was the new contract month. It opened on the first day of trading at 0.8500. So it was a good thing I wasn't still long from 0.9950. In the end, the decision to sell at 1.10 was good for me—and good for the exchange.

Chapter 4

MACRO ACD

In Chapter 1 we discussed the concept of micro ACD, namely, how to plot Point As and Point Cs based on the opening range of a given day. But what does a good A up or a Point C down mean in a larger context? We know that in the microview, an A down is where you'd have a short position/bias and an A up is where you'd have a long position/bias. After the trading day is done, however, what do all those Point As and Cs mean? That's the macro ACD concept.

Simply put, macro ACD looks at 30 trading days in a continuum, based upon what happens on each day—for example, whether an A up was made, a C down was made and so forth. Each day is given a value, anywhere from −4 to +4 depending upon what occurred.

Each day is given a value based on what occurred on that day, such as whether an A up or an A down was made, whether or not a C up/down was made, and where the market settled.

Figures 4.1 through 4.26 depict examples of market activity and possible scenarios, each of which is assigned a particular value.

The market confirmed an **A UP** on the 4th 20-minute bar of the day, from that point until the close, the market never traded below the opening range, and closed above the opening range, giving this day a **Number Line Value = + 2**

A Value: 15 ticks
A Up: 4165 (9:58)
Opening Range: 4085-4150 (9:30-9:50)
Close: 4330 (3:10)

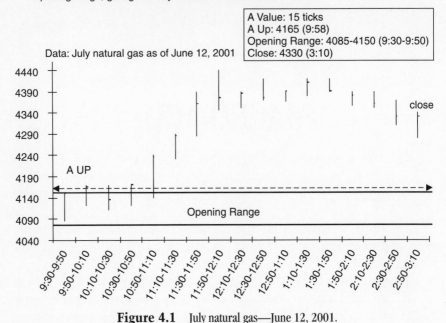

Figure 4.1   July natural gas—June 12, 2001.

The market made an **A DOWN** on the 2nd 20-minute bar of the day, from that point until the close the market never traded above the opening range, and it **closed below the opening range**, giving this day a *Number Line Value = - 2*

A Value: 25 ticks
A Down: 7415 (10:25)
Opening Range: 7440-7580 (9:50-10:10)
Close: 7065 (3:10)

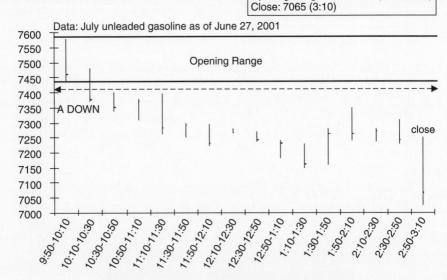

Figure 4.2   July unleaded gasoline—June 27, 2001.

The market made an **A UP** on the 3rd 15-minute bar of the day, however, it failed to close above the opening range, giving this day a **Number Line Value = 0**

A Value: 17.5 ticks
A Up: 1832.5 (10:10)
Opening Range: 1799-1815 (9:30-9:45)
Close: 1801(4:15)

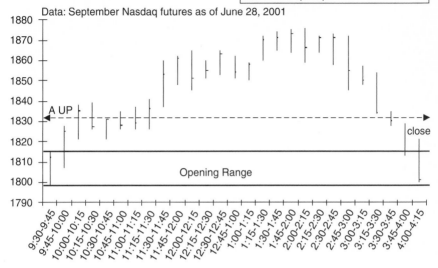

Figure 4.3 September Nasdaq futures—June 28, 2001.

The market made an **A DOWN** on the 3rd 20-minute bar of the day, however, it failed to **close below the opening range**, giving this day a **Number Line Value = 0**

A Value: 33 cemts
A Down: 45.52 (10:15)
Opening Range: 45.85-46.09 (9:30-9:50)
Close: 45.94 (4:00)

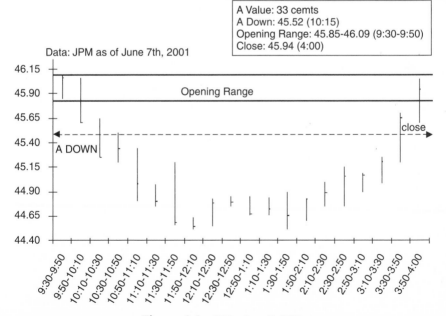

Figure 4.4 JPM—June 7, 2001.

85

The market trades on either side of the opening range never making an **A UP or DOWN,** on the last bar of the day the market makes an **A UP** and **closes above the A UP value,** giving this day a *Number Line Value = + 2*

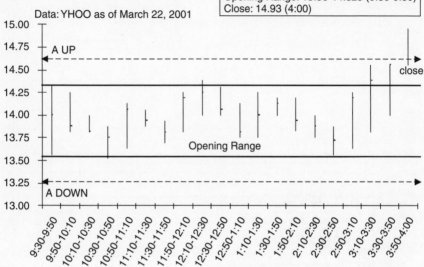

A Value: 27 cemts
A Up: 14.595 (3:52) A Down: 13.29
Opening Range: 13.56-14.325 (9:30-9:50)
Close: 14.93 (4:00)

Data: YHOO as of March 22, 2001

Figure 4.5 YHOO—March 22, 2001.

The market trades on either side of the opening range, never making an **A UP or DOWN,** on the 3rd-to-last bar of the day, the market made an **A DOWN** and **closes below the A DOWN value,** giving this day a *Number Line Value = - 2*

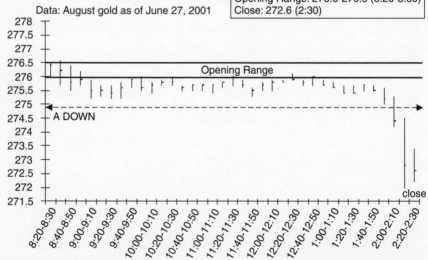

A Value: 1.20
A Down: 274.8 (2:07)
Opening Range: 276.0-276.5 (8:20-8:30)
Close: 272.6 (2:30)

Data: August gold as of June 27, 2001

Figure 4.6 August gold—June 27, 2001.

The market made an **A DOWN** at the 11:30 am bar, on the 2nd-to-last bar of the trading day (12:30 pm), it trades above the opening range and makes a **C UP**, it then **closes above the opening range,** giving this day a *Number Line Value = + 4*

A Value: 4 ticks
C Value: 13 ticks
C Up: 922 (12:48) A Down: 899 (11:42)
Opening Range: 903-909 (9:30-10:00)
Close: 958 (1:20)

Data: July sugar as of June 29, 2001

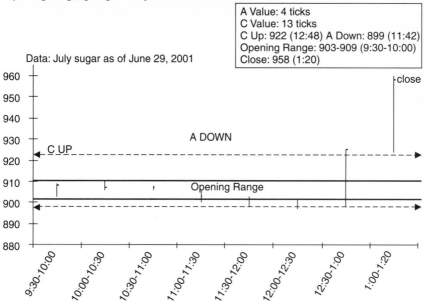

Figure 4.7   July sugar—June 29, 2001.

The market confirms an **A UP** on the 4th 20-minute bar of the day, **on the last bar of the trading day,** it trades below the opening range and makes a **C DOWN**, giving this day a *Number Line Value = - 4*

A & C Values: $1.25
A Up: 96.75 (11:41) C Down: 90.25 (12:24)
Opening Range: 91.50-95.50 (9:30-9:50)
Close: 88.56 (4:00)

Data: GLW as of October 18, 2000

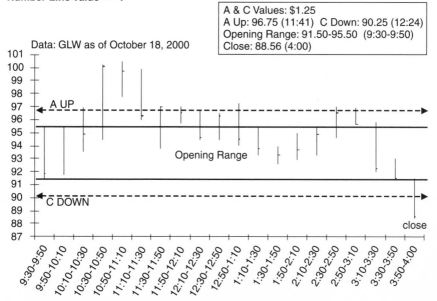

Figure 4.8   GLW—October 18, 2000.

87

The market made an **A DOWN** on the 2nd 20-minute bar of the day, then at the 3:30 pm bar it made a **C UP**, it then **closes above the opening range,** giving this day a *Number Line Value = + 4*

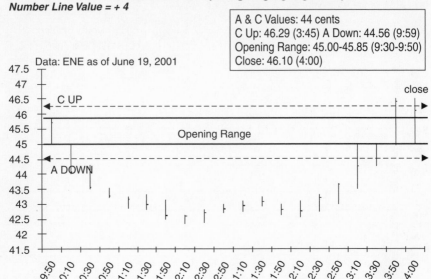

A & C Values: 44 cents
C Up: 46.29 (3:45) A Down: 44.56 (9:59)
Opening Range: 45.00-45.85 (9:30-9:50)
Close: 46.10 (4:00)

Figure 4.9   ENE—June 19, 2001.

The market made an **A UP** on the 2nd 20-minute bar of the day, at the 1:30 pm bar it trades below the opening range and subsequently makes a **C DOWN** at the 1:50 pm bar, it then **closes below the opening range,** giving this day a *Number Line Value =- 4*

A Value: 25 ticks C Value: 85 ticks
A Up: 9805 (10:19) C Down: 9615 (1:59)
Opening Range: 9700-9780 (9:30-9:50)
Close: 9555 (3:10)

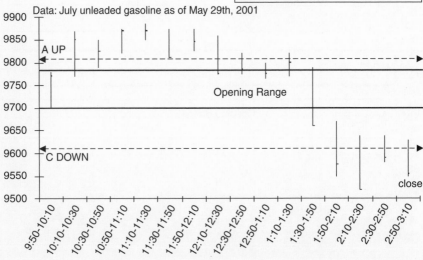

Figure 4.10   July unleaded gas—May 29, 2001.

88

The market made an **A UP** on the 2nd 20-minute bar of the day, at the 2:50 pm bar it trades below the opening range and makes a **C DOWN**, then it **closes back in the opening range,** giving this day a *Number Line Value = 0*

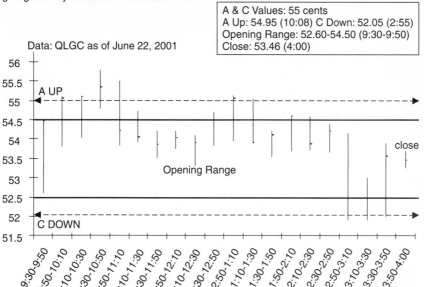

Data: QLGC as of June 22, 2001

A & C Values: 55 cents
A Up: 54.95 (10:08) C Down: 52.05 (2:55)
Opening Range: 52.60-54.50 (9:30-9:50)
Close: 53.46 (4:00)

Figure 4.11   QLGC—June 22, 2001.

The market made an **A DOWN** at the 11:50 am bar, at the 3:10 pm bar it trades above the opening range and also makes a **C UP**, it then **closes back in the opening range,** giving this day a *Number Line Value = 0*

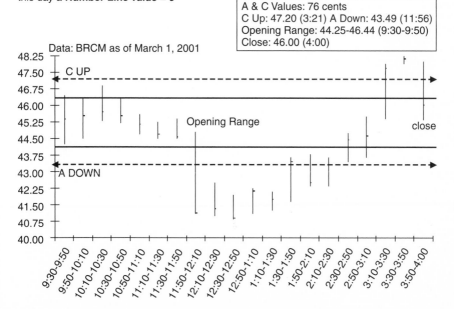

Data: BRCM as of March 1, 2001

A & C Values: 76 cents
C Up: 47.20 (3:21) A Down: 43.49 (11:56)
Opening Range: 44.25-46.44 (9:30-9:50)
Close: 46.00 (4:00)

Figure 4.12   BRCM—March 1, 2001.

The market made an **A UP** on the 2nd 5-minute bar of the day, at the 11:50 am bar it makes a **C DOWN,** and the 1:50 pm bar trades **above the opening range,** giving this day a *Number Line Value = 0*

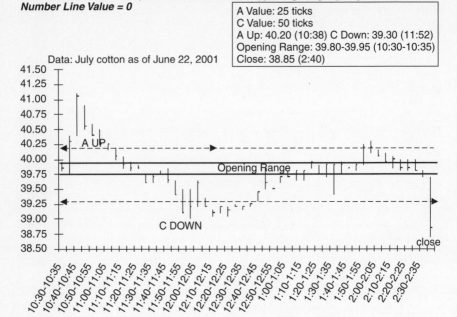

A Value: 25 ticks
C Value: 50 ticks
A Up: 40.20 (10:38) C Down: 39.30 (11:52)
Opening Range: 39.80-39.95 (10:30-10:35)
Close: 38.85 (2:40)

Data: July cotton as of June 22, 2001

Figure 4.13   July cotton—June 22, 2001.

The market made an **A DOWN** on the 3rd 20-minute bar of the day, at the 12:15 pm bar it makes a **C UP**, the 2:30 pm bar trades **below the opening range,** giving this day a *Number Line Value = 0*

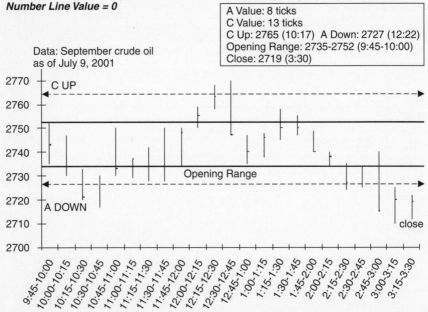

A Value: 8 ticks
C Value: 13 ticks
C Up: 2765 (10:17) A Down: 2727 (12:22)
Opening Range: 2735-2752 (9:45-10:00)
Close: 2719 (3:30)

Data: September crude oil
as of July 9, 2001

Figure 4.14   September crude oil—July 9, 2001.

90

The market confirmed an **A UP** on the 3rd 15-minute bar of the day, at the 1:30 pm bar it trades below the opening range & attempts to make a **C DOWN**, the attempt fails due to the limited time price traded at the "C" price level, the market **closes in the opening range,** giving this day a **_Number Line Value = + 3_**

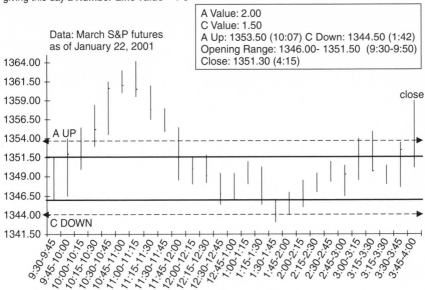

Figure 4.15   March S&P futures—January 22, 2001.

The market made an **A DOWN** on the 2nd 20-minute bar of the day, at the 1:50 pm bar it attempts to make a **C UP** but fails based on the inability of price to trade above the "C" price level, then the market **closes back in the opening range,** giving this day a **_Number Line Value = - 3_**

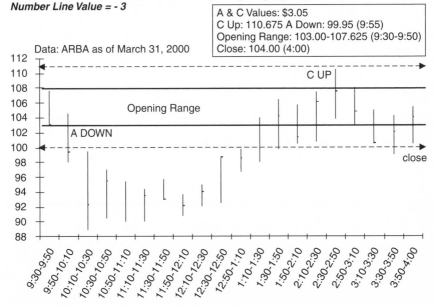

Figure 4.16   ARBA—March 31, 2000.

The market attempts to make an **A UP** on the 6th 20-minute bar of the day, however it **FAILS** due to the inability of price to trade above the A price level, subsequently, at the 1:50 pm bar, price makes an **A DOWN**, the market **closes below the opening range,** giving this day a *Number Line Value = - 3*

A Value: 47 cents
A Up: 73.12 A Down: 71.21 (10:30)
Opening Range: 71.68-72.65 (9:30-9:50)
Close: 96

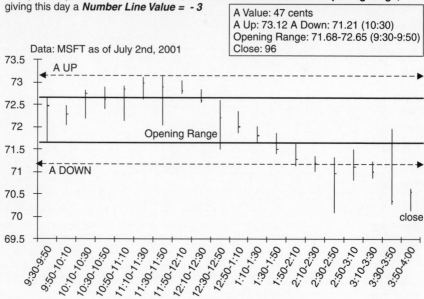

Data: MSFT as of July 2nd, 2001

Figure 4.17   MSFT—July 2, 2001.

The market attempts to make an **A DOWN** on the 4th 20-minute bar of the day, however it **FAILS** based on the limited time spent trading at the A price level, the 2:10 pm bar makes an **A UP**, then the market **closes above the opening range**, giving this day a *Number Line Value = +3*

A Value: 1.79
A Up: 122.353 (2:11) A Down: 113.523 (10:46)
Opening Range: 115.313-120.563 (9:30-9:50)
Close: 127.25 (4:00)

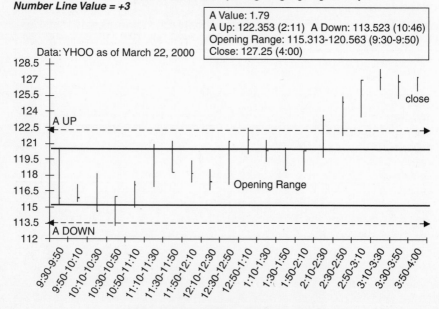

Data: YHOO as of March 22, 2000

Figure 4.18   YHOO—March 22, 2000.

92

The market attempts to make an **A UP** on the 3rd 20-minute bar of the day, however it **FAILS** based on the limited time spent trading at the **A UP** price level, at the 11:10 am bar, it made an **A DOWN**, the market **closes in the opening range,** giving this day a *Number Line Value = - 1*

A Value: 14 ticks
A Up: 22.22 (11:17) A Down: 21.73
Opening Range: 21.87-22.08 (9:30-9:50)
Close: 21.99 (4:00)

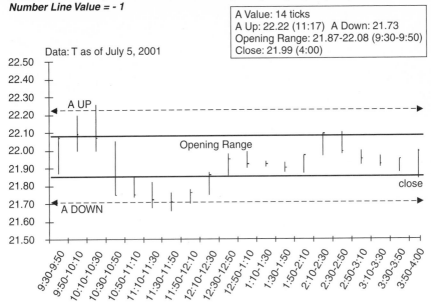

Figure 4.19   T—July 5, 2001.

The market attempts to make an **A Down** on the 11:30 am bar of the day, however, it **FAILS** due to the limited time spent trading at the **A Down** price level, the 1:50 pm bar price trades above the opening range and makes an **A Up**, then the market **closes in the opening range,** giving this day a *Number Line Value = + 1*

A Value: 26 ticks
A Up: 21.71 (1:56) A Down: 20.54
Opening Range: 20.80-21.45 (9:30-9:50)
Close: 21.28 (4:00)

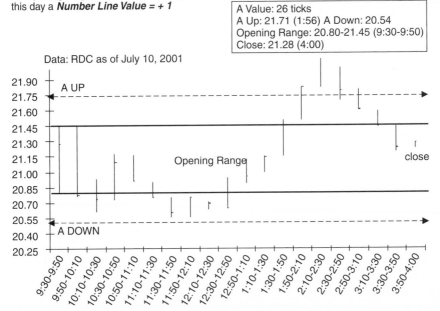

Figure 4.20   RDC—July 10, 2001.

93

The market attempts to make an **A UP** on the 4th 20-minute bar of the day, however it **FAILS** based on the inability of price to trade above the A price level, from that point until the close, price never trades down to the A price level, and the market **closes below the opening range,** giving this day a *Number Line Value = - 1*

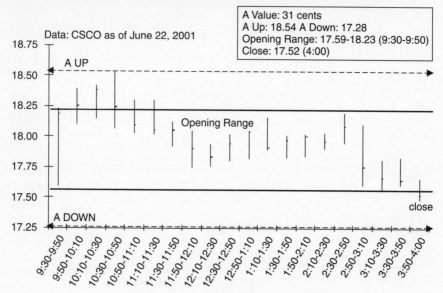

A Value: 31 cents
A Up: 18.54 A Down: 17.28
Opening Range: 17.59-18.23 (9:30-9:50)
Close: 17.52 (4:00)

Data: CSCO as of June 22, 2001

Figure 4.21   CSCO—June 22, 2001.

The market attempts to make an **A DOWN** on the 11:50 am bar of the day, however, it **FAILS** due to the limited time spent trading at the **A Down** price level, from that point until the market close price never trades to the **A UP** and **closes in or above the opening range,** giving this day a *Number Line Value = + 1*

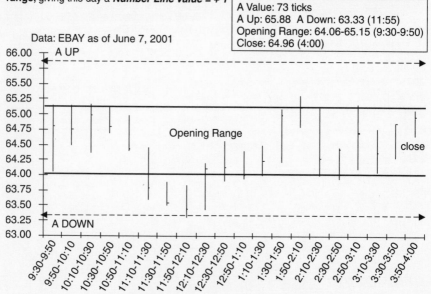

A Value: 73 ticks
A Up: 65.88 A Down: 63.33 (11:55)
Opening Range: 64.06-65.15 (9:30-9:50)
Close: 64.96 (4:00)

Data: EBAY as of June 7, 2001

Figure 4.22   EBAY—June 7, 2001.

The market attempts to make an **A UP** at the 10:55 bar, however it **FAILS** due to the limited time spent trading at the A price level, at the 11:55 am bar the price trades below the opening range and attempts to make an **A DOWN**, which also **FAILS** due to the limited time spent trading at the A price level, the market **closes in the opening range,** giving this day a *Number Line Value = 0*

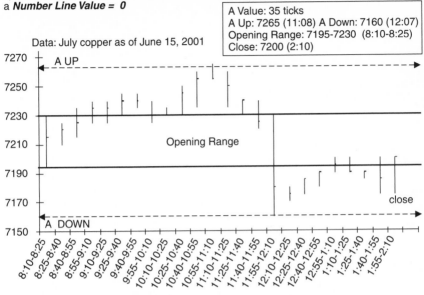

Data: July copper as of June 15, 2001

A Value: 35 ticks
A Up: 7265 (11:08) A Down: 7160 (12:07)
Opening Range: 7195-7230 (8:10-8:25)
Close: 7200 (2:10)

Figure 4.23   July copper—June 15, 2001.

The market attempts to make an **A DOWN** on the 4th 20-minute bar of the day, however it **FAILS** based on the limited time spent trading at the **A DOWN** price level, at the 12:20 pm bar, the market attempted an **A UP** but failed due to the limited time spent trading at the **A UP** price level, the market then **closes in the opening range,** giving this day a *Number Line Value = 0*

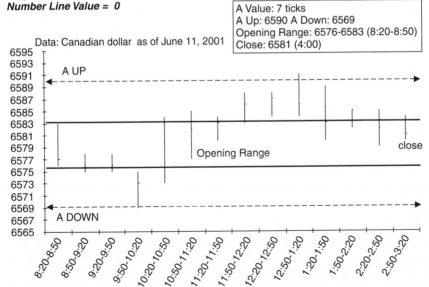

Data: Canadian dollar as of June 11, 2001

A Value: 7 ticks
A Up: 6590 A Down: 6569
Opening Range: 6576-6583 (8:20-8:50)
Close: 6581 (4:00)

Figure 4.24   Canadian dollar—June 11, 2001.

95

The market made an **A UP** at the 11:30 bar, at the 12:10 pm bar it trades below the opening range & attempts to make a **C DOWN**, but the attempt fails due to the limited time price traded at the C down level, and the market **closed above the opening range,** giving this day a *Number Line Value = + 2*

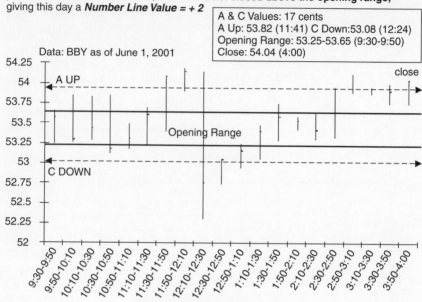

A & C Values: 17 cents
A Up: 53.82 (11:41) C Down:53.08 (12:24)
Opening Range: 53.25-53.65 (9:30-9:50)
Close: 54.04 (4:00)

Data: BBY as of June 1, 2001

Figure 4.25   BBY—June 1, 2001.

The market made an **A DOWN** on the 7th 20-minute bar of the day, at the 1:30 pm bar it trades above the opening range & attempts to make a **C UP**, the attempt fails due to the limited time price traded above the C price level, the market **closes below the opening range,** giving this day a *Number Line Value = - 2*

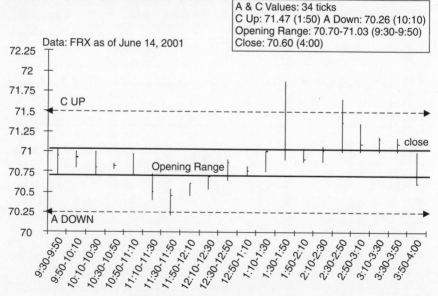

A & C Values: 34 ticks
C Up: 71.47 (1:50) A Down: 70.26 (10:10)
Opening Range: 70.70-71.03 (9:30-9:50)
Close: 70.60 (4:00)

Data: FRX as of June 14, 2001

Figure 4.26   FRX—June 14, 2001.

96

Once you have assessed the values for several trading days in a row, you can begin a number line that reflects the activity of the past 30 trading days. (Remember, the time frame is 30 trading days—not calendar days—with holidays and weekends excluded. And even if the market is open for only a half day, such as before a major holiday, that's still considered a trading day.) The 30-trading-day tally is a cumulative one. On the thirty-first day, when you add the value of the latest day, you eliminate the value of the earliest one.

The main purpose of the number line is to identify a potentially developing trend. That generally occurs when the cumulative tally of the past 30 trading days has gone from 0 to greater or equal to $+/- 9$, a level it must maintain for two consecutive trading days. (As with any part of the ACD system, this applies to both equities and commodities.) The cumulative sum of $+/- 9$ is important because we have found that when the sum of the values of the previous 30 trading days is greater than or equal to $+/- 9$ (on two consecutive trading days) it becomes statistically significant, especially in light of the fact that the number line had started out at 0. In other words, reaching the sum of $+/- 9$ is not the only important element. The fact that the market reached this level, coming from a cumulative sum of 0 over the course of several trading days, is the other critical criteria.

When the 30-trading-day cumulative tally goes from a base of 0 to reach $+/- 9$ on two consecutive trading days, it becomes statistically significant.

Let's take this step by step. First of all, this is a running total of 30 trading days. So, let's say that at the end of the 30 trading days the number line is $+5$ (taking into account all the $+1$s, -1s, $+2$s, -2s, etc.). On the thirty-first trading day, you would not only add the value of the current day to the sum, you would also eliminate the oldest value in the running 30-trading-day tally. Let's say on this particular day the market made an A up. As you can see in the previous figure examples, that's a value of $+2$. Also, let's say that you are eliminating a -2. That's a net change of $+4$. (Eliminating a -2 and adding a $+2$.) Now your cumulative

30-trading-day value on the number line is +9. On the subsequent trading day if the 30-trading-day sum is +9 or greater, then that becomes a statistically significant event to be applied to your trading strategy.

The macro ACD number line concept is a useful indicator for both long-term system traders as well as day-traders. First of all, as I discussed in Chapter 1, the ACD system relies on volatility. In other words, the market has to have sufficient movement, up and down, in order for the A ups and A downs to be profitable. Thus, when the market moves sufficiently above the opening range to make an A up, you establish a long position/bias. When it goes below the opening range to make an A down, you establish a short position/bias. Day by day, the ACD points help you to plot where you'd be long or short.

But what about the broader context? How can you tell what the overall trend is? When is the trend confirmed and when is it reversing? That's how the macro ACD number line can help you. To illustrate, say you were away from the market for three trading days. All you'd have to do is review the market action by looking at the macro ACD values for those days. For example, if you see that crude oil futures (or whatever market you're tracking) had values over those three trading days of +2, 0, and +2, what would you immediately know? You'd see that the market had an A up day (+2), a neutral day (0), and then another A up day (+2). In a broader context, though, these two A up days with a neutral day in between tell you something else: You've had bullish signals on two out of three days and the other day was neutral. Now, you know that heading into the current trading day there is a supportive ACD bias to the market.

Let's assume now that the values of the past three trading days were −3, −2, and then +2. Looking at each trading day individually, you'd see that you had a failed A up and then an A down on one day (−3), an A down on the second day (−2), and then an A up on the third day (+2). In a broader context, you have three sell signals in the first two days—the failed A up and then the A down on the first day and an another A down on the second day. The third day, however, produced a bullish signal. This mix of signals would tell you that, on the next day, there is no suggested ACD bias entering that day's trade.

Examining the values of the past few trading days reveals a bullish, bearish, or neutral ACD bias for the subsequent trading day.

As I mentioned briefly in this opening of this chapter, we have found over the years that when the cumulative value over the past 30 trading days is +/− 9 on two consecutive trading days, the market is likely to have significant momentum in one direction or the other. In fact, there are several significant points at which the market, on a 30-trading-day cumulative basis, likely will see a major move: when the number line reaches −9, 0, or +9. These points are where the market reaches a kind of critical mass at which it's likely to have significant price action. Conversely, when the market is not at one of these critical mass points (such as between 0 and +/− 9) you can determine that the market has a ways to go before making a major breakout.

When the cumulative value over 30 trading days goes from 0 to +/− 9 on two consecutive trading days, the market is likely to experience a significant increase in volatility. For options traders, this projected increase in volatility can assist them in developing their trading strategies. Further, the +/− 9 number line value alerts the trader that a significant trend should be developing. However, keep in mind that this development must occur in conjunction with what I call the *instant gratification rule*. The market movement you're looking for must develop quickly or the signal is invalid, and then there would be a potential for a system-failure trade.

Generally when the market breaks the +/− 9 threshold, it should experience an immediate movement in the direction of that number line value (to the downside if the cumulative value is −9 and the upside if it is a +9). By immediately, I mean within two or three trading sessions. This is in keeping with a similar concept discussed in Chapter 1 that time is more important to a successful trade than price. Remember, if a trade takes too long to develop, it allows the retail bus people to get on board at the same price level you have entered the trade at. How good could this trade really be? As you recall, in Chapter 1 a good A up or A down was made only when the market spent sufficient time at certain price level, but if it languished there, the signal was invalid. Here too, with the macro ACD number line, if after the +/− 9 threshold is reached and with a second consecutive +/− 9 value, if the expected price action doesn't develop soon thereafter, there is a good possibility a system-failure trade has been set up.

Here's an analogy that may help to explain this concept of time and opportunity. As any football fan knows, when the running back is trying for a touchdown, he's looking for that momentary window of opportunity. He's looking for a hole in the defense that will give him a clear shot to make a touchdown. That hole, if it exists, is going to be there for only a split second. If the running back hesitates or if his path is blocked, that hole, or opportunity, won't be there. But if the running back breaks through the hole, then he knows he has a straight shot toward a touchdown.

It's the same concept with the macro ACD trade. What you're looking for is that opening in the market (like the hole in the defensive line), confirmed by two consecutive days at +/− 9. When that occurs, it should theoretically be a touchdown trading opportunity. Similarly, if the macro ACD signal is valid, the market should take off like the running back headed for the goal line. But if the market hesitates or languishes where it is, that opportunity won't stay there. The hole in the defensive line has closed up.

That's what I mean by instant gratification. If the market is going to go in the direction of the macro ACD number line signal, you should know immediately, or at the most within two or three trading sessions. If it's not successful, then look for the system-failure trade.

For the macro ACD signal to be valid, the market must make a move in the anticipated direction immediately—at least within two or three trading sessions.

For long-term traders, the number line serves an additional purpose; it is an excellent indicator for when to participate in the market and when not to. Let's say the cumulative, 30-trading-day number line has been bouncing like a pinball over the past

10 trading days between −4 and +4, as one A up is made and then is eliminated by a new A down. This back and forth, directionless trade is not conducive to a longer-term trading strategy. When the 30-day number line is vacillating on both sides of zero, it's time to stay out of longer-term trades. While there may be some intraday trading opportunities with a +2 day (when an A up is made) or a −2 day (when an A down is made), the market does not have a sustained trend in one direction or the other. In fact, when the 30-trading-day number line is between −9 and +9, you can usually expect a choppy market.

Also for day-traders, the number line purpose discussed above can help you recognize system failures as well as opportunities to fade ACD signals. An opportunity to fade ACD signals occurs when the market keeps challenging that statistically significant area of +/− 9, but a second day confirmation never occurs. Let's say the 30-day sum is +7 one day, +9 the next, and then +7, followed by +8, +9, and then +7 again. In this instance, as a day-trader you would treat this scenario as an opportunity to fade intraday signals until the cumulative, 30-trading-day tally produces two consecutive days at +/− 9.

Remember, too, a system failure occurs if the instant gratification rule is violated. If after two consecutive number line days at +/− 9, the market does not move in the direction you anticipate within two or three trading sessions, then you know that a system failure is developing. If that's the case, you would look to exit the position suggested by the macro ACD signal and potentially find a spot to reverse your position to fade this false breakout.

The macro ACD number line serves several purposes, including helping long-term traders to identify choppy markets, to assist options traders to identify increases in volatility, and to enable day-traders to take advantage of opportunities to fade ACD signals and to recognize system failure trades.

System failures and opportunities to fade aside, remember that the main purpose of the macro ACD number line is to show you where there is the potential for a trend to develop. And the most important opportunities for a trend to develop are when the number line has moved from a base of 0 to +/− 9. At this critical threshold, you look for the confirmation. For example, if the 30-trading-day number line has reached +9, you would need that cumulative sum on a second day to be at least +9 or better. If on the second day the number line is at +10, then you have your confirmation. If the cumulative tally slips to +7 on the subsequent day, then there is no confirmation (and as I explained previously, you'd be on the lookout for a potential system-failure trade.)

Even of more significance than the occurrence of two consequent days at +/− 9 is the time between these events. To illustrate, let's say a commodity had two consecutive +9 days in January, and then the 30-day number line reset to zero in February, and then there were two consecutive +9 days again in March. While notable, this kind of pattern—two confirmed +9 events occurring two months apart—would not be as significant as occurrences that are less frequent. In other words, a more significant event would be two consecutive +/− 9 days occurring in March for the first time since the previous September. A market event may be significant in and of itself, but it becomes even more important if it happens infrequently in a market.

The infrequency of significant market events—such as two consecutive +/− 9 days coming from a 0—underscores their importance. These opportunities are what I call once-in-a-blue-moon trades, such as I experienced in the August 1990 crude oil futures market, which I shared in Chapter 3.

Since the macro ACD number line takes into consideration previous market action (which is known) as well as today's action, it becomes helpful in planning and executing the trades you make today. For example, let's say that the cumulative, 30-trading-day value was +9 at the close of the market yesterday. What's your first assumption? You will look for confirmation of an uptrend developing with another +9, or if that does not occur, you will be on the lookout for a system-failure trade.

Now, going into today you know that the value of the day you are going to eliminate on the 30-trading-day number line was a +1. What does that mean? Automatically—even before today's trading begins—the number line is now a +8 (the previous day's tally of +9 minus the +1 value from the day you are eliminating). Starting at a +8, you know that in order to maintain a cumulative, 30-trading-day sum of +9 (and thus confirm the potential for the development of an uptrend) today's trade activity would have to result in a value of at least a +1.

Let's say that today the market makes an A up, which carries a value of +2 and brings the cumulative, 30-day-trading tally to +10. Since the previous day's tally was +9, this confirms the potential for an uptrend to begin. Now, you have identified a low-risk high-probability trading opportunity.

Since an A up has already been made (+2), the only thing that could lower the sum on the day is if the market were to close below the opening range (which would carry a value of 0). Thus your price risk for this trade is only below the opening range. Any market action above the opening range is in your favor.

Based on this scenario, you would be looking for an opportunity to increase your trading position (maximize size) since market conditions have already minimized your risk. Thus, if you typically traded five futures contracts on a day-trading basis, you would look to increase both size and trade duration. Instead, you would look to add to your position as long as the trade stayed in your favor, perhaps up to 10 futures contracts. Then, at the end of the day, with the market still above the opening range, you would not exit the entire 10-contract position. Rather, you'd hold a few of those contracts overnight in anticipation that a significant uptrend is developing.

When the market confirms a +/− 9 value on the macro ACD number line, traders should consider increasing their trade size, as well as carrying a position overnight in anticipation of a continued move in the direction of the trade.

At this point, let's take a look at a real-world example of how the 30-trading-day number line can be used for a longer-term perspective and managing a trading position. In Table 4.1, you can see the coffee futures market from January through June 1997,

TABLE 4.1

Coffee number line

Date		# Line #	Settlement	Date		# Line #	Settlement
Jan	2	−6	11665	March	7	8	18980
Jan	3	−6	11625	March	10	14	19930
Jan	6	−6	11405	March	11	11	20315
Jan	7	−4	11935	March	12	7	19610
Jan	8	−2	11890	March	13	5	18225
Jan	9	0	11935	March	14	11	18635
Jan	10	0	11960	March	17	9	16865
Jan	13	5	11845	March	18	5	16880
Jan	14	7	12220	March	19	5	16810
Jan	15	7	12260	March	20	9	16915
Jan	16	9	12305	March	21	4	16575
Jan	**17**	**10**	**12400**	March	24	5	16290
Jan	**20**	**10**	**12925**	March	25	5	17930
Jan	21	9	12965	March	26	7	18685
Jan	22	10	13530	March	27	5	18980
Jan	23	9	14005	**March**	**31**	**3**	**19115**
Jan	24	7	13690	April	1	8	19430
Jan	27	9	13660	April	2	8	19315
Jan	28	5	13950	April	3	4	17770
Jan	29	9	14480	April	4	10	17915
Jan	30	9	14030	April	7	14	17940
Jan	31	17	13940	April	8	14	17875
Feb	3	18	14565	April	9	14	18970
Feb	4	20	14745	April	10	12	19105
Feb	5	16	14455	April	11	10	18910
Feb	6	17	15080	April	14	11	19600
Feb	7	15	15105	April	15	6	17465
Feb	10	14	15865	April	16	4	18530
Feb	11	15	16355	April	17	5	18750
Feb	12	17	17185	April	18	9	19415
Feb	13	19	18005	April	21	7	19405
Feb	14	18	17785	April	22	1	18835
Feb	18	18	15725	April	23	3	19340
Feb	19	18	16630	April	24	9	19820
Feb	20	16	16640	April	25	11	19325
Feb	21	14	16185	April	28	10	19640
Feb	24	14	16165	April	29	14	19895
Feb	25	15	16325	April	30	17	21040
Feb	26	15	17285	May	1	20	22290
Feb	27	13	17110	May	2	16	21615
Feb	28	13	17685	May	5	20	21850
March	3	15	18485	May	6	16	21285
March	4	14	19525	May	7	12	21140
March	5	13	20065	May	8	12	21690
March	6	8	19370	May	9	12	21790

Continued

TABLE 4.1 *(Continued)*

Coffee number line

Date		# Line #	Settlement	Date		# Line #	Settlement
May	12	14	22965	May	30	18	27640
May	13	12	24115	June	2	14	25395
May	14	12	24060	June	3	18	26420
May	15	16	25520	June	4	19	25155
May	16	14	25315	June	5	15	23050
May	19	10	24625	June	6	13	23725
May	20	8	24025	June	9	15	25330
May	21	8	25310	June	10	10	21795
May	22	10	26030	June	11	6	20765
May	23	14	25685	June	12	1	19240
May	27	13	27430	June	13	-3	18275
May	28	18	29555	June	16	0	18160
May	29	20	31480	June	17	0	19070

which shows the settlement price and the daily value for each day. As you look at the chart, you'll see that on January 16, the cumulative, 30-trading-day sum reached +9 for the first time. This would have been the initial tip-off of an upward trend developing. But before you could be sure of that, the market would have to prove itself by sustaining at least a +9 level the next day.

January 17, the day being eliminated from the 30-trading-day sum, had a value of −1. That would bring the 30-trading-day number line to +10. Thus, as a longer-term system trader who follows the number line concept, you would look for the market to maintain that level. For example, if the market on that day, January 17, had an A down (with a value of −2), then the trend would not be confirmed. For confirmation of the uptrend, January 17 would have to be either a neutral day (value of 0) or produce a value of +1 or a +2 on the upside, and no more than a −1 on the downside. In other words, if the value on January 17 was no weaker than −1, this would be the signal to establish a long position. As it turned out, the cumulative, 30-trading-day sum advanced to +10 on January 17, and the upward trend was confirmed.

As you're about to see, this information would also benefit the short-term day-trader as well as the long-term position trader. The next trading day, January 20, the trading day being eliminated from the 30-trading-day tally was a +3. That would bring the market back down to a +7. The long-term system trader would have remained in the market with a position established on the close at January 17. But the day-trader would be looking for a good A up (for a value of +2) on January 20.

On January 20, coffee futures opened at unchanged from the previous day at 124.00. At the time, the A value was 100 ticks. (For a list of current A values, see the Appendix.) That would make an A up target at 125.00 and an A down at 123.00.

On January 20, the opening range was 123.35 to 124.00. The low was 123.35. The high was 129.50. The settlement was 129.25. Based on this data, you can see that the market did, indeed, make an A up (at 125.00) and settled above the opening range and near the high of the day. Based on this information what do you think the daily value for January 20 was? If you said +2, you're right!

Now, as a day-trader, you know that +2 value will bring the cumulative, 30-trading-day tally to +9. With this kind of scenario, as a five-contract coffee futures day-trader, you wouldn't sell all your contracts at the end of the day. Rather, you would stay long a couple of contracts going into the next day, especially since you have positive open trade equity in the trade.

Also, to review, with this scenario on January 20, what was your risk as a day-trader to get into this trade? Once you made the A up, your risk was only the penetration of the bottom of the opening range, which for one coffee contract (based on the January 20, 1997 price) was a risk of $619 per one-lot contract. On that day alone with a 129.25 settlement you already netted a profit of $1,600 on one contract!

For a longer-term perspective, take a look at what happened to coffee futures from the end of January through March. Coffee futures began a substantial, unprecedented move higher, from the January 20 close of 129.25 to over 200.00 in March, and settling on March 31 at 191.15. Over those two months, the day-trader experienced good intraday volatility, with plenty of good A ups being made to capture profits on a short-term basis.

Meanwhile, the longer-term system trader, who had established a long position on January 17, should technically have stayed in that position until the cumulative, 30-trading-day number line crosses below 0 for two consecutive days. Or, to manage the trade, the trader might decide to exit the position when he or she saw a sharp, rapid decline in the number line value. For example, on May 29, the number line value was at +20 and the price was 314.80. At this point, the long-term system trader, with a one-contract position established on January 17, would have a profit of $72,000! The day-trader, meanwhile, should have realized a profit of about $125,000 to $130,000 on just the two contracts carried since January 20—in addition to whatever day-trading profits made since then.

Going back to the chart, you can see that the 30-trading-day number line value of +20 was the highest of the six-month period. But within eight trading days, the number line value declined significantly, falling below +9 to a 30-trading-day sum of +6 on June 11. At this point, an experienced, longer-term macro ACD trader would be looking to lock in profits based on the negative activity of the number line. Remember, I said earlier that when the number line moves from 0 to +/− 9, it is significant. In the same vein, it is also significant when the number line moves in the other direction, especially when it is rapidly losing value.

In this example, we see that on June 2, the 30-trading-day number line is at +14. In itself this is not that significant. But take into consideration the fact that, just two trading days before on May 29, the number line had been at 20. Now what gets your attention is the fact that the macro ACD number line has decreased significantly—from 20 to 14—within three trading days. For an experienced long-term macro ACD trader, that would be your signal to exit at least part of your trade and ring the register.

Logical Trader: Midterm

In the past four chapters, you've learned some key concepts in the ACD system including defining Point As and Point Cs, calculating pivots and pivot ranges, assigning a value to the market, and using the macro ACD number line. Now it's time for the review. This midterm is designed not only to assess what you've learned thus far (and don't worry, you're the only one who will know your score) but to reinforce the concepts discussed in the first four chapters.

Write the answers to the following questions on a separate piece of paper. The correct answers appear at the end of this chapter.

Questions

1. The market confirms an A signal. What is the stop signal?
2. The D signal is placed at the opposite side of the opening range as the _____ signal.
3. The C signal established the opposite bias of the _____ signal.
4. Which period or bar on the chart is the most statistically significant for ACD valuation?
5. To find the opening range on a chart, you would identify which bar?
6. Every trade needs a point of reference. What does this mean?
7. What is the macro ACD number line value for a good A down?
8. What is the macro ACD number line value for a good C up?
9. In the ACD system, the D point is the stop for what ACD point?
10. In the ACD system, values are used to calculate Point As and Point Cs. What is the main value difference between stocks and commodities?
11. If natural gas futures have an opening range of 4345 to 4360, a pivot of 4405 to 4430, and a settlement of 4490, what type of day is it?
12. Which two weeks during the first half of the year are considered statistically significant?
13. In a given day, a market has a failed A up and a failed A down. What is its macro ACD number line value for the day?
14. Define a minus day according to the ACD system.

15. Half the duration of the opening range time frame is used to confirm what?
16. What range is considered the meat of the market?
17. You establish a long position on a good A up through the pivot. Where would you place your stop?
18. A failed A up into the daily pivot would be considered a _____-risk trade.
19. A pivot first-hour high or low trade requires the market to close the first-hour within what percentage of the extremes of the first-hour range?
20. A failed C against the pivot is called the _____ trade.
21. How many trading days are utilized to value the cumulative macro ACD number line?
22. If the macro ACD 30-day cumulative tally goes from a base of 0 to reach $+/-$ 9 on two consecutive trading days, it becomes statistically _____.
23. What type of market can the macro ACD number line help long-term traders avoid participating in?
24. The ACD trading methodology can be applied to any commodity, stock, or currency, as long as there is sufficient _____ and liquidity.
25. Trading, as in life, requires you to have a _____.

Once you have successfully answered the first 25 questions, try the following:

1. If there is no B signal, then there cannot be a _____ signal.
2. The market trades at or above the A up for 50 seconds. The opening range time frame is 15 minutes. Is this a good A up or a failed A up?
3. Which is a better trade according to the ACD system: a failed A down or a good C up through the pivot?
4. Calculate the pivot and the pivot range based on the following information: high of 29.00, low of 28.15, settle of 28.65.
5. In one day of trading, a market has a good A up followed by a failed C down. What is its macro ACD number line value?
6. A market has an A value of 15 ticks. The opening range is 35.00 to 35.20. The pivot range is 35.30 to 35.45. The low is 34.95, the high is 37.10, and the settle is 36.25. What type of day is it?

7. Which type of ACD trade traps traders who have losing positions and works best if it occurs closest to the market's close?
8. For a stock such as Vodaphone (VOD), which market should a trader use as the basis for the opening range?
9. If a trader establishes a position and the market doesn't move in the direction he wanted within 40 minutes, what should the trader do with the position?
10. Trading days that have a normal trading range and produce a very narrow daily pivot range for the following day, usually indicates a _____ price range for the following day.
11. The first trading day of the month would be considered an example of a significant _____.
12. In a late day Point C pivot trade scenario, you only go home with a position if the market closes above both the _____ and the _____.
13. When markets are choppy and nonvolatile, it is a good indication that it is time to look for system-_____ trades.
14. For the macro ACD signal to be valid, the market must move in the direction of the signal within _____ trading sessions.
15. The macro ACD number line goes from 0 to +9 and confirms the signal with a second consecutive +9 day. However, the _____ of this occurrence makes the signal even stronger.
16. If the macro ACD daily value is an odd number, what do you know must have occurred that day?
17. Explain the two ways to get a +3 macro ACD value.

Midterm Answer Key

1. B signal
2. B
3. A
4. Opening Range
5. First
6. Points of reference provide traders with price level at which to establish a short or long position/bias, and more importantly a low-risk stop.
7. −2
8. +4
9. Point C

10. For stocks, A and C values are the same. In commodities, the A and C values are different.
11. A plus day
12. The first two weeks of January
13. 0
14. The opening range is above the pivot range, which is above the close. Or, opening range > daily pivot range > close.
15. A "good" A up or A down (as opposed to a failed A).
16. The pivot range
17. Directly below the bottom of the pivot range.
18. Low
19. 15
20. Treacherous
21. 30
22. Significant
23. Choppy
24. Volatility
25. Game plan

Next 17 Questions:

1. Point C
2. Failed A up
3. Good C up through the pivot
4. Pivot = 28.60, pivot range 28.57 to 28.63
5. +3
6. Good A up through the pivot
7. Point C pivot trade
8. The primary domicile market, in this case London.
9. Liquidate the position
10. Large
11. Time frame
12. Point C and pivot range
13. Failure
14. two to three
15. infrequency
16. The market must have had an intraday failed signal.
17. Failed A down and a good A up; or, a failed C down that settles above the top of the opening range.

Chapter 5

PIVOT MOVING AVERAGES

Many trading systems take into account moving averages. The concept of a moving average is that it reflects the average price—on a rolling basis—of a particular stock or commodity over a period of time. For instance, the 200-day moving average is the average of prices for the previous 200 days; the 50-day moving average is the average for 50 days, and so forth. Or moving averages can be based on shorter time periods, from 5 minutes to 30 or 60 minutes. Since it's a moving average, when a new day (or the latest of whatever time frame you're using) is added, the oldest one is eliminated, and so the moving average progresses.

The problem I have with traditional moving averages, however, is that most are based on closing prices. Whether each time period measure is 5 ticks, five minutes, or a day, the price used is the close of that time period. To me, the close is an arbitrary point in time. Moreover, overnight trading, whether in stocks or in commodities, invalidates the concept of the close. I mean, if Stock X closes at 34 a share, but trades overnight up to 35, what is the significance of using 34 to calculate a moving average?

Rather, the moving averages I use are based upon the pivot for each particular day. As you'll recall from Chapter 4, the pivot is calculated based on the high, low, and close for a particular trading day. The resulting price reflects the meat of the market for that trading day. Thus, a moving average that is based upon pivots is far more meaningful and relevant than a moving average that is calculated on the close.

> **The pivot moving average is calculated using the pivots, or the meat of the market, for a certain number of days. This makes the pivot moving average a far more meaningful tool than a moving average that is based upon closing prices, which are arbitrary.**

The second thing about moving averages is that, unlike a lot of traders, I do not view them as a kind of barrier that must be crossed. The so-called conventional wisdom would say that if a stock were below its 50-day moving average it would be a bearish sign. Or, if once it crossed the 200-day moving average that would be a bullish indication. To me, that is not the best use of moving averages as an indicator, especially for a short-term trader.

Rather than focusing on a moving average as a kind of barrier, I look at the pivot moving average line, itself. In particular, what I'm looking for is the slope, or more specifically the change in slope, of that line. Why? Because a change in slope without a large price movement first occurring indicates that there is a change in perception in the market, which is very important.

> **Rather than focusing on the moving average as a barrier to be crossed, I look at the slope of the pivot moving average line. A change in slope is an important indication of a change in perception in the market.**

Think back to what you learned about lines and graphs when you were in school. The slope of a line represented a change in Y (one axis of the graph) over the change in X (the other axis of the graph). The relative changes against the X or Y axis would determine the slope of the line, steeper or flatter, up or down.

Now, apply this concept of slope to the pivot moving average. The points along the horizontal axis reflect time, whether measured in days or minutes. The change along the vertical axis reflects the magnitude of the increase or decrease in value. The greater the change in one direction, the steeper the slope. The smaller the change in one direction, the flatter the slope.

Say, for example, that the pivot on the first trading day is at 34.20, the next trading day it is 34.25 and the third trading day it is 34.30. That would make the pivot three-day moving average 34.25. On the fourth trading day, the pivot is 34.35. Adding the new pivot and eliminating the oldest pivot, you'd have a three-day moving average of 34.30. Now, let's assume that on the fifth trading day the pivot was 34.40. Once again, adding the new pivot and eliminating the oldest, you'd have a three-day moving average of 34.35.

Now you have three pivot moving averages to plot on a graph: 34.25, 34.30, and 34.35. Just by looking at the numbers in this simplified example, you can see that the three-day pivot moving average has steadily increased. When you plot these points on a graph, you get a line like the one shown in Figure 5.1.

The line formed by these three points has a particular slope, in this example it is steadily rising—a classic picture of a market trending upward. Now, let's carry this example forward. Let's assume that on the sixth trading day, the pivot is 34.35, which makes the three-day pivot moving average 34.37 (rounded). On

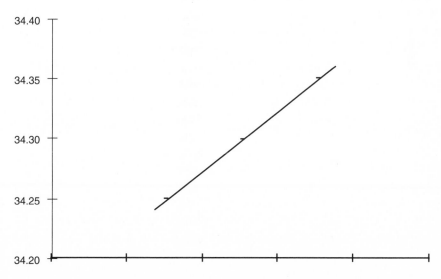

Figure 5.1   Pivot moving averages—increasing slope.

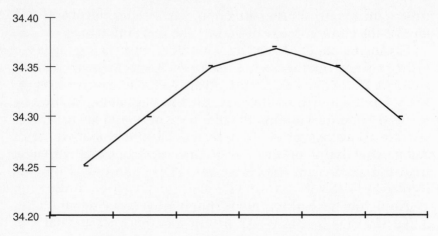

Figure 5.2   Pivot moving averages—change in slope.

the seventh trading day the pivot is 34.30, which makes the three-day pivot moving average 34.35, and on the eighth trading day the pivot is 34.25, making the three-day pivot moving average 34.30. Plotting these moving average numbers on a graph yields an entirely different line (see Figure 5.2).

Clearly, the line curves and begins to slope downward. What this shows you is that there has been a change in market perception. The pivot moving average line has changed from sloping upward to sloping downward, and now the market (as evidenced by the line) is in a downtrend. This simple example shows how the slope of a pivot moving average line can help you to determine the prevailing market trend, and also to determine when there is a shift in the market perception.

In the ACD system, we find that three useful pivot-moving averages to track are the 14-day, 30-day, and 50-day. (Or, on a shorter time frame, you can opt for the 14-bar, 30-bar, and 50-bar pivot moving averages, with each bar representing a certain number of minutes, such as 5, 10, or 30.) Just as you did in the example of the three-day pivot moving averages, the 14-day (or bar), 30-day (bar), and 50-day (bar) pivot moving averages are calculated on a rolling basis. This yields a picture of the market in terms of sentiment, from short-term (14-day/bar) to intermediate (30-day/bar) to long-term (50-day/bar). Using three moving averages, you are able to capture the consensus of opinion of three different time frames, rather than using only one moving average that is representative of just one time frame and one opinion. As in the earlier example, what you are looking for is the slope of these lines—upward, downward, or sideways with no slope at all. Remember, slope measures the rate of change: the steeper the slope, the faster the rate of change. In the case of the slope of the pivot moving average, what you are gauging is the rate of change of people's perception about the market. Thus, if a pivot moving average line shows an abrupt shift in slope, from upward to downward or vice versa, it's an indication that the market also has had a sudden shift in perception. If the slope of the pivot moving average goes from steep to a gradual incline to flat and then to gradually downward, it reflects a gradual shift in perception.

The slope of a line reflects the rate of change. The slope of a pivot moving average reflects the rate of change of perception about the market.

Your goal as a trader is to use the pivot moving average lines to determine the prevailing market sentiment and to detect when that shifts—before a major market move occurs.

One way of looking at the slope of pivot moving averages is to view them as a kind of consensus of opinion. When the pivot moving averages are all sloping in one direction—either upward or downward—the market has a clear trend in that direction. When the slope of the pivot moving averages begins to change—flattening out or shifting suddenly in the opposite direction—then there has been a shift in the overall market perception.

When the pivot moving average lines are moving in different directions—with one sloping upward, one flat, and one downward—then there is no consensus of opinion among the moving average lines. In other words, the market (at least viewed from the perspective of the pivot moving averages) is confused. There is no clear indication of a trend.

It is important to distinguish between moving averages that reflect a confused market versus a neutral market. As mentioned, in a *confused market* the moving average lines diverge (with one moving upward, one downward, and one sideways). In a neutral market, however, the lines are parallel to each other and flat. When the lines are flat, they could very easily turn from, say, neutral to bullish or neutral to bearish. In other words, in a neutral market there is an imminent opportunity for the market to enter a bullish or bearish phase once these parallel, flat lines turn upward or downward. In a confused market, they cannot go directly to bullish or bearish. Rather, the lines that diverge have to align themselves first, and then a trend will emerge as the lines slope in concert upward or downward.

The pivot moving averages are yet another indicator that you can use in conjunction with the ACD concepts that we've discussed in earlier chapters. These various indicators are like layers, one built upon the other, with the ACD concept as the foundation. Here's an example: Let's say the market makes an A up, which as you know from Chapter 1 would give you a bullish bias. The macro ACD number line is at +9, which as discussed in Chapter 4 would indicate that the market is likely to make a significant move. Add to that the fact that the pivot moving averages are sloped upward, which reflects a bullish sentiment. With three indicators moving in concert in this fashion, you would have confidence not only in the bullish signals generated on that day, but also in the potential for a significant move, which would be reflected by the slope of the moving average lines rapidly turning higher. Thus, you may decide to maximize your trade size when the indicators line up in one direction as shown in this example. Or, put another way, this is a time to step on the gas.

Now, let's say that the market has made an A up, which would indicate a bullish position/bias. The ACD number line, however, is at −2, which means it still has a ways to go before it reaches the target of +9 or −9. Meanwhile, the moving averages are sloping downward, which indicates a bearish perception. Given the conflict in these signals, you might not decide to take this trade. Or, you might want to fade the A up, given the fact that other indicators show a bearish to neutral sentiment. If you did decide to take the A up signal with a long position/bias, you would probably trade with a very small position because of a low level of confidence in this trade. In other words, this would be a scenario in which to ride the brake and not step on the gas.

Looking at another scenario, let's say the market is making an A down, which is a signal of a bearish position/bias. Now, let's say that the ACD number line set up is to reach −9. Moreover, the pivot moving average lines are all sloping downward. This is a case in which to hop on that train. You would want to make this trade with maximized size because of your high level of confidence in your chance for making a profit (see Figures 5.3a–h).

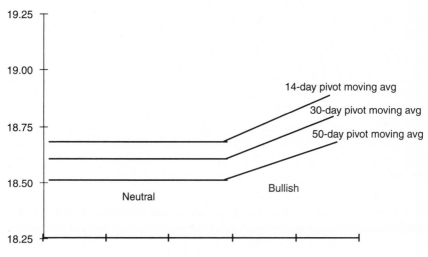

Figure 5.3a   Moving average slope—neutral to bullish.

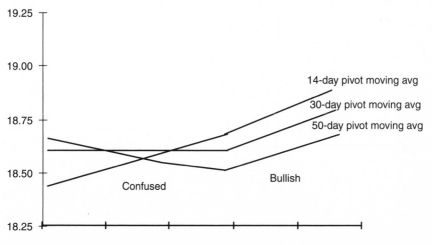

Figure 5.3b   Moving average slope—confused to bullish.

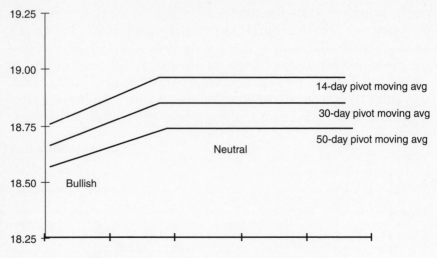

Figure 5.3c   Moving average slope—bullish to neutral.
You can go from bullish to neutral, and back to bullish.

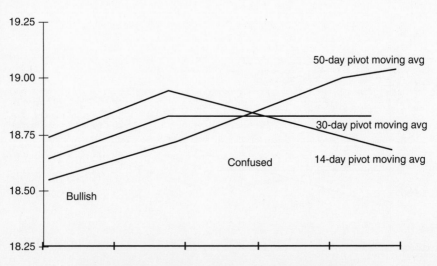

Figure 5.3d   Moving average slope—bullish to confused.

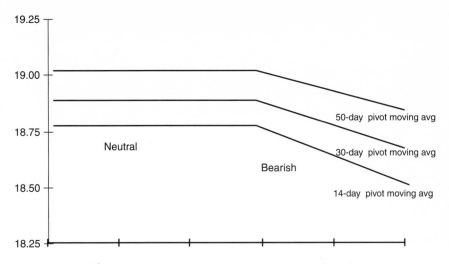

Figure 5.3e Moving average slope—neutral to bearish.

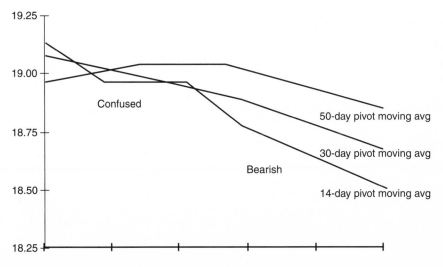

Figure 5.3f Moving average slope—confused to bearish.

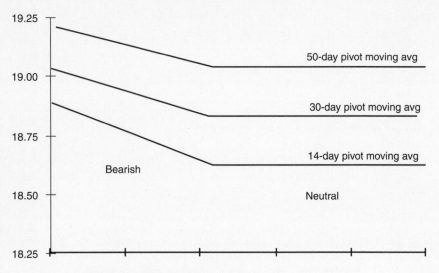

Figure 5.3g   Moving average slope—bearish to neutral.
You can go from bearish to neutral, and back to bearish.

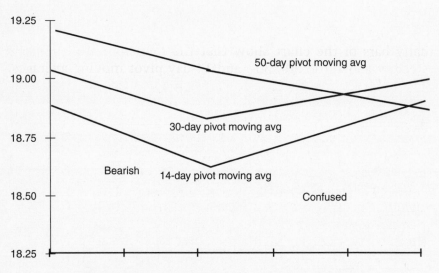

Figure 5.3h   Moving average slope—bearish to confused.

Moving Average Fake-Out

The second strategy using the pivot moving average is the *moving average fake-out* (MAF). To illustrate, look at Figure 5.4, with all three pivot moving average lines sloping upward. The

Data: Natural gas January 2000 contract – from October 5, 2000 until contract expiration December 27, 2000

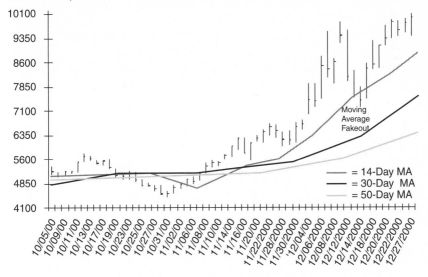

Figure 5.4 Moving average fakeout.

daily bars of the chart show that the market initially climbs steadily above the 50-, 30-, and 14-day pivot moving averages. Then the market dips downward, dropping below the 14-day moving average but remaining above the 30-day. (If the market crosses the 30-day pivot moving average line as well as the 14-day, there is no set up for the moving average fake-out trade.)

Now, even though the lines are sloping upward, you don't have a reason to get long. Rather, you'd wait for the market to bounce and head higher again, crossing the 14-day pivot moving average line. Once the market moves back over the 14-day line, you can resume a bullish bias/position, with the point of reference for this trade being the low of the downmove.

Conversely, assume the pivot moving average lines are sloping downward and the daily bars of the chart are also moving lower. Then the market moves higher and crosses above the 14-day pivot moving average (but does not cross the 30-day line). Even though the lines are still sloping downward, you don't have a reason to get short. Rather, you have to wait for the market to retrace back below the 14-day moving average for your position/bias to move clearly back to bearish. Your point of reference then becomes the high of this move.

As always, you must ask yourself where you'd get out if you were wrong. In this instance, your stop would be the pullback bar. If the market traded lower than the lowest bar of that move, you would exit your long position. Or, if the market traded higher than the highest bar of the up move, you would exit your short position.

In these moving average fake-out scenarios, however, it is important to remember the criteria for making these trades:

- The slope of all three lines is upward, or the slope of all three lines is downward.
- The market trades higher and then reverses, dipping below the 14-day moving average, or the market trades lower, then reverses, rising above the 14-day moving average.
- On the reversal, however, the market never crosses the 30-day pivot moving average. If the market falls below the 30-day pivot moving average (or rises above it in the downtrend), this fake-out scenario no longer applies.
- When the market crosses back over the 14-day moving average line in the direction of the trend, you can establish a position or bias.

Moving Average Divergence Trades

A lot of traders like to fade the market, meaning they pick a top to sell against or they pick a bottom at which to buy. A better strategy, however, would be to identify *moving average divergence* (MAD) patterns to help you to spot opportunities to fade a particular move.

The most important setup for the moving average divergence trade is that the three pivot moving average lines must be either neutral (flat, no slope) or confused (with one sloping upward, one downward, and one flat). In fact, it's best to use the moving average divergence trade when the pivot moving averages are confused. As discussed earlier, when the moving averages are neutral, they can move directly into a bullish or bearish slope. But when the moving average lines are confused, there is less opportunity for a trend to reestablish itself quickly.

The second requirement for a moving average divergence scenario is to have a point of reference (see Figures 5.5a–d). Furthermore, you should enter the trade using either a good or

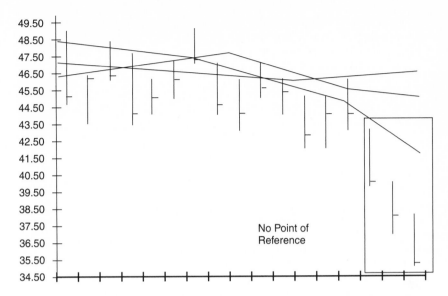

Figure 5.5a   Confused moving averages—no trade, no point of reference.

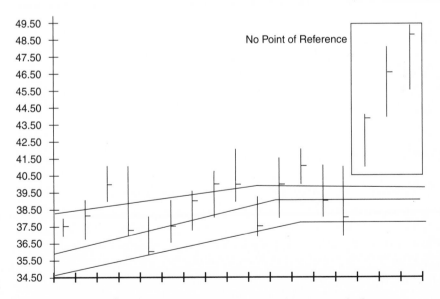

Figure 5.5b   Neutral moving averages—no trade, no point of reference.

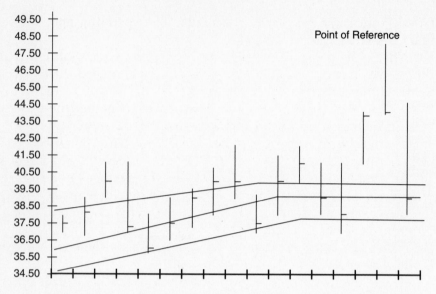

Figure 5.5c   Neutral moving averages—good trade with point of reference.

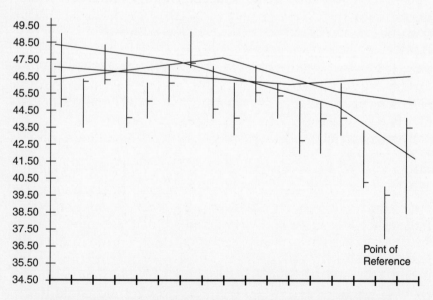

Figure 5.5d   Confused moving averages—best trade with point of reference.

failed Point A or a good or failed Point C, depending upon the market conditions.

What also makes this trade potentially more successful is if the 30-day macro ACD number line is also confused. In other words, if the market has been hovering on both sides of 0—such as from −2 to +2 or from −4 to +4—then this shows that the market is in a state of transition and no clear trend has yet emerged.

In a moving average divergence scenario, what typically happens is the market makes a sharp move up or down away from the moving averages. With the pivot moving averages in a state of confusion, however, there is no sustained trend. Thus any up or down move will be short-lived and eventually corrected. The moment to initiate a moving average divergence trade is when the trader recognizes the move has failed and he or she has a clear point of reference.

One of the market patterns that illustrates this concept is the *Island Reversal Formation*, which is familiar to most technicians and chartists. An Island Reversal Formation occurs when the market has a fake-out to the upside or the downside, leaving two gaps. For example, on Day 1, Commodity X has a low of 15.10 and a high of 15.50. On Day 2, Commodity X gaps open at 15.90 and trades all the way up to 16.50. Then on Day 3, Commodity X gaps lower to 15.70 and trades down to 15.20. What occurred on Day 2 was a fake-out, in which traders believed that the market was going higher, but the move was not sustained. Thus, on Day 3, the market gaps lower and trades back in line with Day 1. What is evidenced by the second gap on Day 3 is that traders are trapped with long positions that have to be liquidated after falsely believing that the market was heading higher (see Figure 5.6).

When the Island Reversal Formation occurs along with the pivot moving averages being either neutral or confused, the market is giving you an excellent high-probability low-risk point of reference to use when executing a MAD trade. The opportunity to execute an Island Reversal Formation/MAD trade exists because, as the confused state of the moving average lines shows, there is no consensus of perception in the market that will lead to a sustained move in one direction or the other. Thus, the probability is high that the uptrend or downtrend is temporary, and picking a top or a bottom could likely result in a profitable trade.

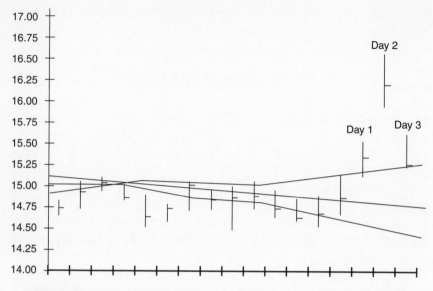

Figure 5.6   Island reversal formation/moving averages (confused) divergence.

Since the ACD system is symmetrical, the same reasoning would apply to a fake-out to the downside. Once again, the setup is with the pivot moving average lines in a neutral or confused state (and confused is preferable). If the bars on the chart have declined steadily and then begin to climb, you have a reference point to pick a bottom to buy the market.

Trading the Number Line with MAD

The pivot moving average lines provide you with yet another point of reference for making a trade. This concept does not replace the micro ACD or the number line. Rather, used in conjunction with these other indicators, you provide yourself with a better, more complete trade setup. For example, let's say the 30-day macro ACD number line is at +7. The pivot moving average lines are sloped upward, although the market has dipped below the 14-day line. Now today the market trades higher, above the 14-day moving average, and makes an A up. The A up, with its value of +2, takes the macro ACD number line to a +9. In addition, the moving average lines are sloping upward *plus* the market has traded back above the 14-day pivot moving average, and in addition made an A up. What's the consensus of all these indicators? Go long—and step on the gas.

The Kindergarten Trader

The beauty of the pivot moving average concept is that it's visual. You can tell by looking what the bias or tone of the market is. If all three lines are sloping upward, it's bullish. If all three slope downward, it's bearish. If they're flat, it's neutral. If one is up, one is down, and one is flat, it is confused. A five-year-old could do this. In fact, we tried this on kindergarten kids and they could tell when all the lines were going up and all the lines were going down. So if they can, so can you. Just don't make this more complicated than it is. Just keep it simple, because it's a simple concept (see Figures 5.7a–d).

Even without price data or daily bars—even without knowledge of the actual commodity—as long as you have the slope of the three pivot moving averages, you can create profitable trading opportunities (see Figures 5.7e–f).

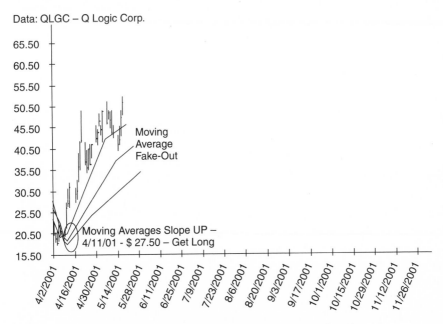

Figure 5.7a   Kindergarten trader—14-, 30-, and 50-day pivot moving averages—4/2/01 to 5/14/01.

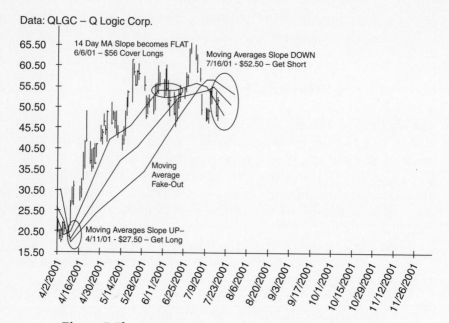

Figure 5.7b   Kindergarten trader—14-, 30-, and 50-day pivot moving averages—4/2/01 to 7/23/01.

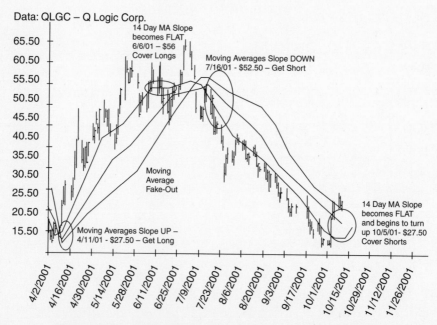

Figure 5.7c   Kindergarten trader—14-, 30-, and 50-day pivot moving averages—4/2/01 to 10/15/01.

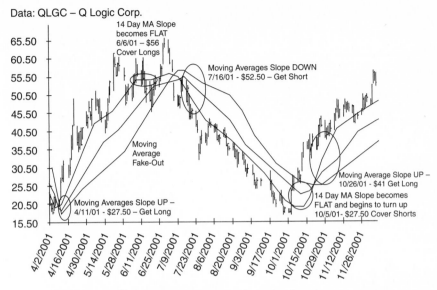

Figure 5.7d Kindergarten trader—14-, 30-, and 50-day pivot moving averages—4/2/01 to 11/26/01.

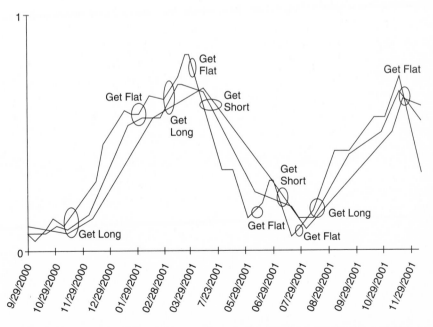

Figure 5.7e Kindergarten trader—no price data or daily bars—9/29/00 to 11/29/01.

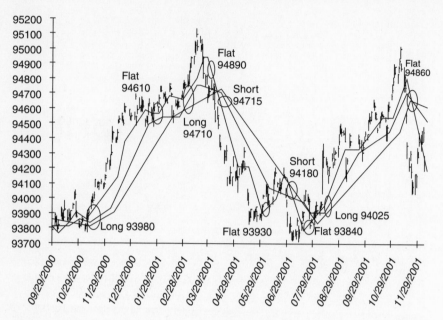

Figure 5.7f   Kindergarten trader—price data and daily bars—Australian bond futures— 9/29/00 to 11/29/01.

Chapter 6

THE ADVANCED TRADER

Many traders have good entry points. But when it comes to profitably exiting a position, that's where they run into trouble. Most traders do not have a consistent exit strategy that allows them to close out profitable positions before they turn into losers. The ACD system not only alerts traders to good entry levels, but it also gives them early warning indicators about when to get out. Furthermore, using these ACD strategies allows a trader to use straight analytics and eliminate the emotional side of trading. In this chapter, I'll discuss various trading strategies that allow you to do just that—exit your trades at the optimal time.

Rolling Pivot Range (RPR)

The *rolling pivot range* (RPR), usually spanning three to six trading days, acts as a reference point for entering and exiting your trades. Perhaps the most important thing about the rolling pivot is not what it tells you to do, but what it prevents you from doing. Namely, it keeps you tied to your winning positions so that you don't get out too early because of some factor that has nothing to do with the market (like a fight the night before with your spouse over your mother-in-law). Using the rolling pivot range can help you manage a position. Further, the rolling pivot range can help short-term traders, who are used to taking quick profits, turn a small, quick winner into an even larger, more profitable one. And, for those traders who tend to hang onto a trade too long, the rolling pivot range will keep them from overstaying their

welcome and get them out before they give back a significant
portion of their profits.

> **For a short-term trader who is not used to holding posi-
> tions, the rolling pivot range gives him the ammunition
> to stay in the trade. For a trader who typically overstays
> his welcome, the rolling pivot range gets him out faster
> than he's used to.**

For a complete definition of the rolling pivot range, refer back
to Chapter 2. Here, I'll discuss using the rolling range in various
trading strategies. On a short-term basis, a daily pivot range can
tell you where to enter the market, such as when you have an A
up through the top of the pivot range, or if the market makes an
A down through the bottom of the pivot range. It's important to
remember that the rolling pivot range—and not the daily pivot
range—can best be used to optimize your exit strategy.
Furthermore, if you're a short-term trader trying to extend the
life of your trade by a day or two, it doesn't much make sense to
use a six-day rolling pivot range. Rather, you'd use only two to
three days. And, if you're a longer-term trader, it wouldn't make
much sense to use a two- or three-day rolling pivot range,
because that would tend to get you out of the market too fast.
Rather, you'd use a five- to six-day rolling pivot range. When
using this strategy, however, you have to be consistent. If you
enter a trade with certain criteria and you are using, for example,
the three-day rolling pivot range as your exit strategy, you just
can't switch—because you're looking for an excuse to stay in the
trade—to a six-day rolling pivot range midway through the trade.

If used properly, the rolling pivot range allows you to stay in
a position through all those crazy economic reports—whether
it's the unemployment report (officially known as Non-Farm
Payroll, typically released on the first Friday of the month) or the
American Petroleum Institute (API) statistics (that are released
on Tuesdays after the close of the energy futures markets). These
reports typically result in short-term random movements in the
market and tend to stop out short-term traders.

Using a rolling pivot range tends to negate the short-term
impact of these reports, and it allows traders to stay in their

positions while the market is digesting the new data. The excep-
tion to this is when there is a dramatic move in the market after
one of these reports (typically a move that is outside one or two
standard deviations of a normal-range day), in which case you'd
want to get out anyway.

The more time you allow the rolling pivot range to
encompass, the greater room or latitude you're giving the
market to move about without stopping you out of your
position. The less time, the less room you are affording
the market to vacillate before stopping you out.

The rolling pivot range can also be used to alert a trader to
exit a position after the underlying market loses momentum
and stalls out, particularly after a long move in one direction or
another. Here's what I mean: Let's say crude oil opens and
makes an A down below the bottom of the four-day rolling
pivot range. You decide to get short because of this and other
ACD factors. You've made up your mind to keep the trade on
until the market reverses and takes out the top of the four-day
rolling pivot range.

Using this concept, there are certain times when the market—particularly after a sustained move in one direction—
tends to go flat or straight-lined. Now, the market has stopped
trending. It's just sitting there. But what happens to the
rolling pivot range that has been sitting above the market? The
rolling pivot range will eventually catch up with the market and
then either get below it (if the market had been trending downward) or above it (if the market had been trending upward). The
market really hasn't moved, but the rolling pivot range has now
caught up to the market or is already on the opposite side of it.
That is an absolute sign of a loss of momentum in the market,
and you should definitely bail out of the trade. Typically, before
the price moves dramatically in the market, the rolling pivot
range bias has already changed. Once the rolling pivot range,
which had been above the market, gets to the market level or
below it, it's time to exit the trade. Or, if the rolling pivot range

had started out below the market and now gets to the market level or above it, it's time to bail out as well.

If the market has made a significant move in one direction and then stalls, when the rolling pivot range catches up to the market and crosses above or below it, that's when it's time to exit the trade—even though the market price may not have moved against you as yet.

Sometimes you get lucky, whether you're trading commodity futures, S&P contracts, or stocks, and you get to ride a short-term trade for an extended period of time—maybe one or two weeks, or in some rare cases three weeks. In other words, you've caught a parabolic move in the market. Initially, the RPR will be far above or below the market because of the magnitude of the move that is being made. Thus, the RPR is not a factor immediately. However, eventually the market loses steam, and the RPR not only catches up with the market, it breaks above or below it

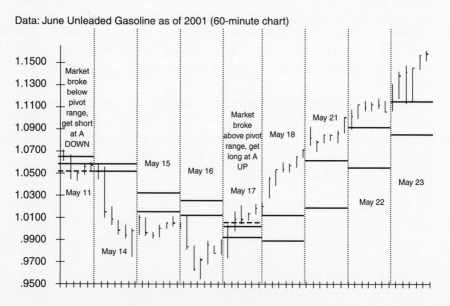

Figure 6.1   Three-day rolling pivot range.

for the first time. That's when it's time to say "Good night, Irene," and get out of the trade ASAP.

In the unleaded gasoline chart from May 2001 (see Figure 6.1), the market begins to stall out, allowing the rolling pivot range to catch up to it. Then, on May 17, the market breaks above the rolling pivot range early in the day. That not only allowed traders to exit profitable short positions at or near the low for that move, but it also potentially allowed them to reverse and go long early in the ensuing rally.

Momentum

When I look at momentum, I examine the close of the market today in relation to the close of the market some period of time ago. I like to use an eight-trading-day comparison. But whether you use 6 trading days, or 8, or 10, it doesn't matter as long as you're consistent with your thinking—just as in the case of the rolling pivot range. You can't change the time frame of this tool just because it would fit the particular trade you're looking at.

Simply put, the momentum shows you who the winners are and who the losers are in the market over this period of time. Let's say that today crude oil futures close at 24, and eight days ago they closed at 25. That results in negative momentum of 100 ticks ($1.00). Obviously, anyone who was short during that time is up those 100 ticks, and anyone who was long would be out those 100 ticks.

Momentum is most useful, however, when the market has had a significant move and now has stalled out with little price movement. If the market experiences a change in this momentum indicator—even a slight one—you know it's time to exit the trade. Here's an example:

Today's close	24.65
Close 1 day ago	24.75
Close 2 days ago	24.50
Close 3 days ago	24.55
Close 4 days ago	24.45
Close 5 days ago	25.00
Close 6 days ago	25.75

| Close 7 days ago | 25.55 |
| Close 8 days ago | 26.00 |

Comparing the close today at 24.65 to the close eight trading days ago at 26.00, you can see that there is negative momentum in the market because today's close is below the close eight days earlier. Now, let's say that for the next three days the market is roughly unchanged at 24.51, 24.58, and 24.52. For all intents and purposes, you could say that, on a closing basis, the market has been basically flat. Then, on the follow day, the market closes at 24.65. Now, a chart of closing prices over eight days looks like this:

Today's close	24.65
Close 1 day ago	24.52
Close 2 days ago	24.58
Close 3 days ago	24.51
Close 4 days ago	24.65
Close 5 days ago	24.75
Close 6 days ago	24.50
Close 7 days ago	24.55
Close 8 days ago	24.45

Now, the current close is higher—by a magnitude of a +0.20 momentum—compared with the close eight days prior. Thus, even though the market has not made a significant move—and actually spent three days at roughly unchanged—this change in momentum from negative to positive means it's time to exit the trade.

A change in momentum—based upon the closing price of a market today compared with prior period—indicates it's time to exit a trade, even if the market has not moved against your position as yet.

The momentum number for various markets is kept every day on the pivot sheets, examples of which are found in the Appendix of this book.

Reversal Trade

Over the past two to three years, the best system I've used—whether trading in open outcry markets such as energy futures or online markets such as OTC stocks—is the *reversal trade*. This is not the typical reversal trade that you have read about in other books or trading publications. The kind of reversal trade that I'm talking about is the one that catches the market with its pants down. In other words, you're trying to capture market failures. Once you've identified that a market failure pattern has occurred, you use the ACD system to enter a trade. Your goal is to be the first one out of the box before everyone else begins to panic and piles into the trade.

Here's what we look for with a reversal trade. First, you must have two consecutive A signals that are in the same direction. Obviously, the fastest time frame for this to happen is two consecutive trading days. As I'll discuss in a moment, you can have two consecutive A signals in the same direction a few days apart—but no other ACD signal can occur in the interim. In other words, if you have an A up on Day 1 and another A up on Day 3, it is a valid setup as long as there was no confirmed ACD signal on Day 2.

Here's an example of a setup: Let's say that today IBM makes an A down at 100 and tomorrow it makes another A down at 100.50. Where IBM settled on either of those days doesn't matter. What you're looking for is the occurrence of two consecutive A down signals—the first at 100 and the second at 100.50.

Now, what you're looking for is whether the next ACD signal is an A up that is above the higher of the two A down values (or, conversely, if you had two consecutive A up signals, you'd be looking for an A down below the lower of the two values). Using this example, let's say that on Day 3, IBM makes an A up at 101.50. This is a reversal trade.

Think about what has happened: There were traders who got short at the first A down at 100 when the market broke down and others who got short on the second A down at 100.50. Now, today, with the A up occurring at 101.50, they're all out money on the trade and will be forced to cover their positions at a loss. Once again, what this reversal trade identifies is when people are trapped in losing positions and have to get out. Hopefully these reversal signals get you into the market before the majority of traders have been able to cover so that you are able to capitalize on the ensuing short-covering rally.

An important caveat to remember: You can only make this trade after two consecutive A signals, followed by an opposite A signal. For example, if you have an A down on Day 3 at 100, and then an A down on Day 2 at 100.50, and then a third A down today at 100.25, this trade is invalid. If you have three A signals in the same direction, then you have to reset the calendar and look for another potential setup. Why? Because short-term traders in the market usually hold positions for as little as four hours or as long as two days. If you've had three consecutive signals in the same direction, those who established a position on the first day are already getting out for a profit on Day 3, and some of those who entered on Day 2 are getting out as well. Thus, there is no reversal trade because too many traders have had the chance to profitably close out their trades.

Or, let's say you get two consecutive A downs and then the market makes a C up on the second day. This also invalidates the count. Further, if you get an A up and then an A down, obviously this isn't a reversal setup as well. Once again, it must be two consecutive A signals (two A ups or two A downs).

As I mentioned earlier in this section, you can have a neutral day in between the two A signals. However, the market cannot make any signal at all—no Point A, B, C, or D. You can potentially have one or two neutral days between the A signals, but if there are too many days between signals then the setup becomes invalid.

Now, going back to the IBM example, let's say that on Day 3 you have an A down at 100 and on Day 2 you have an A down at 100.50 and today you have an A up at 101.25. Is that a reversal trade? Yes. Two consecutive A downs and an A up. But now, let's say that after an A down at 100 on Day 3 and another A down at 100.50 on Day 2, the market suddenly today makes an A up at 104. Which is the better trade?

No question about it. The latter is definitely better because with the gap to 104 traders who got short at 100 and 100.50 are going to be panicking to get out. Also keep in mind that many traders would hesitate to initiate a long position if the market has made such a sudden move higher. In this example, few people would want to buy when the market is $3 to $4 higher. But trading psychology being what it is, what people don't want to do is usually the best thing to do. The larger the differential between the two A downs and the subsequent A up (or two A ups and the A down), the greater the probability of success for this trade. What you're capitalizing on is that people are caught in a sudden move. This is particularly true if the market has gapped open, and traders have remained stubborn and refused to take their losses. Let's say that after two consecutive A downs, IBM gaps higher by $8. A lot of traders will refuse to buy after a gap opening like that. But that kind of scenario often results in a $20 or $30 winner.

The reversal trade uses two consecutive A signals (two A ups or two A downs) followed by an A signal in the opposite direction to identify points in the market in which people are caught. The greater the differential between the two A ups and the A down or the two A downs and the A up, the greater the probability of success for the trade.

The next issue to address with this reversal trade is where do you get out once you put this position on? Since you entered on an A signal, you use straight ACD to manage the trade, including its exit strategy. In other words, stay in the trade until an opposite signal is generated. If you entered on an A up, you'd stay in the trade until you got a C down that day or on the next A down.

I've experienced reversal trades that have lasted as long as two weeks. Once I've put these trades on, the market just kept going my way. I found that reversal trades often work best in immature markets in which there are unsophisticated speculators and traders. My systems have traded the reversal concept in markets worldwide, from U.S. equity and commodity markets, to the German Bund market, the London financial markets, and even as far away as Australia. But remember, you have to follow the basic ACD tenets: Any stock or commodity market that you participate in must have enough liquidity to enable you to trade and enough volatility to make the trade worthwhile.

In short, this reversal strategy works because it preys on human psychology. It looks for market scenarios in which people are being trapped and are going to be forced to liquidate their positions. Figures 6.2 through 6.7 show various trade setups, only some of which fit the reversal trade criteria.

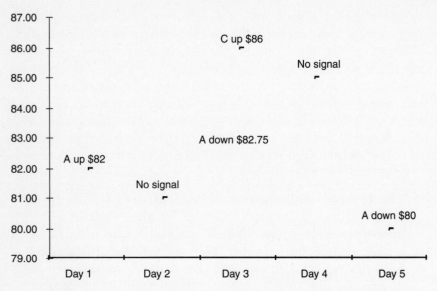

Figure 6.2   Is it a reversal? No—second signal is a C up, not an A up.

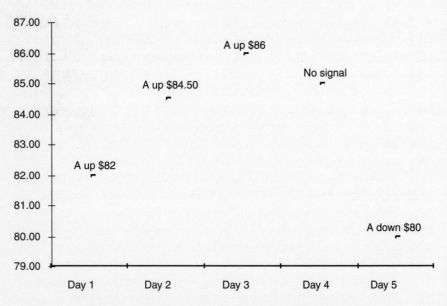

Figure 6.3   Is it a reversal? No—3 consecutive A up signals.

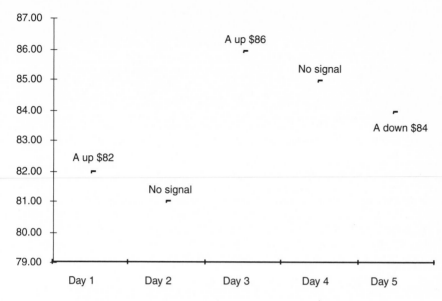

Figure 6.4   Is it a reversal? No—a down price is not below $82.

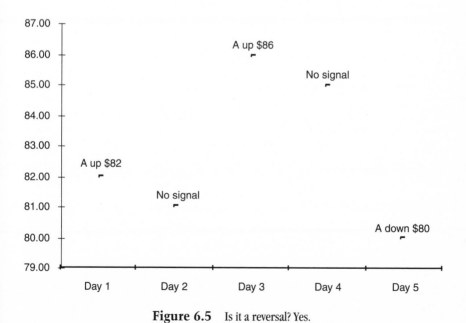

Figure 6.5   Is it a reversal? Yes.

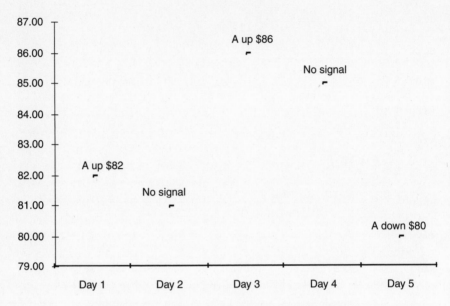

Figure 6.6   Is this a better reversal than Figure 6.7? No.

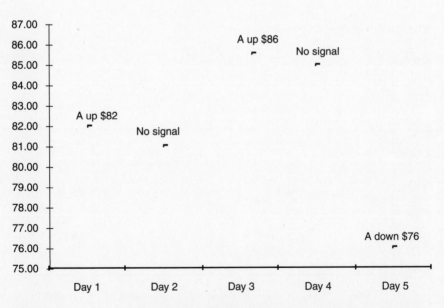

Figure 6.7   This is a better reversal than Figure 6.6! A down price for Figure 6.7 is lower than for Figure 6.6.

Two-Way Swing Area

The next concept is the *two-way swing area*. Let's say that on a chart you can see crude oil futures are rangebound between 24 and 25. The market just keeps bouncing like a pinball between the 24 area of support and the 25 area of resistance. Then some random event causes the market to gap down to, say, 23—below the prior low at 24. Now, let's say that, after some time, the market comes back and tests this 24 area. This prior low of 24 now acts as resistance. Furthermore, the 24 area becomes a two-way swing area. You would want to be a seller until the market moves back through that prior low, at which point that area would act as support.

Figure 6.8 shows the Nasdaq Composite from the April 2001 lows when we put in a support area from 1620 to 1660. After the terrorist attack on September 11, 2001, the Nasdaq Composite gapped below 1620, which turned the 1620 to 1660 area into overhead resistance for the next month as the Nasdaq

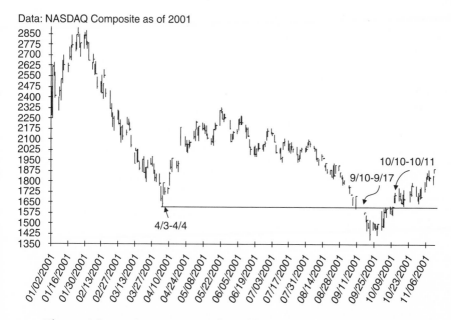

Figure 6.8 Nasdaq composite—1620–1660 swing area—4/3/01 to 11/6/01.

traded to lower levels. Once the market was able to trade back through this area, the 1620 to 1660 zone became support again.

Trend Reversal Trade

Traders love to pick tops and bottoms. It's something I don't really like because it's nearly impossible to do. But if you're going to try to identify market extremes, the best way to do this, in my opinion, is with the *trend reversal trade* (TRT). Basically, when the TRT setup occurs it is a possible signal of a short-term and even long-term change in direction of the market.

For a trend reversal trade setup, the first requirement is a market that has been in a significant uptrend or downtrend for a sustained period of time. A couple of days is not long enough. A couple of weeks may be enough time, but a month is even better—and six months is better yet. Looking at the equity markets that were in a bull phase for basically 10 to 12 years is the extreme example of a sustained trend. The longer the time frame, the better the TRT setup will work.

Once you have identified a market that is in a sustained trend, you first need to have a gap opening in the direction of the trend, particularly after a long weekend or holiday (as we'll discuss further later). Thus, if the market has been in a sustained uptrend, you'd look for a gap open to a new high. Or if the market has been in a sustained downtrend, you'd look for a gap open to a new low.

Using the first example of an uptrend and a gap open to a new high, the next signal you're looking for is for a good A down to be made. This can't be the market just touching the A down and bouncing around, but rather a real, hard A down in which the market trades below the A down level for a period of time.

Before we go any further, let's examine what's going on behind the scenes. The market gapped higher on the opening because the shorts were throwing in the towel. They are willing to pay up to whatever it takes to liquidate in the first 10 to 15 minutes of trading. That's what made the market gap open higher to begin with. At this point, the professional traders step in as sellers. They probably have been riding this trend and now are taking the opposite side of these losers and closing out their long positions, and some are probably getting short as well. The unusual thing that occurs here is that even though the shorts have thrown in the towel as evidenced by the gap-higher opening, the market shortly after the opening trades lower as these professionals liquidate their longs and initiate shorts.

Typically, after the first wave of selling, the market peters out. As soon as the market begins to recover, floor traders and upstairs day-traders who have become accustomed to the bull trend that has existed in this stock or commodity for so long will either initiate new longs or at least get out of their shorts. The trend has ingrained in people's heads that it doesn't pay to be short.

This short-covering rally pushes the market back into or through the opening range. However, the market either fails to make a good C up or never even gets there. Once the market retraces back to the middle of the opening range, it's the perfect opportunity to execute a TRT trade and get short.

Once again, let's see what's really going on. The traders who were short on the first move down are now out of the market. They're not likely to get short again after a failed C up. However, if you get short in the opening range, all you're risking is to the Point C. If you're right, you've caught the top, and your profit potential is enormous because later in the day this market should collapse and settle somewhere near the lows of the session. Longer term this could spell trouble for this market and a reversal to the prevailing trend.

But what happens if, after the market has the failed Point C up, it returns to the opening range and it just sits there? That would allow all the retail bus people to get in at the same level as you did, and as you remember, time is a more important stop than price. The market must move in the direction you anticipate within a reasonable time frame and in no circumstances can this be longer than twice the duration of the opening range. If the market hasn't made a move within that time frame, then the trade is taking too long to develop, and you should just get out.

I sometimes have called this the *walk around the block* trade. When I was pit-trading crude oil futures, if I spotted the opportunity to fade the market at the opening range after a failed C up or down, I would just put on the trade, put my stop in at the C, and go for a 20-minute walk. Upon my return to the pit, if the market hadn't gone my way, I would get out. If the market had gone my way, I would keep the trade on and probably press it.

If I was lucky enough to catch a successful TRT setup, I would not only use the short-term ACD signals to manage the trade, but I would use longer-term indicators—such as the rolling pivot range—to turn this trade from a successful day-trade into a longer-term one. It's not uncommon for the TRT to end up calling the top or the bottom of a move, and catch a significant reversal.

If you're lucky enough to catch a TRT trade, you don't want to get out for just a few ticks. Rather, you want to at least wait for the market to make a new low for the day. For example, let's say that on a Friday, crude oil futures close at 32.00. On Monday, it opens at a three-month high of 32.50 and then makes an A down at 32.25. After this, it rallies up to 32.60, which is just short of a Point C up, and then it retraces back to the opening range around 32.50. Now, let's say that you get short there, at 32.50. And let's suppose that the low for the day, thus far, is 32.10. On a short-term basis, you'd want to stay short until the market at least reached 32.10, because 9 times out of 10, it will settle at or below that prior low of the day. Further, you'd probably want to keep a position on with some of the contracts and use a longer-term ACD concept such as the rolling pivot range to manage the trade.

Again, one of the key concepts in the TRT is to understand the psychology of the market at these times. After the market has gone through gapping open to a new high, selling off to make an A down, reversing to a failed Point C up, and then returning to the opening range, there will be very few traders who would be willing to sell at this point. Even people who made money earlier, such as when they got short after the gap higher open and then covered after the A down was made, would be hesitant to make another trade. They're just happy that they were able to make some money initially. They don't have the wherewithal to go short again. But with an understanding of the TRT setup, you know you have a low-risk high-probability trade, in this case, to get short in the opening range. Remember, the hardest trades to make are usually the best ones to make.

After the gyrations of a gap higher, a good A down, a rally to a failed Point C, and then a sell off to the opening range, few traders would have the wherewithal to establish a short position/bias. But the hardest trades are the best ones to make. (Obviously, the TRT trade is a symmetric formation, and in a sustained downtrend, you'd be looking for a gap lower opening, good A up, failed C down, and then attempt to buy the market when it gets back into the opening range.)

Let's just review this trade:

1. The market gaps open to a new high (low) after a sustained up (down) trend. At this point those traders who have been wrong for so long are just getting out.
2. The market makes a good A down (up). This is the result of the smart money getting out, taking their profits after a long, steady upward (downward) trend.
3. After a lull the market begins to trade higher (lower) again. The short-term traders who had gone short (long) intraday near the A down (up) get stopped out. As they cover their short (long) positions and establish some new long (short) positions, the market moves higher (lower)—all the way to the Point C level but fails.
4. This failed C up (down)—at a new high (low) for the day—triggers selling (buying) that brings the market back to the opening range.
5. At this point, if you're a trader, you've had a wild ride. You've seen the smart money sell (buy) early, then traders go short (long) only to get stopped out as the market rallies (breaks) to new highs (lows). Then you witness the market fail again at the Point C extremes. You're just happy to get out of there without losing the shirt off your back!
6. Is the typical trader going to initiate a new position once the market retraces back to the opening range? Not likely. But this brings us to one of the biggest lessons of trading.

Once again, the hardest trades to make are always the best ones to do.

An excellent example of a TRT setup occurred on March 10, 2000. The Nasdaq Composite settled on Thursday, March 9, 2000, at 5046. Then, some high-flying dot coms and technology stocks released positive earnings, which sparked a gap higher opening on Friday, March 10, at 5080 to 5100. The market then traded lower to make an A down at 5063 and establish an intraday low at 5055. After that low was put in, the Nasdaq Comp rallied back up through the opening range to approach the Point C up at 5135, but instead failed and never got higher than 5132.52. After that Point C failure, the market returned to the opening range and traded steadily lower, eventually making a new low for the day at 5039. The Nasdaq Comp that day settled at 5048.

If you had recognized this as a TRT, not only would you have gotten short after the failed C up at the opening range of 5080 to 5100 in anticipation of a new low for the day, but you probably would have held a portion of this short position for the longer term. Believe it or not, you'd still be short today!

The I'm Mad As Hell and Can't Take It Anymore Trade

The I'm *mad as hell* (MAH) trade combines the concept of the TRT along with a long weekend or a holiday, such as Memorial Day, Thanksgiving, or Labor Day. As with a TRT trade, the MAH trade requires the market to have been in a sustained trend. And as we know from the psychology of the TRT, when the market has been in a sustained trend, there are traders who have made numerous attempts to pick a top and have gotten their clocks cleaned (vice versa for a bear market). Now, the long weekend comes. The traders are sitting at home over Memorial Day or July 4th and they're miserable about how they've been on the wrong side of the market for so long and how much money they've lost. Maybe their spouses are now even giving them market advice! They've reached the point where they can't take it any more. They say "uncle" and are resolved to get the hell out of their losing positions as soon as the market reopens. If they've been short in a rising market, they're going to buy the opening. If they've been long in a falling market, they're going to puke on the opening.

At this point, when human emotion is capitulating, the result is that you're going to see in the market gap up or down in the direction of the prevailing trend. Those traders who are frantically trying to achieve peace of mind are basically creating that gap. Then after these people have finally thrown in the towel, lo and behold, the market retraces back to the prior session's trading range. The top or bottom that they've been trying to pick for so long is finally in, and they're no longer involved.

For example, in 2000, Qualcomm Inc. (QCOM) had a trading range of 640 to 660 on a Friday prior to a long weekend. Over the weekend, some analyst predicted that Qualcomm would eventually trade 1,000. After the long weekend, Qualcomm gapped open higher and traded to between 680 and 685. However, later in this day the stock retraced back into Friday's range of 640 to 660. Qualcomm never traded higher.

Combining the TRT concept with this MAH trade, what you're looking for is a gap to a new high, followed by an A down, then a failed C up and then, finally, a retracement into the prior trading day's range. When the market retraces back into the prior trading day's range, it's time to put on a short position if you haven't put one on already.

What makes the MAH and TRT setups so effective is that the history tends to repeat itself in the market. People tend to panic and make the same mistakes over and over again. Identifying when these setups occur can help you anticipate changes in market direction and profit from other people's misery.

Change in Trend

In addition to the TRT, MAH, and other early warning indicators we look at, we generate computer programs to predict trend changes. In our databases, we have collected more than 15 years' worth of price data on individual commodities and individual stocks and analyze them to determine the average duration of time that a specific trend should last. What we try to determine is how long these trends—big or little—last statistically, on average. Then based upon this pattern recognition, we make projections for the month forward. For example, at the end of each month we run this analysis and make our projections for what trend changes should take place in the following month. This analysis identifies two or three days during the month when any established trend could easily reverse. It's another proprietary indicator that should help you get out of a position if it shows up on this monthly change-in-trend radar screen. (Further statistics on this change-in-trend program are available in the Appendix.)

Sushi Roll

Despite the name *Sushi Roll*, this indicator has nothing to do with Japan, raw fish, or anything else connected with sushi. But it so happens that when we were first discussing this indicator we were at a Japanese restaurant and someone order sushi. One thing led to another, and that's how this particular early warning indicator of a change in market direction got the name sushi roll.

Now, here's what this early warning indicator does. First of all, everyone knows what the textbook definition of a reversal day is: The market makes a new high above the prior day's high and then takes out the prior day's low and closes below the prior day's low. Or, the market makes a new low, takes out the prior day's high, and settles above the prior day's high. The problem with this kind of reversal trade is that it's obvious. Anybody with any type of trading screen sees this. Since it's readily apparent and everyone can easily detect it, it can't really have any value. (Remember, if everybody is making the same trade or looking at the same information, how good can it be?)

That's where the sushi roll comes in. Instead of looking at just one day, we substitute five rolling trading days. Or, for a shorter-term perspective, you can use five 10-minute bars. Whatever your time frame, as long as you're consistent, the object is to compare the latest five increments of time to the prior five increments of time. If you're short and the market in the latest five bars of time trades below the prior five-period bar low, and now settles above the prior five period high, it's a sushi roll and it's time to get out of your shorts.

Here's an example of using the sushi roll concept on a 10-minute chart for crude oil futures. Let's say that crude oil rises from 20.70, and now the market is at 21.20. You're long and the market has gone your way. Now, in the next 50 minutes (measured by five 10-minute bars) the market ranges from 21.20 to 21.36, which is only 16 points. Then, in the next 50 minutes, the market trades above the high at 21.36 and then takes out the low of 21.20 and settles below on the last bar at 21.10. (Remember, it's not enough for the market to just make a new low, it must also close that last period below the prior five-bar low.) At this point, would you get short? Maybe, maybe not. But would you liquidate your long position from 20.70? Absolutely.

Figures 6.9, 6.10, and 6.11 depict different scenarios of sushi roll setups.

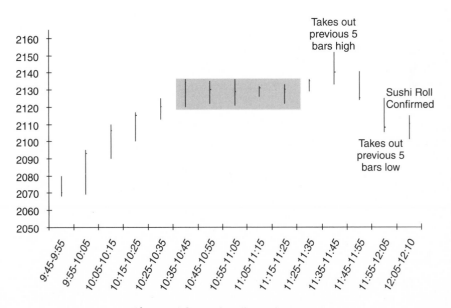

Figure 6.9　Sushi roll—10-bar setup.

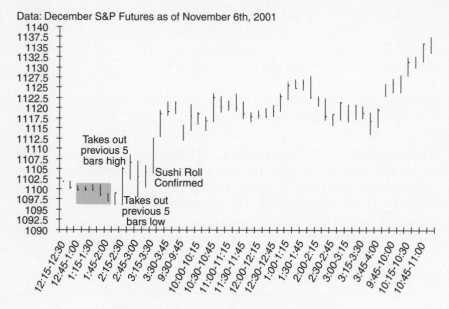

Figure 6.10   Sushi roll—extremes of the day.

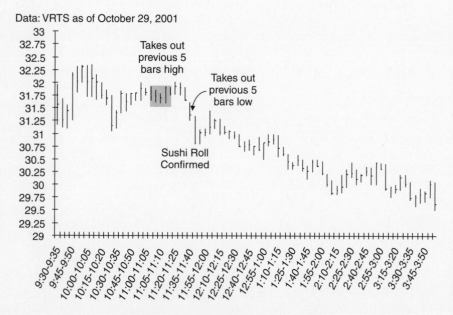

Figure 6.11   Sushi roll—middle of the day.

Outside Reversal Week

An *outside reversal week* applies the concept of the sushi roll over a Monday-through-Friday time period. This weekly reversal tends to work well, but monthly reversals work even better. While I've never seen a yearly reversal, I would guess that if one did occur, it would probably be unbelievable. An outside reversal week uses last week's Monday-through-Friday range as the first five trading days, while this week's Monday-through-Friday range is considered to be the second five days. In order for an outside reversal week to occur, this second week would have to take out the prior week's low and then take out the prior week's high and settle on Friday above it. (Or, take out the prior week's high and then take out the prior week's low and settle below it on Friday.)

The question may arise as to why I use five trading sessions as the basis for outside reversals, and not four days, six days, or seven days. The short answer is, I'm the most comfortable with the five-day time period. I suppose you could use four or six days. But whatever time frame you use, you must be consistent with it. When an outside reversal week occurs, it's a high-probability low-risk trade that can identify significant market tops and bottoms.

Here's an example of an outside reversal week. In the table below, the open, high, low, and closing prices are listed for Enron (ENE) for a two-week period in the spring of 2001.

Date	Open	High	Low	Close
Week 1				
April 23	60.77	61.70	**60.32** (4)	61.65
April 24	61.95	62.95	61.60	61.87
April 25	61.62	62.99	61.18	62.88
April 26	63.01	**63.99** (2)	63.01	63.66
April 27	62.80	63.61	62.18	**63.50**
Week 2				
April 30	63.20	**64.75** (1)	62.26	62.72
May 1	63.60	63.60	61.80	62.41
May 2	63.40	63.40	**59.50** (3)	60.50
May 3	59.60	60.20	57.05	58.35
May 4	58.54	59.70	58.46	**59.48** (5)

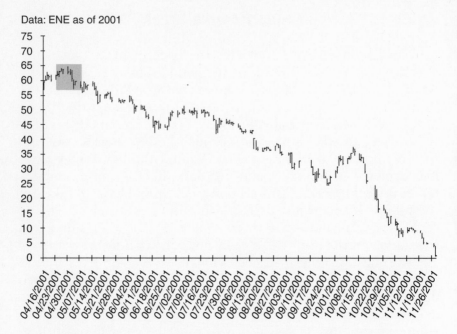

Figure 6.12   Enron (ENE)—outside reversal week—4/30/01 to 5/4/01.

Examine the high, low, and close data in the table. What stands out from these two weeks? As the bold numbers clearly show, the first thing that occurred is the market made a high in Week 2 at 64.75 (1) that exceeded Week 1's high of 63.99 (2). Subsequently, the market lost its upside momentum and reversed. On May 2, it made a low of 59.50 (3), which was below the previous week's low of 60.32 (4). It then confirmed the outside down reversal week by settling on May 4 at 59.48 (5), which was below the previous week's low of 60.32. This was a classic example of an outside reversal week. Over the next several months, the stock steadily declined. In December 2001, ENE traded under 50 cents a share and the company filed for bankruptcy (see Figure 6.12).

The Crash of '29—Almost the Perfect Trade

Let's look to see how these ACD concepts would have applied themselves to the stock market in 1929. From 1925 through 1929 the stock market enjoyed a long, sustained uptrend. It

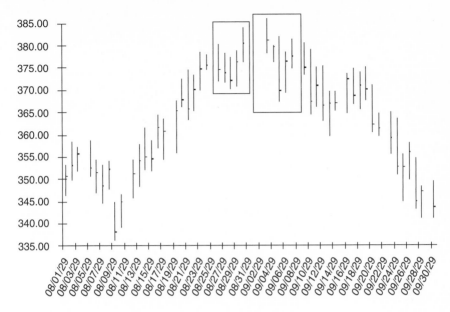

Figure 6.13   Dow Jones Industrials—1929.

closed out the month of August 1929 on its absolute high. (Back
then the market traded six days a week and closed only for
Sundays and holidays, see Figure 6.13).

Dow Jones Industrial Average

Date	High	Low	Close
8-26-29	380.18	372.09	374.46
8-27-29	378.16	371.76	373.79
8-28-29	377.56	**370.34** (2)	372.06
8-29-29	378.76	370.79	376.18
8-30-29	**383.96** (1)	376.16	**380.33** (3)
8-31-29		Holiday	
9-01-29		Sunday	
9-02-29		Holiday	
9-03-29	**386.10** (4)	378.23(5)	381.17 (6)
9-04-29	380.12	376.33	379.61
9-05-29	382.01	**367.35** (7)	369.77
9-06-29	378.71	369.46	376.20
9-07-29	381.44	374.94	**377.56** (8)

As you can see the high of the last week of August 1929 was 383.96 (1), the low was 370.34 (2), and the close was 380.33 (3), the all-time weekly high close. Then came Labor Day weekend. Traders who had been short and getting killed in the market finally decided to capitulate (the MAH trade). On the following trading session, September 3, 1929, the market gapped open to a new high at 385.20. It then proceeded to make an A down around 382.80 and rallied back to fail a C up at the new all-time high of 386.10 (4). The market then traded all the way back down to a new intraday low of 378.23 (5), and settled at 381.17 (6)—a *perfect* trend reversal trade (TRT) setup.

Now look what happened the rest of the week. As we said, the high of the week of September 3 to 7 was 386.10 (4), which exceeded the prior week's high of 383.96 (1). The low put in on September 5 of 367.35 (7) was below the prior week's low of 370.34 (2). The week closed at 377.56 (8), which was below the prior week's all-time high close of 380.83 (3). However, this was not a perfect reversal week because the market did not settle below the prior week's low of 370.34 (2)—but it was pretty damn close! After the week of September 7, the market really began to collapse. On Saturday, September 14, the market settled at 367.01, on September 21 it settled at 361.16, and on Saturday, September 28, the Dow Jones settled at 347.17. In fact, this setup marked the beginning of the end for the market of 1929 and basically foreshadowed the crash.

Hopefully, if you and I had been trading back then and we knew then what we know now about ACD, we would have liquidated our longs and avoided the crash. Or maybe we even would have been lucky enough to be short!

Since I keep telling you that the ACD system is symmetrical, it's important to note that what worked back in 1929 at the top also worked well at the bottom in July 1932. The outside reversal setup in 1932 did not occur exactly after the long July 4th weekend, but rather one week later. Still, the July 1932 scenario is an important one to examine (see Figure 6.14).

The market, obviously, had been in a sustained downtrend. Any trader who had been trying to pick a bottom during this time had faced a losing battle. The same index that had traded at 380 back in August 1929 had lost almost 90 percent of its value and was now trading in the 40s.

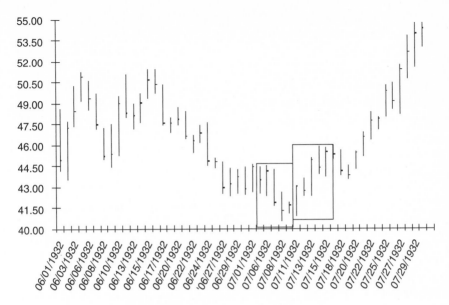

Figure 6.14   Dow Jones Industrials—1932.

Dow Jones Industrial Average

Date	High	Low	Close
07-05-32	44.43	42.53	43.47
07-06-32	**44.50** (1)	42.31	44.08
07-07-32	44.26	41.63	41.81
07-08-32	42.61	**40.56** (2)	41.22
07-09-32	41.89	41.08	**41.63** (3)
07-10-32		Sunday	
07-11-32	43.03	**40.92** (4)	42.99
07-12-32	43.65	42.36	42.68
07-13-32	45.05	42.35	44.88
07-14-32	45.85	43.91	44.34
07-15-32	**45.98** (5)	45.02	**45.29** (6)

The week of July 5 to 9, the market had a high of 44.50 (1), a low of 40.56 (2), and an all-time weekly low settlement on July 9 at 41.63 (3). The following week, on July 11, the market opened on the dead low at 40.92 (4), which while it was not below the prior week's low of 40.56 (2) was very close. It then put in a high at 45.98 (5) on July 15, which was well above the prior week's high of 44.50 (1). The market settled at 45.29 (6), far above the 41.63 (3) settlement from the prior week.

A perfect sushi roll? A perfect outside reversal week? No. But an indication of a possible turn in the market? Yes. In fact, the market never looked back. By the end of July 1932, the market closed at 54.26. In fact, the market never exhibited this reversal weekly pattern again until midway through the 1990s. So if you were just using this strategy to trade the market from 1932 through the 1990s. . . .

Wishful thinking aside, the important point of this exercise using the Dow Jones Industrial Average examples of August 1929 and July 1932 is to show you that history does repeat itself. Our grandparents made the same trading mistakes that we are making today. These historical market moments are not perfect ACD setups. But is anything in life a perfect setup? No, but if you look at these examples, you can see they're both pretty damn close.

Picking the Right Time Frame

If you're a short-term trader, then long-term trading indicators mean next to nothing. And if you are a long-term trader, you would not initiate a trade based on a one-day event like an A up through the pivot. This brings into focus the contrast between trading ACD intraday and using longer-term indicators.

If you're a short-term trader, you're going long at A ups and short at A downs, and then you're neutral at Point Bs above and below the opening range. Or, you're bearish at Point C down, and you're neutral at Point D. But all of these are intraday indicators and intraday market guidelines.

From a longer-term perspective, what happens intraday doesn't really concern you. Rather, you would look at an analysis of the final day's outcome and value the day from a number line perspective. The intraday movements mean little if anything. For example, if you try to capture moves when the market goes from 0 to +/− 9 and then you hold that position until the market resets at 0, you don't really care much about intraday movement. All you want to know is the final ACD score for that day. If the market made an A up and settled above the opening range, that day is a +2. Even if the market made an A up, then went below the opening range to Point B and stopped out the day-traders in the process, you wouldn't care—as long as the market eventually traded back above the opening range to settle there. Then it's a +2, and all the intraday gyrations don't mean anything from this perspective. (As long as a C down wasn't reached.)

Thus, you need to decide what trading time frame suits you and your trading style, and also what indicators have the most impact on your trading time frame—and stick with them.

Chapter 7

THE ACD VERSION OF "RIPLEY'S BELIEVE IT OR NOT!"

When I started writing this book, I initially thought I'd include one chapter on risk management and another on trading stories. I hoped to weave into these chapters other ancillary trading techniques that I currently employ. However, as the book developed, it became evident that most of the trading antics that I remember the clearest somehow all involved risk management. Therefore, I am simply combining these two ideas into this one chapter.

Hopefully these stories are entertaining but also offer some educational value. Some may seem unbelievable, but I promise you that they are all true. Just like that famous TV show from the past, in some cases the names have been changed in this chapter to protect both the innocent and the guilty. I think that you'll find that this chapter is aptly titled the ACD version of "Ripley's Believe It or Not!"

A Plumber Named LIZA

When it comes to trading in today's markets, you don't have to be a genius. In fact, I think that too much information keeps you from properly dissecting and analyzing what's really important. I have many trader friends who utilize only one or two simple concepts to trade and yet have been very successful.

Take the example of a trader I'll call LIZA, a close personal friend of mine. Before trading, LIZA used to be a master plumber at one of the major ballparks on the East Coast. Somehow he ended up on the Nymex trading floor and has become very successful. Without taking anything away from his success or his unique style of trading, it's fair to say that he does not have an MBA or a dual degree in business and law; he isn't even a college graduate. What he does possess is an innate ability to quickly grasp what's going on around him and a tremendous amount of self-discipline and confidence in his own decision-making ability.

So one day while I'm letting him buy me a tuna fish sandwich, I asked him what was the method to his madness. What made LIZA tick? What he told me was simplistic in nature, but very revealing: He never trades the opening because he feels there is too much random movement in the first hour of trading, and he can't get a good handle on the market. Rather, he comes to the trading pit after the mid-afternoon lull. He looks around a bit, and he observes those traders who are smiling. Then he looks around a little more and sees those traders who are frowning. And he simply follows those who are smiling and he fades those who are frowning.

Now mind you, I have tremendously understated LIZA's trading ability because he has tremendous pit skills. Yet, his approach to the market works. Believe me, there are many other traders who spend their entire lives on the trading floor armed with graphs, charts, and technical gadgets that I have no idea what they even are, and they struggle to make a living. At the end of the day, these people are usually scratching their heads, while my buddy, LIZA, always seems to have a smile on his face.

Good News/Bad Action

The trading concept of *good news/bad action* is straightforward in nature, but it requires some counterintuitive thinking. Let me first share with you an experience I've had on numerous occasions as a guest lecturer to aspiring freshman at the Wharton School of Business at the University of Pennsylvania where I received my MBA. These future leaders of America possess both high S.A.T. scores and usually high opinions of themselves.

In short, a lot of them think that, at 18 years old, they know everything. Typically, I start my lecture with a hypothetical trading story. I tell them to imagine that they're watching the "CBS Evening News with Dan Rather," and he's standing in some Midwest cornfield up to his knees in water, reporting that the Mississippi River has overflowed and the corn crop is decimated. Dan Rather then goes on to interview a couple of farmers who are suffering tremendous financial losses.

Furthermore, I tell them that the next day at the Chicago Board of Trade, where corn futures are traded, corn is expected to open limit up—meaning 10 cents a bushel higher. However, when trading begins, instead of opening limit up, the market is only 6 cents higher, and within an hour it's trading unchanged on the day. The question that I ask the students is, what would they do? How would they capitalize on the situation? Would they buy or sell corn futures?

Almost to a person, every one of them says that they would be a buyer. These geniuses figure that the market is affording them an incredible buying opportunity and has yet to digest the impact of the flood on the supply of corn. They think only in terms of supply and demand. Wrong answer! Obviously, this hypothetical story is a perfect example of good news/bad action. The good news—at least in terms of market pricing—is that a flood has occurred that will reduce the size of this particular harvest. The bad action is evident by prices not meeting the opening call and quickly trading back to the prior day's level. In this instance, you would want to be a seller. For whatever reason, the market has run out of steam, and the buyers have run out of bullets.

Typically, those buyers who got long the market because of this supposed good news are the first ones to get stopped out of their long positions at the first sign of weakness. Usually the market will continue to trade lower for a couple of days, and these traders have no idea where they went wrong. What they've missed is the possibility that the crop damage was already priced into the market, meaning prices had already advanced in anticipation that the flood would take out a certain amount of acreage. Or, maybe the corn crops that were damaged were not even deliverable against the CBOT contract. Who knows? Whatever the reason, this is a clear example of a good news/bad action situation.

Markets That Don't Meet the Call

Astute traders often monitor markets that trade on overnight, after-hours electronic platforms such as the Chicago Mercantile Exchange's Globex or the New York Mercantile Exchange's Access system. What they're looking for are markets that make significant moves overnight but then don't see that same follow-through when the regular trading session reopens in the morning. For example, let's say that natural gas trades up 10 cents overnight on Access to a new 20-day high. However, when the market opens for floor trading at Nymex the next morning, it never meets this call and opens up only 6 cents higher. When markets don't meet their original call, it's usually an early-warning sign of trouble, and the market is likely to reverse course.

As a follow-up, assume for the moment that S&Ps on Globex closed at 9:15 EST 10 handles higher, which would bring the S&P into new nine-day high territory. But on the regular opening at 9:30 EST, they're only five to six handles higher and immediately begin to sell off. This is another case of a market not making the call. However, keep in mind that if, between the time that the overnight system ended (in this case 9:15 EST) and the day session began (9:30 EST), an economic report or some breaking news item was released this would obviously invalidate the scenario of a market not meeting its call.

I remember back in August 1991 when Gorbachev was placed under house arrest during the Russian coup. Brent crude oil in London traded up 4 on this news. However, when New York crude oil opened later that day, the market came in only 2 higher. Such a significant disparity between New York and London was an early-warning signal that something was just not right. At the end of the day, oil futures had traded all the way back down to unchanged.

Most of the time a trader discovers why the market never made its opening call only after the fact. Instead of worrying about specific particulars and why one thing may or may not have impact on the market, it's much easier just to react to the price action exhibited by that commodity or stock. If Company XYZ announces earnings that look spectacular, but instead of opening up $2 higher as indicated, the stock XYZ opens only $0.50 higher, sell it. Later on, let some analyst tell you that stock

XYZ's earnings were not as good as they looked. Or, if OPEC reaches a production-cut agreement and crude oil is supposed to open higher and instead comes in lower the next day, sell that too. Let some oil guru tell CNBC later on that two or three oil-producing nations were already cheating on the new quotas.

I Have No Clue

Let's say that a market has been trending in one direction for a significant amount of time, and you ask traders that you respect why they think this is happening. Maybe natural gas prices are trending higher because of a prolonged bout of cold weather. Or, crude oil prices are climbing in anticipation of an OPEC summit. Perhaps S&P futures are tanking because Federal Reserve Chairman Alan Greenspan is speaking at yet another luncheon. If a market is making a substantial move and traders seem to understand why, this market trend is not going to last very long. However, if the market is moving in one direction and nobody has a clue as to why, then the trend is going to be prolonged. When a market goes up or down for no apparent reason, it tends to go a lot further in that direction than people can imagine.

Finding a Trader's Achilles' Heel

When trading, figuring out the market is only part of the battle. A far bigger challenge is dealing with yourself and your personality quirks and emotional demons. Most traders have a hard time keeping their trading ego in check. The best trader in natural gas (we'll call him MVP) happens to work for MBF and is like a brother to me. This is a man who would never gamble more than $50 or $100 on a hand of blackjack at a casino. I think that if he ever lost more than $500 or $1,000 in Atlantic City or Las Vegas, he would kill himself. Yet, this same person thinks nothing of trading hundreds of natural gas contracts at a time and doesn't bat an eye over having hourly profit and loss swings in the six figures.

When it comes to taking on risks, he's Jekyll and Hyde! He wouldn't bet more than $50 at the craps table, but when it comes to trading, he'll take on a 500-contract position like it was nothing.

How do you deal with a psycho like this? Since MVP works with me at my trading firm, I had to figure out a way to rein him in. At first, I attempted to rationally explain to him that it's a lot more fun (and made more sense) to piss away money in the real world while remaining under control in the pit. I would preach over and over, trade when the market needs your liquidity. Trade when it's volatile and not because you just need your daily market fix. I tried as gently as I could to tell him that his out-of-control pit theatrics were taking a severe toll on his physical and mental well-being.

When that didn't seem to work, I decided that it was time to stoop to guerilla-warfare tactics. I needed to find his Achilles' heel. One afternoon I spent some time with MVP and his dad. Being with the two of them, I could tell that his father was the most important person in my friend's life. It's not that he didn't love his wife and son, but I could clearly see the love, admiration, and respect he had for his father. Although he was a grown man in his thirties, his dad was the one person he most wanted to please.

Then, it hit me. The next time he was in the process of losing $250,000 in two short trading hours, I summoned my friend to my office and proceeded to call his father, a retired executive living in the Chicago area. "John," I said, "your son is out of control."

My friend's face turned ashen. I finally had gotten to him. I had found his Achilles' heel. Is he in control every day? No. Does he still go over his loss limits on occasion? Yes. But I found a way to keep him on a leash. All I have to say is, "I'm going to call your Dad."

The next trader I decided to perform some of this mental magic on was a man we'll call NOT-I, who is one of the most beloved traders in the business. He always has a smile on his face, but he too has a tremendous discipline problem. I tried taping a picture of his son to the back of his trading pad. I tried explaining how much money he was giving away due to his lack of discipline. He still couldn't stop himself from racking up big losses. One day he stopped by and complained to me about the amount of alimony he was forced to pay to his ex-wife every month. "Why couldn't she get a job? The whole divorce system in the United States is insane and unfair."

As he complained, a light bulb went off in my head. Like all of the traders who work with me, NOT-I had loss limits that he was supposed to adhere to. I told him that the next time he exceeded his limit, I would take $500 out of his personal account and send it to his ex-wife with a note explaining that she must spend this money on herself, preferably shopping. I warned him that each time he went over his limits, I would double the amount that I would send her from his account.

He never thought I would do it. The next thing you know, I sent $500. Two days later, I sent her $1,000, and then $2,000, and it was all coming out of his pocket. Finally, after I had sent his ex-wife $4,000, he finally caved in. Does he still go over his limits occasionally? Yes. But have we found an effective way of risk-managing him? Absolutely.

Taking a break when you've reached your loss limit is good advice for any trader. Until the tragic events at the World Trade Center, our office was adjacent to a 16-screen movie theater. My risk managers were instructed that if anyone continually violated his or her trading limits, they were to hand that trader a movie pass. You can't imagine how much those $10 movie passes have saved the firm's bottom line!

Managing traders over the years, I can tell you that what goes on in someone's personal life will definitely have an effect on their trading P&L. In this case, the best thing to do is to find someone to talk to. Clear the air and clear your head in the process. That's what I found worked with a trader, who I'll call Lucky. This outgoing, jovial guy had suddenly turned introspective, and his trading was definitely off. After a little nudging, I got him to open up. He told me that his wife had just given birth to their fifth child, and his home life was proving to be more than he could handle. "My oldest is in high school, and my youngest is two months old," Lucky confided in me. "I've got problems ranging from pot to colic."

I couldn't make Lucky's problems go away, but just by listening, I helped him regain his focus and get his trading back on track.

A Dose of Reality

Everybody in life has his or her struggles, both personal and professional. As traders, we run the risk of becoming so self-absorbed in the market and in our trading performance that we lose our perspective on life. We fail to appreciate just how fortunate we are to have the opportunity to trade. Whether on the trading floor or off the screen, traders set their own hours and work for themselves. That's an opportunity that, frankly, not many people can enjoy.

When you have a bad streak in trading, you can't fall into the trap of feeling sorry for yourself. If you do, you'll become introspective and most likely miserable. Sometimes, you may need a strong dose of reality to bring you to your senses.

Self-pity had become a problem for one of my traders when he had a string of losing trading months. I needed to find a way to get him back on track. He had forgotten what life was all about and needed a wake-up call. I figured that it was my responsibility to deliver this message to him. One day, I arranged for my driver to show up at his apartment, unannounced. My driver, all 320 pounds of him, "persuaded" this trader to surrender his wallet, his credit cards, and the keys to his apartment. Call it intervention. Call it kidnapping. This trader was in for the eye-opener of his life.

Unbeknownst to him, I had rented a one-bedroom tenement apartment for him in Harlem for one month. Instead of trading, he was to spend half his day working at a homeless shelter and volunteering at a pediatric AIDS ward. Every day, my driver brought him $25 to live on. It was a lesson in tough love. He needed to see how people who were less fortunate and in many cases completely helpless lived. The trader adjusted to his new environment and even embraced it. Unfortunately, he developed a case of lice. After he shaved his head, I figured he had suffered enough and allowed him to return to the trading pit and to his apartment. But he came back a changed man. Today he's still a regular volunteer at this homeless shelter, and he has turned around both his personal life and his trading career. He is, in short, a new man.

My First Deal

Many people ask me, what's the secret of my success. I have no secret—I'm an open book. Being in the right place at the right time, being a disciplined trader, and coming to grips with who I am have helped me to get where I am today.

Everything in life, to some degree, depends on luck and timing. I was 12 years old when I first noticed that my next-door neighbor kept coming home with nicer and nicer cars. Being a curious, greedy, and nosy little kid, I kept trying to figure out what this man did for a living. When I finally got up the nerve to ask him, he told me that he was a silver broker on the Commodities Exchange (Comex). My neighbor had three sons. One of them was my friend, but he attended public school while I went to private school. Although he was a tremendous athlete, it's safe to say that he was not very academically inclined.

Using this to my advantage, I decided one afternoon to negotiate what turned out to be my first—and most fortuitous—business deal. I promised my neighbor that if he allowed me to become a clerk/intern at his brokerage firm, even though I was only 13 at the time, he could transfer his son to my school, and no matter what it took, I would guarantee that his son would graduate from high school.

When we shook hands on that deal, little did I know that I was going to work for the largest commodities silver broker in the world, who executed a large portion of the Hunt Brothers' business. (Years later, the Hunt Brothers would gain notoriety for their attempt to corner the silver market.) I guess being nosy pays off once in a while.

I remember vividly one snowy day when school was out for Thanksgiving break. My neighbor asked me if I could come help out at work since he knew that his firm would be short on staff. I jumped at the chance. Previously, I had spent my time at the exchange writing up trading cards for brokers, along with doing other odd jobs and errands. But on this day, I was pressed into service. Due to the snow, our desk, which was usually staffed by more than 30 people, had only six bodies. In the main silver booth there were three colored phones—blue, beige, and red. "If one of these three phones rings, don't pick it up! Come get me," my neighbor told me, and then he went to the pit to trade.

Fifteen minutes into the trading day, one of these phones rang. Everyone was tied up on other phone lines, taking orders and handling reports. I panicked. I ran to the side of the trading ring and said to my boss, "The blue phone is ringing!" He looked me squarely in the eye. "Okay, pick up the phone and answer the man's questions. If he figures out that you're only 14 years old, you're fired!"

The phone was still ringing when I got back to the booth. An imposing voice asked me where my boss was. "He's tied up in the ring," I told him, which looking back was probably not the best thing to say—how could anyone be too busy for the Hunts?

"Who are you?" the gentleman asked.

"I'm Mark." So far, so good.

"How come I never heard your voice on this phone before?"

I had to think fast. "I'm just helping out in silver today because we're short-handed due to the snow storm. Usually I'm working on the gold desk."

That sounded good to me, and apparently it sounded good to him, since he then asked me, "So what do you think of the silver market today?"

I was completely flabbergasted! Here was one of the Hunt brothers who dominated the world's silver market, asking a 14-year-old little punk what he thought of silver. You couldn't make this stuff up if you tried!

Discipline

In terms of discipline, one of the things that has really helped me in terms of trading was that I grew up in a strict kosher environment. That meant I could not eat certain foods, nor could I mix meat and milk products together. When my friends would go to McDonald's and order a cheeseburger, I was stuck with boring fish fillet sandwiches. Even though I now bend a little with the dietary laws, being kosher for almost 22 years instilled in me the same discipline that I have needed to follow my trading tenets.

Have I had a bad day and lost my mind on occasion? Of course, I'm a human being, not a robot. But what has kept me in check is my personal greed factor. ACD has worked for me for so long that I know if I just stick to the game plan and continue to be the house (a concept I'll explain later in this chapter), I'm going to make money.

I can't stress this concept of discipline strongly enough. If you don't have the wherewithal to keep yourself in check, the concepts, ideas, and methodology that I have presented in this book can all be thrown out the window.

Lastly, I know who I am. Everybody wants to be something he or she is not. Basketball is my true passion. I would love to coach the New York Knicks. Some of my best friends are prominent NBA and college coaches. But that's not me. The same way, I'm not George Soros. Coming to terms with who I am as a trader, knowing my limitations, and doing what I do well—and not doing those things that I have no clue about—has brought me continued success. Too many people want to be who they are not, and professionally—whether in trading or in another field of business—that's where they run into trouble.

Summer Internship at MBF

And now I've come full circle: I got my start in trading because I was willing to tutor someone else's son. Now, I'm tutoring again, both the traders who work at MBF and the readers of this book. There is an old saying, "those who can do and those who can't teach." Hopefully I am one of the few who can do both.

I get an immense amount of satisfaction from the success of traders that I've taught over the years. I think that I live vicariously through each and every one of them. Perhaps it's my way of giving back out of gratitude for the opportunity that was given me. (If I hadn't been such a nosy 13-year-old, who knows where I would have ended up!) MBF's summer internship program is one of the best on Wall Street, if not the best. We combine teaching market theory along with practical hands-on trading and clerical experience. (For more information about our trading internship program, see our website at *www.mbfcc.com.*)

In this program, I try to attract kids from both high school and college who are all over the map in terms of their educational and socioeconomic backgrounds. We have students who are matriculating at Ivy League schools such as Princeton, Yale, and Penn, as well as inner-city kids who are just looking for a chance. In fact most of the underprivileged students know that they know nothing and therefore they have no preconceived notions about the market. As a result, they are easier to teach. Furthermore, since I have a lot of friends who are coaches at the high school and college level, each summer I include several of their athletes in our program, which leads to some pretty interesting lessons—both about trading and life.

It's a unique situation when you can pair up a finance major from the Wharton School of Business with the starting point guard for the University of Virginia, or someone going to John Hopkins University with the starting quarterback from Notre Dame. You may have a five-foot-seven finance major teamed up with a six-foot-eight basketball player, and he knows that if his Michael Jordan wannabe partner acts up in class, it's the little guy who gets into trouble. That has led to some comical confrontations, such as when I had to separate a six-foot-eight athlete from the chokehold of his five-foot-seven trading partner. Many of these summer interns have gone on to develop close personal friendships.

Hopefully, by dedicating all these resources to this program, I'll find my next RN. RN was my first summer intern almost 15 years ago. Currently, he trades more crude oil futures contracts in a day than most Wall Street firms trade in a week. He is widely recognized as the largest crude oil pit trader in the world. His success has provided me with a great deal of pride and personal satisfaction. At the end of each summer we conduct a mock trading session for these interns in the pit after the close of trading. No matter what his P&L was for the day—good or bad—RN always finds the time to participate and mentor these kids.

Being a Risk Manager

As I've taught and trained traders over the years, I've come to realize that just because someone can't manage him or herself in trading, it doesn't mean that they're not cut out for this business. My head risk manager, let's call him TOE, who oversees 65 proprietary traders and various black-box trading systems, could not control himself when he was trading for his personal account. TOE would repeatedly violate his self-imposed limits. But what he couldn't do for himself, he can quite successfully do for others. He can easily identify with other traders making the same mistakes that he used to make. TOE is able to spot the early warning signs that a trader is about to become unglued before it happens. He's the perfect risk manager. TOE is an example of someone who has turned an unfortunate personal trading experience into a very successful career at MBF.

Sentiment Divergence

There are several published indices that attempt to gauge the overall sentiment prevalent in a particular market. Typically, the higher the reading, the more bullish the underlying sentiment is. Even though it could never happen, at its extreme, a rating of 0 would indicate that everyone is bearish; conversely a rating of 100 would indicate that everyone is bullish.

For as long as I can remember, MBF has subscribed to one such service, the daily sentiment index (DSI Index) (for more information about the DSI Index, contact www.trade-futures.com). Over the years I have observed that markets can sustain a very high or low reading for a prolonged period of time. Therefore, trying to fade the market based solely on extreme readings usually doesn't work. However, what does seem to work well is when a daily sentiment index divergence pattern develops. It makes sense that if the market exhibits positive performance in a trading session, the percentage of market participants who are bullish should increase. Likewise, if a market exhibits weakness during the trading day, the percentage of market participants who are bullish should decrease. This holds true whether you are trading U.S. government bonds, crude oil, Boeing, or S&P futures. In all cases human nature acts and reacts the same way.

If crude oil yesterday settled at 23.50 and today settled at 24.00 and sentiment increased from a prior reading of 30 to let's say 42, this should not be a surprise: This is exactly what should happen. However, if crude oil rallied the same 50 cents, but the sentiment reading went from 30 to 20, that should catch your attention. In the latter case the market has rallied, but for some reason—as evidenced by the declining sentiment—there are many market participants who don't believe in the move the market just made. Either they think that the top has been set by today's action, or that the 50-cent rise in the market was really an aberration. Let's add to our trading example that tomorrow morning the market gaps open higher at 24.40, a 40-cent gap higher opening from the previous 24.00 close. Those traders who thought yesterday's market rally was just a bogus move are now caught and will quickly move to cover their short positions.

If the market had opened this day unchanged at 24.00 or lower, at say, 23.75, there is no trade to be made here. What you are trying to capitalize on is the market making a substantial move in one direction while at the same time a large number of market participants don't believe the move. In order for this trade to work, you need a gap higher opening so that these traders who sold into the market yesterday are trapped. The trade to make in this case is to buy the gap higher opening and get on board before these traders have a chance to cover. Obviously, the same would hold true if the reverse had occurred where the market had declined and most traders thought it was a bottom.

The more significant the opening, the greater the probability of success is for the trade. If the market opens up 1 dollar higher rather than 40 cents higher, this is a better trade. Furthermore, if the gap higher opening places the market at new contract high territory, as opposed to just opening in the middle of its range, this also increases the probability of success.

Black Monday

Years ago, I had a terrific young lady work for me as a clerk on the trading floor. She was organized, intelligent, and worked well under pressure. However, she did have one expensive vice: When she went shopping, she couldn't leave a store or the mall until her credit card was completely maxed out.

The Friday before, the crash had been options expiration, and many market participants went home that weekend thinking that the worst was over and expecting the stock market to stabilize in the coming week. On Black Monday—the day of the crash in 1987—I was trading in the silver futures pit, having a particularly bad day. However, on Monday morning, the S&P futures recorded their largest gap lower opening since the inception of the contract. I was fortunate to have gone home on Friday short S&P futures. Since I was getting killed in the silver pit, my instinct was to close out my profitable S&P trade and offset my silver losses. I didn't have any logical reason to liquidate my S&P position, I just wanted to ring the register and recoup my moronic silver trading losses. Obviously, I had failed to realize the significance of the monumental DSI divergence that was occurring right before my eyes.

So I said to my shopaholic clerk, "Do me a favor. Get me out of my S&P position, will you?"

She looked back at me with a puzzled expression and said, "Mark, the S&P DSI Index settled in the 30's on Thursday and higher on Friday. With this gap lower opening, isn't this a perfect example of a DSI divergence trade?"

I knew she was right the minute she said it. Here was the student telling the teacher what to do. I said to myself, if I don't go ahead and listen to her, what good are the lessons I'm teaching? I had to follow my own trading rules.

"Okay," I agreed. "Don't cover me at the market. Sell another five S&P contracts and put a stop in on all 25 at the Point C up. Let's see what happens."

What ensued next was the Crash of 1987. Three hours later, I bought back all my S&Ps for a big profit. Huge, that's all I'm going to say about the trade. I was also happy that I, the teacher, had taken my student's advice. She had recognized the DSI divergence trade unfolding in the S&P market and prevented me from closing out the trade prematurely.

Needless to say, after the close of trading that day I called my shopaholic clerk into my office. I told her, "Give me all your credit card bills" and right there I paid them all off.

Taking on Size—And Sizeable Traders

Some 10 years ago, I remember an incident that took place in the sugar futures pit. Back then, the New York Cotton Exchange, the New York Coffee, Sugar and Cocoa Exchange, the Commodities Exchange, and the New York Mercantile Exchange all shared one common trading facility at 4 World Trade Center. It wasn't until late 1997 that the Nymex and Comex moved to their own trading facility adjacent to the World Financial Center. (The terrorist incident on September 11, 2001, leveled 4 World Trade Center, forcing the Coffee, Sugar and Cocoa Exchange and the Cotton Exchange to relocate to a backup facility in Long Island City.)

Even though I owned a gold badge that allowed me to trade in any pit in New York, I spent most of my time in crude oil. However, if I spotted an opportunity in another market on the floor and crude oil was quiet, I would not hesitate to stroll over and get involved. One afternoon, crude oil was slow and I noticed that sugar had just reversed direction and was set up for a late-day Point C pivot trade. When I went into the sugar ring, it's fair to say that I was not welcomed with open arms. If it weren't for this ACD opportunity, sugar would be the last pit that you would find me in.

Back then, the sugar market closed around 1:45 EST. In sugar resided a very large local trader—both in terms of his trading size and his physical dimensions. He was consistently able to intimidate the market not only by trading in large quantities, but with his enormous physical presence. Around 12:30 that afternoon, sugar, after making a good A up earlier in the day, had reversed course and was about to make a good C down through the bottom of the daily pivot and three-day rolling pivot. I knew that I was risking only 15 to 20 ticks on the trade (to the Point D level).

Before me lay a tremendous risk/reward opportunity. I started selling like there was no tomorrow—200, 400, and finally about 700 contracts. As usual, relying on my ACD indicators had once again given me self-confidence to put on a large-scale position. The sugar trader whom I previously mentioned happened to find himself on the opposite side of the market. The more I sold, the more he bought, and the market just kept going lower and lower. He began shouting at me from across the pit, calling me every vulgarity known to mankind. I thought to myself, should I answer back? No, I decided. I was a guest in his pit. Besides, he was about 16 times my size. I was making money and he was getting annihilated. If he wanted to scream and yell, what did I care?

It was a couple of minutes before the 1:45 P.M. close and I covered my short position. The market had dropped some 40 to 50 cents since I had first initiated my shorts. Our large sugar trader on the other hand must have incurred losses well into the six figures, and he had steam coming out of his ears.

This monster, who had been cursing at me for the past hour, then turned to me and made a comment that combined the "F" word with a reference to my ethnic background. With that, I decided the time had come to reply, saying something about him and crack dealing in lower Manhattan.

The next thing I knew, this rhinoceros was charging at me, and what transpired next disrupted the entire close. The market had to be suspended for a half hour as approximately 10 order decks (consisting of stacks of trading cards with customer orders written on them) belonging to various floor brokers had been knocked over by our rhino.

Eventually, both of us were brought up before the exchange's business conduct committee on trading decorum charges. To be honest, I was a little unsure of how this would turn out. After all, I was a virtual stranger to the sugar pit. To the rhino, sugar was his home. But much to my surprise, the business conduct committee fined me only for use of vulgar language and did not suspend my trading privileges. My "wild kingdom" adversary got a fine twice as large as the one I had to pay, plus a three-day suspension—on top of losing all that money. In the end, the only reason that I had gone to that pit and confronted that big monster was because that good Point C pivot trade was an opportunity too good to pass up.

Getting Lost

The best way to learn how to trade a system like ACD is to get a little lost. When you're new to a city, whether it's New York, Chicago, or Los Angeles, you're never going to learn your way around if you just drive from Point A to Point B. But if you drive around, get lost, and then find your way home, you'll get to know the city a lot better. It's the same thing with trading. Whether you're in the pit or trading off the screen, you want to start out trading small, let yourself get lost in the market, and see if you can extricate yourself from whatever trading mess you find yourself in. From these early trading debacles you'll be able to determine whether you have the sufficient mental fortitude and the drive necessary for a successful trading career.

A case in point: A father-son trading team came to me a number of years ago with a proposition. The father suggested that both he and I back his son on Nymex. After I spent a couple of minutes with his son it was obvious that he possessed a rare intuitive trading gift. After shaking hands on the deal in my office, the father abruptly had a change of heart. He was nervous and told his son that he wasn't going to enter into this trading partnership with a madman like me, whom he called the Crazy Eddie (remember the lunatic electronics salesman in the television ads?) of the commodities world.

The next day, I called his son back into my office. I decided I'd back him myself because I thought he possessed that rare trading gift. I told him, "Screw your father. I'll teach you some basic ACD concepts, and then you'll go into the pit and just find your way."

Well, finding his way turned out to be a little more expensive than I had first imagined. Three days into his crude oil trading career, he lost $50,000 in one afternoon after an unfortunate set of circumstances. To make matters worse, he liquidated his position opposite other locals who really took him to the cleaners. His father came back to see me again and said, "Well, I know that you don't want to back my son any more."

"You're not involved with this deal," I told him.

Despite the losses he had racked up, I knew this kid possessed great pit skills and innate ability. It just so happened that his getting-lost adventure was a little more expensive than most. I made his father a new proposition: In six months time, we would evaluate his son's trading. If his son was down $100,000 in net trading, I would write the father a check for an additional $100,000. But, if the son was up $100,000, the father would have to write me a check for $100,000.

Luckily for his father, he didn't shake hands on that deal. His son went on to become one of the most successful crude oil traders in the pit. He is currently in the process of starting a multimillion-dollar hedge fund, and people are throwing money at him left and right.

Gartman's Rules

The stories that I have conveyed in this book have all illustrated some valuable insights into trading, whether it's the need to control your emotions, keep your ego in check, or learn from past mistakes. Hopefully you can identify with one or more of these trading weaknesses. Although ACD can help you refine your trading methodology, unless you have the proper mental approach, trading success will be impossible to achieve.

Dennis Gartman, author of the daily market commentary, The Gartman Letter (see *www.thegartmanletter.com*), also publishes once or twice a year "Gartman's 20 Ridiculously Simple

Rules of Trading." These rules can be found in their entirety in the Appendix. I think that if you review them, you'll find at least a couple of them to apply to your own trading. Among my favorites are: We must think like fundamentalists, but must trade like technicians. We must understand that markets can remain illogical far longer than any of us can remain solvent. We must understand that margin calls are the market's way of telling us that our analysis is wrong. And, finally, keep our technical systems simple.

Fear and Greed

Several years ago, I established a commodity trading advisory (CTA) business and named it F&G Commodities. I asked various people what they thought the F and the G stood for. Some guessed F for Fisher and G for someone else. Others just thought that I had randomly chosen two letters of the alphabet. What F and G symbolized are the two key ingredients that every trader needs to possess in the right combination in order to be successful—namely, fear and greed.

Whether you are trading stocks, futures, currencies, or anything else, you need to have enough fear in you, meaning a healthy amount of respect for the market that you are participating in. Allowing yourself to believe that you are always right, especially when the market is clearly dictating that you are dead wrong, is a sure path toward trading disaster. You need to be like the Sergeant Schultz character from the old TV sitcom, "Hogan's Heroes," who professed on numerous occasions, "I know nothing!" However, fear is not enough. A trader must also have a healthy amount of greed. You must be willing and able to press winning trades and allow these once-in-a-blue-moon occurrences to develop into large-scale winners. Sometimes it takes an iron will and a great deal of patience to be able to max out on these particular trades.

In 1990, during the Gulf War, trading in crude oil was treacherous. If you found yourself on the wrong side of the market, but stubbornly held onto your losers, the market made you pay dearly. At the first sign of trouble, you needed to recognize that you knew nothing and liquidate your position ASAP. During this time, there were two large futures brokers who stood on the top step, directly behind me in the crude oil ring. They worked for a major wire house and were constantly busy. On many occasions I took the opposite side of their orders—some small, some very large.

One day during the crisis, crude oil opened sharply higher but immediately began to sell off. After opening around 35, the market quickly broke below the bottom of the daily pivot range. As the market continued lower, these brokers were trying to execute large sell orders (along with everybody else in the pit). Each time I bid for crude oil, they tried to whack me with big size, but I wasn't biting. If they offered me 100 contracts, I'd buy 10 or 20, but then I would keep selling right along with them. I wasn't about to get in the way of this freight train.

These two brokers were terrific at their jobs and normally never lost their composure. But as wave after wave of selling kept hitting the market, they became unnerved. In the midst of all this chaos, a runner from their wire house came up behind them and handed them a huge stack of order tickets. It didn't take a genius to figure out that those orders were going to be sell stops that would be elected if the market went any lower. When I saw the utter look of panic and frustration on the faces of these two brokers, my greed instinct took over. As the market continued to trade lower and lower, I just kept selling. They kept asking me for bids, but I still would buy only 10 or 20 contracts, far less than the 100, 200, or 300 contracts that I would usually take off their hands. Both of these brokers frantically began to hit any bids that they could find. They just wanted to fill the orders and be done with this nightmare.

At that moment, I saw that the last print on the board was 30 cents lower than the prior print. Most of the time, brokers would just shout out the last digit of the price at which they were trying to execute. If crude oil was trading at 32.85, a broker could say, "At five." Or, as in this case, if the market were trading at 32.80, he could say "At 0." The confusion in this case was the result of the last trade taking place at another 0—33.10 and the current trade being done at 32.80. When one of these two brokers shouted out that he was offering "at 0," I wasn't sure just what 0 he meant. At this point, I was short 350 contracts and felt that the market was reaching a support area, a prior pivot on gap day point. It was probably, I thought, a good place to cover.

However, I needed to make sure what price the broker was offering. I grabbed the collar of his trading jacket and screamed at him, "What 0 are you selling at?"

He looked at me with a straight face and with sweat pouring down his shirt. With all sincerity, he replied, "Any f . . . ing 0 you want."

I proceeded to cover my short position and actually got long at 32.80. The market eventually declined even further, but the point of this story is not to show you how much money I made or lost. I had basically pressed on the gas when human emotion had gotten the best of even these two phenomenal brokers and was sure to milk this opportunity for all it was worth.

Be the House

It's amazing the misconception that people have about gambling in a casino. Most are shocked to learn that casinos have only a 1 to $1\frac{1}{2}$ percent statistical advantage over the player in both blackjack and craps but are still able to generate huge profits. Furthermore, these gaming establishments must spend millions of dollars on luxurious attractions and outlandish accommodations. Only in Las Vegas can you find volcanoes, shooting springs, replicas of the New York skyline, the Eiffel Tower, and the Venice canals.

On the other hand, if you have been able to digest ACD and incorporate it into your existing trading philosophies, you are now in a position to become "the house" when it comes to trading the markets. Hopefully, you have created a situation where instead of enjoying only a $1\frac{1}{2}$ percent advantage, your edge (after taking into account slippage and commissions) is closer to 5 percent.

If you've ever spent any time in a casino, you are familiar with the term *comp*. The casino rewards its patrons primarily for the amount of time they spend at the tables and not for the size of their wagers. The house knows that the longer they can keep the player gambling, the greater the chance that their statistical edge will kick in. Basically, the more time you spend at the tables, the more bets you are going to place, and the greater the probability that you will eventually walk out of the casino as a loser (one of the infamous bus people).

The casino would rather not have someone make a single large wager for $100,000 and, win or lose, immediately walk away. Although the house has a small statistical edge in blackjack or craps, any one hand of cards or roll of the dice is completely random. What the house wants is for you to keep playing. The passage of time is the casino's best friend and the player's worst enemy.

Applying this concept to the markets, if you can develop this 5 percent trading edge, you would want to act just like the casino. Can the house lose 10 hands of blackjack in a row? Of course it can. Can you have a string of 10 losing trades in a row? Absolutely. However, if you spread out your trading bets over many independent situations and bet small enough on each one, a run of bad luck will not put you out of business. You are simply trying to identify as many ACD setups as possible and place these bets. As long as you are able to identify low-risk high-reward trading opportunities, you'll always live for another day. In the end, you will be one of the survivors. And in this business, those traders who survive are the ones who are successful.

If the odds are in your favor of making a profit with your trading system, then keep your trade size consistent, cut your losses short, and know that, over time, you'll be successful.

Measuring and Monitoring Risk

The proprietary traders who work at MBF fall into one of two categories: They are either discretionary traders or they are traders who develop black-box systems. The systems group is far easier to manage. Each trade requires a particular setup and has specific risk-reward criteria. Furthermore, each system portfolio has individual position stops, as well as the portfolio having an overall dollar risk limit. The discretionary group presents a far greater challenge to manage, since we are now dealing more with trading personalities than trading positions.

Floor traders in the various energy and metal trading pits along with off-floor, short-term, seat-of-the-pants traders make up this discretionary group. To them, long term is never more than a few trading hours. Short term may be as little as five seconds. Our job is to help these traders find their own comfort level. One trader may have the psychological makeup and discipline to trade 50 or 100 contracts at a clip, in let's say, natural gas. While another may feel more comfortable trading spreads.

We set each trader's position limits based on three different types of trade scenarios.

1. Is it a trade that will be initiated and liquidated within a matter of seconds, "a scalp trade," or will it be longer term?
2. Is it a spread or outright trade?
3. Is it a trade that will be closed out by the end of the day or it will it be a position held overnight?

Obviously, a trader who scalps the market with 100 lots at a time probably has the same risk profile as someone who trades one-third of this size but keeps the position on for 10 to 15 minutes. Furthermore, a 50-lot trader in let's say, natural gas, fits a different risk profile than a 50-lot trader in crude oil, just as someone who trades 3,000 IBM at a clip takes a different level of risk than someone who trades 3,000 Yahoo.

In the appendix are exhibits of the daily pivot sheets for both stock and commodities. The column labeled $ risk is a proprietary measure of the inherent risk across all futures contracts and all stocks. Ten S&P contracts have a lot more risk than 10 natural gas contracts, which have a lot more risk than 10 Comex Gold contracts. For example, this $ risk measurement tells us how many natural gas contracts to trade for every one S&P contract. If the S&Ps have a daily risk of 6,000 while natural gas has a risk of only 1,000, for each S&P contract that you put on, you would have to trade six natural gas contracts in order to get the same risk equivalent position.

No matter how large or small the trader is, MBF follows the same risk guidelines. Since most traders have type A personalities and are goal oriented and very competitive, we provide incentive to them by allowing them to trade on a bigger scale if they meet certain intramonth profitability levels. This is our way of letting a trader who is on a hot streak step on the gas. We are trying to allow this trader who is in the groove to go for doubles and triples, not just singles. Conversely, if a trader is going through a slump, we will cut his position size. Sometimes as little as a one-third, or as much as a one-half or even two-thirds, to prevent this slump from becoming a black hole from which he can never recover. Remember, those who survive their bad runs are the ones who are successful in the end.

At the end of each month, whether a trader has had his position size increased or decreased throughout the month, we erase the blackboard and start the following month at his original position limits. The rationale being that the trader who has been on a roll is eventually going to cool off and we want to bring him back to his normal size before he gives back a significant amount of his profits to the market. On the other hand, the rationale for the trader who has been in a slump is that if you believe that nothing has fundamentally changed in this person's trading ability, forcing him to remain at minimal position levels for too long will make it almost impossible for him to recoup his losses and return to profitability.

Lastly, we encourage our traders to trade bigger when the markets are busier and volatile. This is exactly when a floor trader or a short-term trader can best capitalize on their trading edge. However, most traders do the exact opposite. Out of fear they decrease their size when the markets are volatile and increase their size when the markets are dead.

It Can Never Happen . . .

My family loves to ski. I like to sit in the sun. My objective when we travel to Colorado is summed up by the *Saturday Night Fever* theme song, "Staying Alive." While my family is off skiing, I'm happy just to sit in the lodge or ride up and down the gondola. One day, while I was just hanging out, I struck up a conversation with a gentleman who turned out to be the head trader of a large Boston-based energy-trading firm. As you can guess, our discussion eventually turned to trading.

He explained that his firm's strategy involved trading *cracks*. Crack trading involves trading heating oil or gasoline versus crude oil. (In a refinery, both heating oil and gasoline are produced by being cracked out of crude oil.) Their trading methodology was straightforward. When they felt that the crack spreads were overvalued, they would get short; when they felt the spreads were undervalued, they would get long.

I asked him, "But what happens, the one time out of 20, when the crack spread blows out ridiculously for no apparent reason? What happens when that once-in-a-blue-moon set of events occurs, and the crack goes to astronomical levels for absolute no apparent economic reason?"

"It can never happen to us," he informed me. "We have the financial backing of two large banks in the Northeast, giving us enough ammunition to withstand any trading aberrations while we wait for the market to come back to reality."

I didn't feel it was my place to disagree or offer any advice. After all, I had just met the man. But I can tell you the first thing that I did when I got back to New York was to walk up to a broker who worked for this firm and tell him to start looking for a new job. I told him the entire ski lodge story and warned him that eventually his firm was going out of business; it was just a matter of time. The broker laughed.

That following winter, the crack spread blew out from 3.00 to 10.00. My Nostradamus prediction had come true. That well-capitalized trading firm was forced to liquidate their positions at absolutely the worst possible time. In fact, some bank executive with no clue about trading instructed this floor broker to liquidate over 6,000 crack spreads in a three-hour period of time! Of course, I made sure I was in the pit to capitalize on this opportunity.

The moral of this story is, it doesn't matter how much money you have, or how smart you think you are, the market can outlast—and outsmart—you.

Another case in point is Metallgeselschaft, better known as MG, which used to be the largest single player in the energy markets. MG's problem was that they traded at a size that was too big for the market to absorb. You want to be a market participant; you don't want to be the market.

MG, however, had become the target of every energy-trading firm on the street. Every firm knew the size of MG's positions, which had to be rolled from month to month. In this book, I've stressed over and over that in order to trade successfully, you need a market that has sufficient volatility and liquidity. MG's size was three times as large as the market's liquidity would allow for. I wrote a letter to the Nymex compliance department, telling them of my fears about MG's size and the way they were managing their positions. Needless to say, my warnings went unheeded. Within a year of my letter being sent to compliance, MG went broke.

Next!

No doubt you've heard the expression "no pain, no gain." I guess that means in order to be successful in trading you must be able to endure all the emotional abuse and financial pain that the market can inflict upon you while waiting for losing positions to become winners. To me, that's total nonsense. If there is anything that you've learned from this book, it's that successful trading is a matter of seeking out immediate gratification. If the market doesn't move your way within a short time of putting on a trade, just get out.

Imagine a single guy going to a bar, looking to get lucky, and there are only four hours before closing time. If he walks up to a girl and discovers that there is no chemistry between them, is he going to waste his time with her? No. He is going to say to himself, "Next!" and move on. The same holds true for trading. Don't waste your time. There is no reason to endure significant market pain or frustration. Allow time to act as a stop in forcing you to liquidate stagnant and losing positions. Remember, if everyone can get into a trade at the same level that you did, how good can the trade really be?

I have asked countless brokers and phone clerks this question: How many times has a customer initiated a position and instructed you to stop him out if the market doesn't go anywhere within, let's say, a half-hour? The answer invariably is "nobody." Most people trade just with price stops and not with time stops. They think they have to endure some initial pain. You, however, should not.

An important rule of trading is that time is much more important than price.

ACD also helps you to capitalize on trading opportunities when markets become ridiculously volatile and all over the map. Those are the times when you really need to keep your wits about you and trade as objectively as possible. The ACD indicators and ideas that have been explained in this book allow even the most discretionary of traders to have some systems-based foundation.

Psychologically, using ACD as a foundation for one's trading allows a trader to take personal credit for all his success, while at the same time, allowing him to blame all his bad days on some stupid system.

Losing the Value of a Dollar

There are many businesses in which successful people over the years make a hell of a lot more money than those in trading. However, I do not know of a single business where a person can make or lose as much money in such a short period of time as in the trading world. The greatest danger that one faces after being exposed to the markets is the loss of their personal monetary value system.

In the summer internship program, I warn all parents of this potential risk. While working in the trading environment is a tremendous learning opportunity, these interns will likely lose their perspective on money. As interns they are assigned as clerks to a particular trader. It is not uncommon for them to witness these traders make or lose 5,000 to 10,000 in a matter of minutes. Now suppose at the end of that day the intern is at the mall, shopping for a shirt. He finds one priced at 29.99 and another one priced at 39.99. Subconsciously, regardless how grounded or disciplined his background, in the back of his mind he is eventually going to ask himself, "What's 10?" I just saw some lunatic lose 5,000 in about five seconds.

In my opinion, that exhibits the biggest drawback of entering a trading career. No matter how well grounded or disciplined you are, your value system will suffer. If you are successful at trading, it's not so bad. However, if you are unsuccessful, not only do you have to deal with your financial losses, you also have to return to the real world with a diminished respect for money. Furthermore, people who fail as traders tend to view themselves as failures in life. No matter how much I try to impress on them that trading success is only a very small part of someone's overall success in life, it's a hard pill for them to swallow.

Harry the Hoof

Take the example of a very successful speculator whom I'll call Harry the Hoof. This trader has three main passions in life: his family, trading, and horse racing. Back in 1999, when the equity markets were rocking and rolling, it was not uncommon for him to have equity positions in the millions of dollars. One afternoon, after suffering what turned out to be his worst day of an otherwise very successful year, he came to see me after the close. I figured that he would just want to "lie down" on my trading couch for a while and lament over his seven-figure loss for the day. However, that afternoon, the 1,000,000 that he had just lost was not foremost on his mind. Harry the Hoof was more frustrated that he could not watch the Aqueduct racing channel from his office than he was upset about his trading debacle. The value of a dollar had become so trivial to him that he could no longer relate to the amount of money he had just lost. All he cared about was some four-legged animals galloping down some racetrack. Luckily for him, both his sense of value and his blood pressure returned to normal the next day.

Hopefully, these stories that I've shared with you in this chapter have taught you an important lesson. You don't need complicated Einstein formulas to make money in the markets. You do need to be disciplined and comfortable with yourself. No matter how good of a trader you think you are, the markets are always going to screw with your head and test your mental fortitude. Remember, the survivors are also the ones who make up the market's success stories.

Chapter 8

TRADER INTERVIEWS

For seven chapters, I've explained the ACD system and how its lessons can be applied to any trading methodology—from ultra-short-term day trading to long-term positions lasting weeks or even months. It can be used whether you are trading on the floor or off the screen. The question probably has come to your mind: "How do other people use this?" In this chapter, you will read about how other professional traders use ACD as part of their trading strategies. Some of the traders interviewed work with me; others are customers of my clearing firm. All of them are successful, both in terms of their annual trading profits and their longevity in this business.

Casey—Getting Out When You're Wrong

Before Casey traded crude oil futures on the floor of the New York Mercantile Exchange, he had been an options trader at the American Stock Exchange. At one time he was the youngest specialist, making markets in very active options such as Motorola (MOT) and Digital Equipment (DEC). Casey traded on the stock exchange floor during the Crash of 1987. Motorola closed on Black Monday at $52. It opened the next day at $60. A half-hour later, Motorola plummeted to $30. For a while there was absolutely no bid for the stock! Despite this frontlines market experience, when Casey moved to crude oil futures to try his hand in a futures pit, he was not prepared to handle the chaotic and volatile pit environment, compared with the orderly specialist system that prevailed in options. While he possessed strong market intuition, he had entered an entirely different universe, one in which he would have to learn new skills (including ACD) to plan, execute, and manage his trading. Here's how Casey describes his transition and how ACD helped him:

> Trading commodities, compared with trading options, was so dramatically different. When you're a specialist in options, you always know who your customers are. The brokers who transacted the orders worked for Morgan or Merrill or another of the large houses, and when they asked for a quote on a particular option, you knew what they had done in the past. So you knew what they were probably going to do now—if they were adding to a position, if they were buying outright, or selling covered calls or covered puts.
>
> In commodities, you're standing in an open outcry pit. The same broker could be buying for 15 minutes for one customer and then selling for the next 15 minutes for another customer. It is a very volatile environment. When I started out in crude oil, I was a spread trader. I was making markets in the back months—ignoring the first two months that were very active. I remember doing a spread one day. I bought 20 contracts of a back month, and then I had to lay off the other side in the front month to create a spread. I was so focused on just getting that spread on, that I offered the front month way below the best bid. One trader in that pit gave me such a dirty look that he made me want to go to the bathroom and cry!
>
> Still, Mark had faith in me. He knew I was a good trader and he supported me—even on a day when I lost about $75,000 and I was sure that he was going to fire me. Before I met Mark, I always thought that I knew which way the market was going. That's not the problem with trading. What you do, how you react when you're wrong, and how you limit your losses is the hard part. For that, ACD is the perfect system in the world for me.
>
> I don't think you can totally rely on just a mechanical system to trade and be successful. So much of trading is emotion and intuition. What distinguishes Mark from everybody else is his discipline, his money management skills, and his lack of emotion when he's wrong—all of

which he has incorporated into ACD. He doesn't care about losing, and I don't care about losing. Too many people just focus on being right. All they care about is being right. For me, what I want to do is make money.

If I showed you five traders and each had two trades on, I can tell you that four of those five would get out of the winning trades too early and wait for the losers to become winners. As for me, if I'm in two positions and one of them is going against me, I get out of the loser. It doesn't matter if I lost $75,000 on that trade. I just get out of it and go on to the next one. By hanging on to losers, traders are wasting other opportunities to get into new profitable trades.

The bottom line is, who cares if you're right or if you're wrong? In the end all you're trying to do is make the most amount of money while taking on the least amount of risk. If the first five trades are loser, loser, loser, loser, and loser, you still have to know where you are going to get out of the next trade if you're wrong, and that's what ACD does for me.

ACD has also taught me that there is no such thing as price. During the 1990 Gulf War, I watched Mark walk into the crude oil pit and every day he got long. I used to say to myself, "Hasn't the market gone up enough?" But watching Mark, I learned that when the market is going up, it's going up. And when it's going down, it's going down. The price doesn't matter.

I can tell you a story about the Nasdaq in early 2000. I sensed that the market was going to crash. But you have to be right on your timing—not just on your idea. I was short the Nasdaq futures, which were trading near 5000. Then P&G pre-announced earnings before the open—and S&Ps were up five handles (500 points). I couldn't understand it! The Nasdaq was up about 60 points. I had come in short the Nasdaq, and I was down about $120,000. I added to my short position by selling 50 S&Ps. When the stock market opened, the Dow dropped something like 400 points, and the S&P dropped 30 handles. I immediately covered my S&P position. Then I foolishly decided to sell another 20 Nasdaq futures. At that point, the Nasdaq was down 60 points. I was up $500,000 or maybe

$600,000. Then the market reversed and exploded! The Nasdaq ended up closing that day up 100 points! I lost all the money back and more. The moral of this story is, once again, there is no such thing as price in trading. When a market is going up—it's going up. As Mark says, if you find a market that's going up and you don't know why, stay long until you find out the reason.

If anybody thinks that trading isn't anything more than a form of gambling, they're kidding themselves. However, in trading, you're able to cut your losses and maximize your profits. If you lose 5 or 8 cents when you're wrong, but make 1.5 or 2.5 times that amount when you're right, you shift the odds to your favor. Then you don't even have to be right more times than you're wrong!

The other thing about trading is you have to be consistent, which is another ACD rule. If you change your style of trading every day, you're not going to make much money.

Today I use ACD to validate my ideas or at least to give me reference points at which to get out if I'm wrong. If I love crude oil today and it closed above the pivot, then I'm going to buy 100 contracts and risk to the A down, or whatever. If I come in and I'm bullish on crude oil and it makes a good A up or a C up, then I use ACD as a back-stop. In extremely volatile markets, ACD works the best.

ACD is more than just A ups and A downs. I think it's a philosophy of trading. There are a lot of traders who buy and then pray while the market goes against them because they think that it will eventually go their way. Most traders average down and just wait for the market to turn their way. Trading my way, I always have a defined amount of money that I am willing to lose. I let the market decide how much money I'm going to make.

RN—Learning the System from the Beginning

RN learned the ACD system from day one. A college student at the time, RN was the first intern ever hired by MBF. At the time, ACD was a system in the making. His assignment was to man-

ually graph the minute-by-minute price action in the silver futures pit. "I knew the system worked because I was the one who
first charted the whole thing," he recalls. Today, RN is one of the
largest crude oil locals at Nymex. RN has tailored ACD and its
pivot concepts to help him trade thousands of crude oil contracts
on a daily basis:

> I'm a very active trader/scalper, and I am involved from
> the opening bell. I can't wait for 20 minutes to go by be-
> fore formulating an opinion. I use a one-minute opening
> range, but I base it on the second active trading month in
> crude oil futures and not the front month. I find that by
> using the second month, it eliminates a lot of the "noise"
> in the market, and it gives me a clearer picture of what's
> really going on. Instead of using an A value of 8 cents and
> a C value of 13 cents, I use 15 cents to determine
> my Point As and 20 cents for my Point Cs.
>
> With my style of trading, using an 8-to 9-cent Point A
> value, I found that I was getting caught and stopped out
> too often. I had to find a time frame that would work bet-
> ter for me. Using a 15-cent A value off a 1-minute open-
> ing range has turned out to work unbelievably well.
>
> I don't wait for an ACD signal. Rather, I use ACD to
> help me determine whether I'm right or wrong. Some-
> times I use the system to help me make a decision
> whether I should take on a momentary large scalp posi-
> tion, while at other times I use it to give me a bias for the
> entire day's action.
>
> For example, if coming into the trading session I know
> that I'm bearish, I'll get short right on the opening. Then
> if the market sells off and makes an A down, I would
> probably add to the position since I know that ACD is
> confirming my initial opinion. However, if I get short on
> the opening and the market makes an A up, I'm not going
> to be stubborn. I take my loss and go on.
>
> Keep in mind that I may trade in and out of a position
> a thousand times a day. I'm constantly getting in and out
> of the market very quickly. Let's say that the opening
> range was 25.90 to 26.00, and the market makes an A
> down at 25.74. If I'm already short and the market goes

down to 25.60, I would probably cover my short position and get a little long in anticipation of a bounce. If I'm right and the market rallies back to the 25.74 A down area, I'd probably cover that long position and get short again. If the market never bounced from 25.60, I would just sell out my long position for a small loss.

As you can see, I use the A points in ACD as a scalping tool, both for entry and exit. I don't use the Point Cs very much. Usually, Point Cs don't occur until late in the trading day, and by that time I probably have dug myself into a position one way or another. But if I'm flat and the market does make a good C up or C down late in the day, I would go with it.

I also use the pivot range to determine reference points for my trading. Let's say that the market makes an A down at 25.74 and the pivot is 20 cents below that at 25.54. If the market gets down near the pivot, say at around 25.58, I would typically cover and wait to see how the market reacts around this area. In this example, I'm looking to see whether the pivot will hold and act as support.

I have often found the pivot turns out to be the high or low for the day. Let's say the opening range for crude oil is 25.15 to 25.20, and the pivot range for the day is 25.22 to 25.28. If I have any inkling that the market is going to sell off, I'll get short right off the bat, because I'm only risking about 10 ticks up to top of the pivot range. It's a low-risk trade with the opening range being right below the pivot. I'm selling with the expectation that the pivot will turn out to be the high of the day.

I also use the pivot concept when I'm trading from off the floor. A few days before the Thanksgiving 2001 holiday, I was short the Nasdaq. I needed to decide if I was going to get out of my position or stay with it. The pivot in the Nasdaq futures for that day was around 1622, and the Nasdaq opened around 1615. With that scenario, I decided to stay short, figuring that the pivot could mark the high for the day. It turned out to be a wise decision—the pivot was the high for the day and the Nasdaq settled 73.50 points lower. In general, I use ACD and the pivot ranges to reinforce my convictions or to tell me when I'm just plain wrong.

Speedy, the Scalper

For Speedy, when it comes to trading, a few minutes might as well be an eternity. A former floor broker and now natural-gas futures local, he has spent his entire career on the floor of the New York Mercantile Exchange. As a local he attempts to take advantage of momentary market opportunities, making scalp trades that get him in and out of the market in a matter of seconds. For him, ACD is a point of reference not only for entering trades, but for exiting as well. With his ultra-short-term style of trading, Speedy uses mostly micro ACD—Points A, B, C, and D—to plot his trades:

> I tend to use the ACD system on a micro basis because my trading is very short term. While I am aware of many longer-term indicators, I really don't incorporate them into my trading. Maybe once or twice a year I'll put on a long-term position, typically in options. But most of the time, as a short-term trader, the long-term indicators aren't going to make a difference for me. In the time it takes for a long-term indicator to flash a signal, I could be in and out of the market hundreds of times.
>
> Whether you trade on the floor or at the screen, you have to know what kind of trader you are. I don't like to sit and analyze the market. When I'm trading, my strength is understanding what's taking place in the pit and reacting to the market action in a split second. I try to sense whether the market is overvalued due to greed or undervalued out of fear.
>
> These are my skills. That is the way I trade on the floor and make a living. Other people may look at one market and its relation to another market and decide that the relationship between the two is out of whack. Someone else might see the big picture and plan out a trade that takes a week to unfold. That's not me. I try to determine how everyone is going to react to the market's second-by-second movements and try to be a quarter of a step ahead of them.
>
> I tend to use ACD as a confirmation tool. I always feel comfortable if I have an opinion and the ACD bias is in

the same direction. It's easy to use ACD when it's confirming what you already think is going to happen. It's much tougher for me to use it as a risk-management tool when I think the market is going one way, but ACD is telling me it's going the other. There are at least several times a week when I'll have a market opinion that is contrary to ACD and it always ends up biting me in the ass. I get an idea in my head that the market is going up and instead it makes a good A down. Instead of getting out, I just hang on. The hard part of trading is admitting when you're wrong. I wish that I used ACD to stop me out of my losing trades as often as I use it to confirm my winning ones.

ACD is not a black-box system that you can only use by itself, and that's the beauty of it. It works with other short-term indicators that you might use. I look at a lot of other indicators that aren't part of ACD: previous highs and lows for the week, the one-minute moving average, and so forth. ACD is complementary to anything else you may be using.

Look, I'm a trader for MBF, working here in The House of ACD. If we all did the same thing, if we all made the same trades, then the P&L sheets for the 20 of us in natural gas would be exactly the same! The truth of the matter is, that's not what happens. We all have our own opinions and sometimes we fight against each other in that trading ring. In the final analysis, we all use ACD in our own unique way. The best way for me just happens to be in risk managing my trades.

RIBI—Staying Out of the Penalty Box

RIBI, the largest natural-gas futures trader at Nymex, trades mostly spreads—meaning taking positions based on the differential between two months. He does not use ACD for entering and existing his spread positions. Rather, he uses the ACD system when he trades the market outright, particularly as a kind of life preserver to keep from drowning in a bad position:

The reality is that I wish I could use the ACD system more. I think it's an amazing money-management system. When I get myself in trouble trading, I look at the ACD numbers—particularly points like a good C up or C down—to figure out where I had better bail out.

Ninety percent of what I do is spread trading; I trade zillions of spreads every day. Because of that, I can't use the ACD system as much as other traders. I do use it, however, when I'm in a position—especially when it turns against me. When that happens, I look to ACD to find out just how bad it's going to be. I look to see if there is a Point A or a Point C coming up—and if that's really going to put the nail in my coffin.

For example, let's say the market is coming off, but I've been trading from the long side. If the market is going to make a Point C down, it will change my mind about scaling into a long position—or at least it should, if I haven't lost my discipline. When the market does make those Point C downs, I can really feel the push. And if I've been on the wrong side of the market, that's where I will feel the pain.

ACD lets me see what's up ahead for me in the market. It's like the storm finder that I have on my boat. Using that storm finder, I can determine if the weather is going to get really bad and I better head to shore, or if I can wait it out. The same way, when I'm stuck in a position—particularly because I have lost my discipline—ACD lets me see how bad it's going to get.

I can tell you this, if you have discipline and you apply ACD to your trading, you will absolutely—no question about it—make money. Where the breakdown occurs is if you don't have discipline. That's 90 percent of the problem. Or if you have no idea how to manage your positions, what this system does is show you how to manage them. The key to the whole puzzle is discipline; the more you have, the better you'll trade.

The best traders have incredible amounts of discipline when they have a trading position on. They cut their losses and run. That's the hardest thing in the world for a lot of other traders. Maybe you're bullish on the market, but your indicators say to get out. After you do, the market goes up this one time. Then you question your system. But if you stick with the system, you'll be a lot better off.

That's the challenge for me. I take these big hits, and then I have to take some time off and search for a way to regain my discipline. When I'm in the penalty box, I realize that I either have to get a grip on myself or spend more time away from trading. Using a system like ACD and keeping your discipline—that's what really works when it comes to trading.

Vernon—Finding the Bias for the Day

For Vernon, who trades commodities, stocks, and currencies both on and off the floor, ACD is a valuable tool for determining the bias of the day for both his day trades and for establishing longer-term positions. Like other traders, Vernon incorporates ACD with other trading systems that he uses, giving him a consensus of opinion:

I like to use the ACD system to get my bias for the day. If an A up is made, you have a bullish bias for that day. With an A down, it's a bearish bias for the day. And when you have a Point C—and that doesn't happen very often—that's a powerful indicator. When that occurs, that's an absolute step-up-and-press-your-bet situation.

When I'm day trading, the ACD system gives me my overall bias. So if the market has made an A up, I'm going to be looking to buy the dips when they occur. Or, if the market has made an A down, I'm going to sell the rallies. I will hold that bias until the market breaks through to the other side of the opening range.

For longer-term trades, I'm using different kinds of charts and indicators. But what the ACD system does is give me the day structure for entering a trade. But if the market has made an A down, that's not the day I'm going to enter that long position. The day structure is always in control, regardless of whether you like a market or you don't like a market. You're not going to enter that trade until the day structure is right.

If you have a bullish bias, you may have to wait two days while the market makes an A down and then another A down. But on the third day, when the market makes an A up, that's when you want to establish that long position.

I especially like to use ACD when it generates a signal late in the trading session. In the markets that I trade, those late-day signals tend to have significant follow-through. The opening range (the point of reference for determining the Point As, Bs, Cs, and Ds) can vary. For the longest time, I used to use a half-hour opening range. Now I use 20 minutes. It doesn't matter, as long as you're consistent. Find the time frame that works best for you and stick to it.

Dove—Adapting ACD

DOVE, a crude oil futures trader, is making the transition from trading exclusively on the floor to trading both on the floor and off the screen. Over the years, his trading methodology has developed into what he calls a modified version of ACD, using the opening range and the pivot range as his guide for both day, trades and position trades:

I have followed the ACD system for years. In the beginning, I used it to a T. But over time, I modified it to suit my trading. For example, when it comes to the opening range time frame, I use a half hour. Others may use 5 minutes, or 15 minutes or 20 minutes. But I have found—at least until the crude market was disrupted after the events of September 11—that the first half hour was the perfect time frame for me.

Based on that, you could see who was going to play in the game that day. If the funds were going to do anything, they would be there in that first half hour. Because of that, most of the time I found that the first half hour would either be the high or the low of the day. Once the market broke out of the first half hour range, I would go with the trend.

For example, let's say the high of the opening range was 30 and the low was 15. If the market went through 30, I would get long, and that would make the opening range the low of the day. But if it went through 15, I would get short.

Another concept that I use has to do with the ACD pivot range. This range basically shows where the bulk of the trading has occurred in the previous session. Let's say the range is 60 down to 25. If the market stays under 60, then I would expect it to fill that whole range. I would not look to sell 60 and then buy back at 55. I would look for a larger move to be made in that range. I tend to trade a little more long-term than a scalper would.

Here's another way that I use both the pivot range and the opening range. Let's say the market gaps open lower below the prior day's low and rallies from the opening range. Then I would get long. If the market is able to get back into the previous day's range, I would look for it to continue to rally to the pivot range since that's where most of the trading took place from the day before.

But I have to say that one of the things I've learned, particularly when I was at MBF, is discipline. I realize that trading is 30 percent technical and 70 percent discipline. There are times that your system may not work for three days in a row. You're tempted to say, "That's it. It doesn't work anymore." But you have to stick with it and be consistent. And if there is one thing that ACD stresses, it's discipline.

Granite—Trading off the Floor

Granite trades all energy futures from upstairs, eliminating the emotion, noise, and confusion that pervades the trading ring. A former energy desk trader for a major Wall Street firm, Granite sees the trading floor as the perfect place for making very short-term scalp trades. But for system day trades or position trading lasting several days, an upstairs trading office away from the pit is a better venue for him. To enter and manage his trades, Granite uses the opening range and pivot range as reference points for his trading system:

The opening range gives me a point of reference to use as a gauge to see how the market reacts around this level. For example, if most traders are bearish and the market opens and immediately trades lower, you will tend to see a lot of short-covering if the market begins to retrace back towards the opening range. At that point, if the market doesn't go through the opening range, I would sell against the top of this range, expecting that the market should come off again. But if the market does rally above the opening range, then you may have a bad news, good action situation. In that case you would want to reverse and get long.

I use the pivot range in a similar way to the opening range. Basically both ranges give me a point of reference for my trading.

Trading a system is better when you're off the floor. In the trading pit, it's very difficult to trade a system because you get caught up in the emotion around you. When I do go to the floor, I use ACD to scalp a few cents here and there. Being on the floor, it's easier to feel the order flow and sense what's coming. But it's almost impossible to use a system on the floor. It goes against your human nature. With all the emotions of the pit, you automatically get out of your positions faster.

I trade almost exclusively off the floor, both day trading and position trading. The reference points of the opening range and the pivot help me to manage my positions. Sometimes you have to day trade around your position or protect your position. These reference points help me to do that.

Let's say you have a long-term short position on, but on a particular day the market is strong and on a good A up. While the short-term movement of the market may not have changed your long-term view of it, you would have to day trade from the long side to protect your longer-term short position.

As you can see, all the traders interviewed in this chapter possess two common traits.

1. They all use the opening range and the pivot range as reference points. Regardless of whatever other systems they use,

these traders look to ACD as a confirmation tool or a barom-
eter of market activity and sentiment.

2. Emphasis is on discipline (the second and more important trait).
    There have been two traders who have worked with me at MBF
    who should have retired by now with millions of dollars in the
    bank. One of them knows the ins and outs of ACD better than
    anyone. The other was probably the fastest and most proficient
    pit trader I had ever seen. Yet, both no longer trade and never
    fulfilled their potential. In the end, their lack of discipline and
    their failure to control their emotions led to their demise.
    Whether a short-term scalper or a position trader, whether on
    or off the floor, successful traders knows that discipline is what
    allows them to enter their trades when the odds are in their
    favor and, more importantly, to get out when they're wrong. As
    Casey says, being right is not the problem. What you do when
    you're wrong is the crucial issue.

APPENDIX

TABLE A.1

ACD system—commodities
First trading
day of the month
Monday, December 3, 2001

Comm.	Month	High	Low	Close	Pivot	+/−	Pivot Range	
CRUDE	F	2050	1938	2009	1999	5	1994	2004
CRUDE	G	2073	1965	2039	2026	7	2019	2033
NAT GAS	F	2690	2555	2634	2626	4	2622	2630
NAT GAS	G	2785	2670	2746	2734	6	2728	2740
UNL GAS	F	5670	5390	5602	5554	24	5530	5578
UNL GAS	G	5755	5505	5695	5652	22	5630	5674
HEAT	F	5690	5430	5577	5566	6	5560	5572
HEAT	G	5750	5510	5659	5640	10	5630	5650
S&P	Z	113600	112500	112950	113017	33	112984	113050
NASDAQ	Z	159200	156300	156700	157400	350	157050	157750
GOLD	G	2787	2755	2779	2774	3	2771	2777
SILVER	H	4250	4145	4227	4207	10	4197	4217
US BOND	H	10408	10319	10403	10331	1	10330	10400
SUGAR	H	768	751	764	761	2	759	763
COFFEE	H	4700	4560	4610	4623	7	4616	4630

Appendix

TABLE A.2

Commodities—first two weeks of January 2001

Symbol	High	Date	Low	Date	Close	Date	Pivot Low	Pivot High
Aussie Bond March	94695	1010103	94485	1010104	94610	1010112	94590	94603.3
Corn March	232	1010102	218.25	1010112	219.25	1010112	221.208	225.125
Cocoa March	870	1010112	752	1010103	860	1010112	811	843.667
CRB Index	23091	1010111	22411	1010103	22954	1010112	22751	22886.3
Cotton March	6180	1010102	5910	1010105	6112	1010112	6045	6089.67
DAX Index	655694	1010104	617244	1010103	649405	1010112	636469	645093
German Bund March	10978	1010105	10837	1010112	10850	1010112	10869.2	10907.5
Dmark March	4925	1010103	4760	1010103	4867	1010112	4842.5	4858.83
USDollar March	11040	1010103	10804	1010103	10932	1010112	10922	10928.7
Euro Curr March	96150	1010105	92870	1010104	95190	1010112	94510	94963.3
Euro$ March	94810	1010108	94135	1010102	94545	1010112	94472.5	94520.8
Coffee March	6800	1010108	6200	1010109	6500	1010112	6500	6500
Brent Crude March	2572	1010105	2390	1010109	2556	1010112	2481	2531
Lumber March	22620	1010103	20960	1010110	21280	1010112	21450	21790
Live Cattle March	8025	1010112	7605	1010109	7957	1010112	7815	7909.67
Footsie March	63035	1010102	60380	1010103	61860	1010112	61707.5	61809.2
Gilts March	11666	1010103	11465	1010112	11481	1010112	11509.2	11565.5
Live Hogs Feb.	5775	1010105	5545	1010111	5670	1010112	5660	5666.67
Nasdaq March	265000	1010105	210800	1010103	254000	1010112	237900	248633
OJ March	8250	1010105	7490	1010104	7660	1010112	7730	7870
Pbellies March	6830	1010102	6377	1010111	6612	1010112	6603.5	6609.17
Bpound March	15100	1010103	14752	1010112	14786	1010112	14832.7	14926
Crude Oil Feb.	3015	1010112	2665	1010102	3005	1010112	2840	2950
Gold Feb.	2738	1010102	2639	1010111	2646	1010112	2660.17	2688.5
Copper March	8440	1010112	8020	1010103	8415	1010112	8230	8353.33
Heating Oil Feb	8900	1010102	8020	1010109	8421	1010112	8434	8460
Unl. Gas Feb	9050	1010112	7800	1010102	9008	1010112	8425	8813.67
JapYen March	8907	1010103	8525	1010112	8533	1010112	8594	8716
Nat Gas Feb.	9870	1010109	8140	1010103	8472	1010112	8649.67	9005
Platinum April	6400	1010111	6045	1010102	6331	1010112	6222.5	6294.83
Swiss Franc March	6304	1010103	6160	1010103	6204	1010112	6213.33	6232
Silver March	4675	1010112	4535	1010103	4655	1010112	4605	4638.33
S&P March	137000	1010103	128750	1010108	133030	1010112	132875	132978
Sugar March	1049	1010109	996	1010112	1000	1010112	1007.5	1022.5
Beans March	510	1010102	477.25	1010112	482.5	1010112	486.208	493.625
US Bonds March	10620	1010103	10408	1010112	10414	1010112	10423	10514
Wheat March	294.5	1010111	275	1010102	289	1010112	284.75	287.583

TABLE A.3 Commodity number line sheets—for 12/12/01 use

S&P's

	10/30	10/31	11/26	11/27	11/28	11/29	11/30	12/3	12/4	12/5	12/6	12/7	12/10	12/11	30	29
S&P's 9:30 - 4:15	118050	106070	115520	115050	112930	114450	114000	112970	114750	116850	116850	116050	113950	113650		
net	118050	-11980	220	-470	-2120	1520	-450	-1030	1780	2100	0	-800	-2100	-300		
BIAS	N	s	b	b	b	b	b	N	N	n	n	n	n	s		
Sentiment	57	22	**80**	73	35	61	60	52	69	87	83	73	33	28		
plus-	-2	-1	0	0	-3	1	-2	0	3	2	0	0	-4	0	1	9
ABCD	0	0	0	0	0	0	-2	2	1	2	2	0	-2	-4		
12 day Cum +/-	4	-1	6	6	3	2	-6	-4	-1	1	-2	0	-2	-8		
12 day Cum ABCD	0	0	0	0	0	0	1	-1	1	1	1	2	1	-1		
30 day Cum +/-	2	-1	0	0	0	1	1	1		1			1	1		
30 day Cum ABCD		4	23	19	16	18	16	16	17	23	21	17	11	9	0	—
# needed to +/-9		3														

11/1

CRB

	10/29	10/30	11/26	11/27	11/28	11/29	11/30	12/3	12/4	12/5	12/6	12/7	12/10	12/11	30	29
CRB 10:00-4:00		118050	18953	19023	18896	18930	19266	19251	19048	18986	18912	18957	18858	18891		
net	0	118050	-59	70	-127	34	336	-15	-203	-62	-74	45	-99	33		
BIAS		N	b	b	b	b	N	n	n	n	n	n	n	s		
Sentiment		57	44	45	33	45	77	75	63	61	55	58	55	57		
plus-		0	-1	1	-1	-2	2	0	-2	-2	-3	4	0	2	2	3
ABCD		2	2	4	2	2	2	0	-2	-1	0	-5	-1	-1		
12 day Cum +/-		0	8	10	4	2	2	0	2	-1	-7	-5	-5	-3		
12 day Cum ABCD		-4	2	3	2	2	2	2	2	-2	2	2	2	2		
30 day Cum +/-		0	2	3	4	2	2	4	0	0	-3	2	2	3		
30 day Cum ABCD		-20	0	1	4	0	2	4	0	0	-3	1	1		0	0
# needed to +/-9																

Nasdaq

	10/30	10/31	11/26	11/27	11/28	11/29	11/30	12/3	12/4	12/5	12/6	12/7	12/10	12/11	30	29
Nasdaq 9:30 - 4:15	118050	136900	161800	161500	155900	160500	159800	156800	164000	172000	172400	167700	164750	165555		
net	118050	18850	3850	-300	-5600	4600	-700	-3000	7200	8000	400	-4700	-2950	805		
BIAS	N	n	b	b	s	N	n	n	n	n	n	B	b	b		
Sentiment	57	**24**	75	70	31	63	60	47	71	90	**80**	75	41	**40**		
plus-	-2	-3	0	0	-3	2	0	1	2	2	-2	-2	-1	0	3	-3
ABCD	0	0	2	0	-3	-3	-3	-1	1	1	-1	-1	2	1		
12 day Cum +/-	0	0	2	0	-3	3	3	-1	1	3	-1	-5	2	2		
12 day Cum ABCD	10	3	-4	0	-3	3	0	-1	1	1	-1	-1	2	1		
30 day Cum +/-	0	3	-4	0	-3	3	-1	1	3	3	-1	-3	3	-3		
30 day Cum ABCD	10	0	2	2	4	6	6	2	3	4	3	3	3	3		
# needed to +/-9	10	9	11	7	4	8	6	2	2	0	3	-4	-5	-3	0	0

Continued

TABLE A.3 Commodity number line sheets—for 12/12/01 use (Continued)

	10/29	10/30	11/26	11/27	11/28	11/29	11/30	12/3	12/4	12/5	12/6	12/7	12/10	12/11	30	29
US Bonds 8:20 - 3:00	Z	Z	10312	10321	10220	10330	10322	10404	10500	10221	10116	9915	9931	10012		
net	0	0	-3/32	9/32	-1 1/32	1 5/16	-1/4	7/16	7/8	-2 11/32	-1 5/32	-2 1/32	1/2	13/32		
BIAS			H2	Z	Z	H2	H2	H2	H2	H2	H2	H2	H2	H2		
Sentiment			s 11	s 14	s 17	61	56	63	72	12	9	s 4	s 15	s 18		
plus-	0	2	0	3	0	2	0	0	0	-2	0	-2	0	0	0	0
ABCD	0	0	-1	-1	-1	-1	-1	-1	-1	-1	-1	0	-3	0		
12 day Cum +/-	14	16	-15	-14	-11	-7	-7	-5	-1	1	-1	-5	-3	-1	0	
12 day Cum ABCD	0	0	0	0	0	0	0	1	1	-1	-5	-4	-6	0	-10	
30 day Cum +/-	16	18	3	6	4	4	2	2	6	2	0	-3	1	-10		
30 day Cum ABCD															12/11	
# needed to +/-9																

	10/29	10/30	11/26	11/27	11/28	11/29	11/30	12/3	12/4	12/5	12/6	12/7	12/10	12/11	30	29
Euro$[ED] 8:20 - 3:00	Z	Z	97890	97978	98015	97940	97950	97965	97965	97800	97780	97890	97985	98055		
net	0	0	5	88	37	150	10	15	0	-165	-20	110	95	70		
BIAS			Z	Z	Z	H2	N	H2	n	H2	H2	n	B	b		
Sentiment			s 35	41	43	49	59	60	61	44	41	69	73	74		
plus-	0	0	1	1	2	2	2	2	2	-2	2	2	2	2	2	0
ABCD	0	0	1	2	2	3	2	1	1	2	2	6	9	14	-9	
12 day Cum +/-	8	6	2	2	2	-1	1	2	1	2	0	2	9	14		
12 day Cum ABCD	0	0	-16	-11	-7	-1	2	2	1	2	0	2	2	2		
30 day Cum +/-	12	12	-13	-13	-13	-11	-11	-13	-13	-15	-13	-11	-11	-9	11/16	
30 day Cum ABCD																
# needed to +/-9																

	10/29	10/30	11/26	11/27	11/28	11/29	11/30	12/3	12/4	12/5	12/6	12/7	12/10	12/11	30	29
Cocoa 7:30AM - 9:00AM	Z	Z	1303	1286	1292	1347	1339	1307	1271	1277	1274	1246	1221	1285		
net	0	0	43	-17	6	55	-8	-32	-36	6	-3	-28	-25	64		
BIAS			b	b	b	N	b	b	b	n	b	b	N	n		
Sentiment			87	78	75	91	86	78	61	65	63	58	36	77		
plus-	0	0	0	-1	0	2	-2	-1	-2	3	0	0	-3	0	2	0
ABCD	0	2	2	2	2	2	6	5	2	4	2	2	2	2	14	
12 day Cum +/-	2	2	15	11	9	8	2	5	3	4	2	2	-1	-1		
12 day Cum ABCD	0	0	3	2	2	2	2	2	2	2	2	2	2	2		
30 day Cum +/-	-4	-4	19	17	19	19	15	14	14	17	15	17	14	14	11/9	
30 day Cum ABCD																
# needed to +/-9																

208

	10/26	10/29	11/26	11/27	11/28	11/29	11/30	12/3	12/4	12/5	12/6	12/7	12/10	12/11		30	29
Coffee			4970	4650	4615	4550	4620	4610	4530	4590	4560	4650	4685	4770			
9:30AM - 11:00AM	Z	Z	H2	H2	H2	H2	H2	H2	H2	H2	H2	H2	H2	H2			
net	0	0	−40	−320	−35	−65	70	−10	−80	60	−30	90	35	85			
BIAS			n	n	S	s	s	s	s	s	s	s	s	s			
Sentiment			33	14	13	7	11	**13**	10	18	**19**	25	25	28			
plus-			−1	0	0	−1	1	0	0	1	−1	1	0	0	2	0	0
ABCD	−2	−2	−2	0	0	0	0	0	0	0	0	0	0	1	−3		
12 day Cum +/−	0	0	−1	−1	0	−1	0	0	−1	0	−2	0	0	0			
12 day Cum ABCD	−4	−4	−4	−4	−4	−2	0	0	−2	0	−2	0	−2	−1			
30 day Cum +/−	0	0	1	1	1	0	1	1	1	2	1	2	2	2			
30 day Cum ABCD	−8	−12	−6	−4	−4	−4	−4	−6	−6	−4	−4	−4	−4	−3	9/28		
# needed to +/−9																	

	10/26	10/29	11/26	11/27	11/28	11/29	11/30	12/3	12/4	12/5	12/6	12/7	12/10	12/11		30	29
Cotton			3630	3712	3778	3900	3920	3774	3706	3678	3793	3734	3634	3711			
1:30PM - 3:00PM	Z	Z	H2	H2	H2	H2	H2	H2	H2	H2	H2	H2	H2	H2			
net	0	0	17	82	66	122	20	−146	−68	−28	115	−59	−100	77			
BIAS			b	b	b	b	b	b	b	b	b	b	N	n			
Sentiment			63	66	81	87	**84**	63	61	55	64	60	58	62			
plus-			0	1	0	0	0	0	0	0	1	−1	0	0	0	0	0
ABCD	0	0	0	4	0	2	−2	−3	0	−1	2	−2	−2	0	10		
12 day Cum +/−	0	0	0	1	1	1	1	1	1	1	2	1	1	1			
12 day Cum ABCD	−8	−6	6	10	8	14	8	3	3	4	4	4	0	−2			
30 day Cum +/−	0	0	−1	0	0	0	0	0	0	0	1	0	0	0			
30 day Cum ABCD	−20	−22	4	10	8	14	12	9	13	12	14	12	10	10	11/27		
# needed to +/−9			3														

	10/26	10/29	11/26	11/27	11/28	11/29	11/30	12/3	12/4	12/5	12/6	12/7	12/10	12/11		30	29
Orange Juice			9550	9600	9530	9470	9500	9490	9480	9415	9115	9010	9145	8990			
3:30PM - 5:00PM	Z	Z	F2	F2	F2	F2	F2	F2	F2	F2	F2	F2	F2	F2			
net	0	0	130	50	−70	−60	30	−10	−10	−65	−300	−105	135	−155			
BIAS			n	n	n	B	b	b	b	N	n	S	s	s			
Sentiment			64	65	54	49	53	**55**	55	47	15	14	31	25			
plus-			0	0	0	0	1	0	0	0	0	0	1	0	−2	0	0
ABCD	0	0	0	0	0	0	0	0	0	0	−2	0	0	0	−2		
12 day Cum +/−	0	0	−4	−4	−4	−4	−2	−1	0	0	0	1	2	2			
12 day Cum ABCD	4	4	2	2	2	2	2	2	2	2	−2	−2	−2	−2			
30 day Cum +/−	0	0	−4	−4	−4	−4	−3	−3	−3	−3	−3	−3	−2	−2			
30 day Cum ABCD	−8	−10	4	4	4	4	4	4	4	2	−2	−2	−2	−2			
# needed to +/−9																	

Continued

TABLE A.3   Commodity number line sheets—for 12/12/01 use (Continued)

Sugar — 11:30AM - 1:00PM

	10/29	10/30	11/26	11/27	11/28	11/29	11/30	12/3	12/4	12/5	12/6	12/7	12/10	12/11	30	29
net		0	755	757	754	768	765	764	769	779	784	775	750	734		
	Z	Z	H2	H2	H2	H2	H2	H2	H2	H2	H2	H2	H2	H2		
			3	2	-3	14	-3	-1	5	10	5	-9	-25	-16		
BIAS			b	b	b	b	N	b	b	N	b	b	b	N		
Sentiment			76	75	73	79	76	73	75	71	73	75	63	54	0	0
plus-			0	0	0	2	0	2	0	2	2	0	-2	-2		
ABCD	0	2	3	0	0	2	2	2	2	2	2	0	2	2	-1	0
12 day Cum +/-	0	2	2	3	3	7	7	7	5	7	9	9	9	5	9	
12 day Cum ABCD	-6	-4	5	3	-1	-1	7	7	5	7	9	9	9	5		
30 day Cum +/-	0	0	-1	-1	-1	-1	-1	5	5	-1	-1	-1	-1	-1		
30 day Cum ABCD	-16	-14	-1	1	1	3	4	4	2	9	11	9	9	9	12/5	

DXY — 9:30AM - 4:15PM

	10/30	10/31	11/26	11/27	11/28	11/29	11/30	12/3	12/4	12/5	12/6	12/7	12/10	12/11	30	29
net	0	11490	11717	11682	11617	11627	11546	11600	11605	11625	11566	11618	11650	11587		
		N	-30	-35	-65	10	-81	54	5	20	-59	52	32	-63		
BIAS		N	b	b	b	b	N	n	s	N	n	n	n	s		
Sentiment		63	90	83	71	69	54	67	65	70	63	77	79	73	6	0
plus-		2	0	-1	-3	2	-2	2	0	2	0	0	-2	-4		
ABCD	3	2	2	-1	-3	3	-3	2	3	3	-2	1	0	0	6	7
12 day Cum +/-	7	5	2	2	-1	3	-3	3	1	3	1	1	-1	-7		
12 day Cum ABCD	7	7	5	5	3	3	3	3	1	3	1	1	6	6		
30 day Cum +/-	0	0	6	2	-1	-1	5	5	5	6	3	6	6	6		
30 day Cum ABCD	0	11	6	5	13	15	13	13	13	15	13	13	11	7	10/31	

EURO[EUUS] — 2:30AM - 3:00PM

	10/31	11/1	11/26	11/27	11/28	11/29	11/30	12/3	12/4	12/5	12/6	12/7	12/10	12/11	30	29
net	9001	9027	8807	8823	8881	8885	8961	8918	8901	8883	8948	8896	8909	8915		
		26	29	16	58	4	76	-43	-17	-18	65	-52	13	6		
BIAS	n	0	s	s	s	N	B	b	b	N	B	b	b	N		
Sentiment	83		21	25	46	49	68	35	33	17	59	21	23	25	6	0
plus-	-1	0	0	0	4	0	1	-1	0	-1	2	-1	0	0		
ABCD	-2	-2	2	0	2	2	3	-3	1	-2	1	-2	-1	-1	2	
12 day Cum +/-	-1	0	2	0	2	2	3	2	0	0	2	0	-1	-1	14	
12 day Cum ABCD	-4	-1	10	8	8	12	11	8	8	8	10	8	6	6		
30 day Cum +/-	-1	-4	3	3	3	3	4	3	3	8	2	8	2	2		
30 day Cum ABCD	-12	-10	1	1	12	14	19	18	20	18	20	18	16	14	11/28	

210

Table (continued) — currency data grid.

EUROCURR[EC] 8:20AM - 3:00PM

	10/29	10/30	11/26	11/27	11/28	11/29	11/30	12/3	12/4	12/5	12/6	12/7	12/10	12/11	30	29
8:20AM - 3:00PM			87970	88160	88710	88830	89540	89410	88970	88350	89180	88630	88620	88810		
net			200	190	550	120	710	-130	-440	-620	830	-550	-10	190		
BIAS	Z	Z	Z	Z	Z	Z	Z	Z	Z	H2	H2	H2	H2	H2		
Sentiment	0	0													0	0
plus-																
ABCD	0	0	-2	1	0	0	0	0	0	-1	0	0	0	0	-1	
12 day Cum +/-	0	0	2	2	2	0	2	-2	0	-2	2	-2	2	0		
12 day Cum ABCD			-5	-3	2	2	2	2	2	-4	-2	-4	2	2		
30 day Cum +/-			-5	-1	-1	-1	1	-2	-2	0	0	0	0	0		
30 day Cum ABCD																
# needed to +/-9	-12	-12	-4	-3	-1	-1	1	-1	-1	-3	-1	-3	-1	-1		

Sfranc 8:20AM - 3:00PM

	10/29	10/30	11/26	11/27	11/28	11/29	11/30	12/3	12/4	12/5	12/6	12/7	12/10	12/11	30	29
8:20AM - 3:00PM			6011	6029	6072	6049	6090	6044	6047	6016	6071	6028	6011	6044		
net			-28	18	43	-23	41	-46	3	-31	55	-43	-17	33		
BIAS	Z	Z	Z	Z	Z	Z	Z	Z	Z	H2	H2	H2	H2	H2		
Sentiment	s	N	s	s	s		n		n		n	n		n	0	0
plus-	61	57	19	22	41	25	55	22	25	14	45	18	21	25	1	
ABCD	0	0	0	1	0	-1	1	0	0	-1	0	0	0	0		
12 day Cum +/-	0	-1	0	2	0	-2	2	-2	1	-1	2	0	2	3		
12 day Cum ABCD	4	0	2	1	2	2	3	2	6	0	2	0	0	0		
30 day Cum +/-	0	-1	0	6	8	10	12	8	1	2	0	0	0	5		
30 day Cum ABCD				1	1	0	1	1	1	2	0	0	0	0		
# needed to +/-9	-10	-11	0	-2	-2	-6	-4	-6	-6	-8	-6	-4	-2	1		

Sentiment box value under 12/10 (boxed): **21**

British Pound 2:30AM - 3:00PM

	10/31	10/30	11/26	11/27	11/28	11/29	11/30	12/3	12/4	12/5	12/6	12/7	12/10	12/11	30	29
2:30AM - 3:00PM	14554	14554	14114	14144	14253	14270	14257	14253	14217	14165	14286	14332	14356	14383		
net	14554		10	30	109	17	-13	-4	-36	-52	121	46	24	27		
BIAS	N	b	s	s	s	N	N	Z	Z	H2	H2	B	b	b		
Sentiment	57	70	10	13	29	41	25	25	21	19	58	62	63	66	0	+
plus-															1	
ABCD	0	1	-2	2	2	0	0	0	0	-1	1	3	0	0		
12 day Cum +/-	2	2	-1	0	2	-1	-1	-1	0	-2	2	0	0	3		
12 day Cum ABCD	1	1	-12	-8	-1	-1	-4	-2	0	-1	0	3	5	8		
30 day Cum +/-	0	2	0	0	0	0	0	0	0	0	0	0	0	0		
30 day Cum ABCD	8	1	-11	-7	-5	-5	-3	-1	1	-1	1	2	0	1		
# needed to +/-9	-1	12														

Continued

TABLE A.3 Commodity number line sheets—for 12/12/01 use (Continued)

Japanese Yen 9:00PM - 3:00PM

	10/30	10/31	11/26	11/27	11/28	11/29	11/30	12/3	12/4	12/5	12/6	12/7	12/10	12/11	30	29
(price)		8167	8058	8064	8121	8078	8098	8059	8054	8052	8016	7970	7936	7927		
net	0		16	6	57	-43	20	-39	-5	-2	-36	-46	-34	-9		
BIAS	N	s	s	s	s	s	s	s	s	s	s	s	s	s		
Sentiment	57	39	9	13	34	18	22	16	15	17	12	10	9	14		
plus-													0	0	0	0
ABCD		-4	0	0	0	-1	1	0	0	0	-1	0	-2	3	0	-13
12 day Cum +/-	-4	0	-11	3	2	-4	4	-4	0	0	-2	-2	-2	-1		
12 day Cum ABCD	-12	-18	-11	-10	-1	-2	-1	-8	-4	-2	-7	-7	-7	-2		
30 day Cum +/-	0	0	1	1	1	0	1	-1	1	1	0	0	0	0		
30 day Cum ABCD	-34	-36	-19	-18	-16	-20	-16	-16	-14	-12	-10	-14	-16	-13		
# needed to +/-9														11/15		

Canadian $ 8:00AM - 3:00PM

	10/29	10/30	11/26	11/27	11/28	11/29	11/30	12/3	12/4	12/5	12/6	12/7	12/10	12/11	30	29
(price)			6249	6270	6311	6324	6356	6349	6363	6358	6356	6350	6331	6342		
net	Z	0	-6	21	41	13	32	-7	14	-5	4	-6	-19	11		
BIAS	0	0	n	Z	Z	Z	n	n	B	b	b	b	b	H2		
Sentiment	N	N	15	21	41	13	32	-7	14	-5	H2	H2	H2	11		
	61	57	15	23	44	47	60	62	66	62	43	37	23	24		
plus-	0				0	0	0		0	0				N		
ABCD	0	-2	0	-2	1	2	2	2	0	0	0	-1	-2	2	1	-5
12 day Cum +/-	2	0	0	1	1	0	2	0	0	0	0	0	-2	2		
12 day Cum ABCD	-2	-2	0	1	-2	2	-2	1	-2	-5	-1	1	0	2		
30 day Cum +/-	0	-2	-9	-7	1	0	-2	0	0	1	-2	0	0	0		
30 day Cum ABCD	-14	-16	-11	-11	-11	-11	-9	-7	-9	-7	-9	-7	-9	-5		
# needed to +/-9														11/9		

Gold 8:20 - 2:30

	10/29	10/30	11/26	11/27	11/28	11/29	11/30	12/3	12/4	12/5	12/6	12/7	12/10	12/11	30	29
(price)			2733	2742	2750	2745	2749	2778	2763	2746	2750	2747	2730	2729		
net	Z	0	-8	9	8	-5	4	29	-15	-17	4	-3	-17	-1		
BIAS	0	0	s	s	s	G2	G2	G2	G2	G2	G2	G2	G2	G2		
Sentiment	N	N	15	20	23	25	4	29	-15	-17	4	-3	-17	-1		
	61	57	15	20	23	25	27	53	49	45	44	43	35	33	n	n
plus-	0	0	0	0	0	-1	0	0	0	-2	0	0	-2	-1	-2	-8
ABCD	0	0	0	0	0	0	0	2	0	-1	0	-1	-2	-1		
12 day Cum +/-	4	2	-4	-4	-2	-2	-1	0	-1	-1	-1	-1	-2	-2		
12 day Cum ABCD	4	2	-4	-4	-2	-2	-1	2	-1	-1	-1	-1	-2	-2		
30 day Cum +/-	0	0	-1	-1	-1	-2	-4	-2	-2	-2	-2	-4	-8	-8		
30 day Cum ABCD	2	2	-2	-4	-4	-4	-6	-2	-4	-4	-4	-3	-1	-1		
# needed to +/-9																

Silver

	10/29	10/30	11/26	11/27	11/28	11/29	11/30	12/3	12/4	12/5	12/6	12/7	12/10	12/11	30	29
8:25 - 2:25	N	N	4050	4065	4140	4090	4157	4215	4153	4200	4238	4268	4243	4275		
			H2	H2	H2	H2	H2	H2	H2	H2	H2	H2	H2	H2		
net	0	0	-20	15	75	-50	67	58	-62	47	38	30	-25	32		
BIAS	s	N	s	s	s	N	n	n	n	B	b	b	b	b		
Sentiment	61	57	15	19	35	31	39	61	57	60	63	65	60	63		
plus-	0	0	-1	0	0	-1	0	1	0	1	2	0	0	0		
ABCD	0	-2	0	0	2	-2	0	2	0	2	2	0	0	2	0	0
12 day Cum +/-	2	0	-1	-1	-1	-2	-2	-1	-1	0	0	6	6	8		
12 day Cum ABCD	0	0	0	0	0	0	0	0	0	0	4	0	0	0		
30 day Cum +/-	2	-2	-2	-2	-2	0	-3	-2	-2	-1	-1	-1	-1	-1	-1	
30 day Cum ABCD	0	-2	-8	-10	-8	-10	-10	-6	-8	-6	-4	-4	-4	-2	-2	
# needed to +/-9														11/8		

Platinum

	10/29	10/30	11/26	11/27	11/28	11/29	11/30	12/3	12/4	12/5	12/6	12/7	12/10	12/11	30	29
8:20 - 2:30			4397	4384	4360	4430	4491	4570	4542	4536	4633	4700	4744	4607		
			F2	H2	F2	F2	H2	F2	F2	F2	F2	F2	F2	F2		
net	0	0	-23	-13	-24	70	61	79	-28	-6	97	67	44	-137		
BIAS	s	N	b	b	b	b	b	b	b	b	b	s	b	b		
Sentiment	61	57	45	44	42	56	63	75	70	66	73	77	78	55		
plus-	0	0	0	0	0	0	2	0	-1	0	0	2	1	0		
ABCD	0	0	1	1	0	0	2	2	-1	-1	-1	-1	0	0	4	0
12 day Cum +/-	-4	-6	4	4	4	4	4	6	4	4	6	6	8	8	4	14
12 day Cum ABCD	0	0	4	4	4	2	2	0	4	3	3	3	0	0		
30 day Cum +/-	-6	-6	4	4	4	4	4	6	6	8	3	3	8	8		
30 day Cum ABCD	-3		2	-2	-2	2	3	1	1	1	10	12	14	14	12/6	
# needed to +/-9																

Copper

	10/29	10/30	11/26	11/27	11/28	11/29	11/30	12/3	12/4	12/5	12/6	12/7	12/10	12/11	30	29
8:10AM - 2:00PM	N	N	6910	7130	7145	7235	7320	7135	7090	7030	6965	6855	6850	6890		
			H2	H2	H2	H2	H2	H2	H2	H2	H2	H2	H2	H2		
net	0	0	55	220	15	90	85	-185	-45	-60	-65	-110	-5	40		
BIAS	s	N	b	b	b	b	b	b	b	b	b	N	n	S		
Sentiment	61	57	77	89	85 [boxed]	85	88	45	44	42	38	32	35 [boxed]	39		
plus-	0	0	0	0	1	0	0	0	0	0	-1	-2	1	0		
ABCD	0	2	-3	0	2	2	2	-3	0	1	-2	0	0	0	0	0
12 day Cum +/-	-14	-8	0	0	1	1	1	1	-3	-3	-5	-5	-3	-1	0	-4
12 day Cum ABCD	0	0	0	0	1	2	2	-3	1	1	0	0	0	0		
30 day Cum +/-	0	0	0	0	1	1	1	1	-3	-3	-5	-5	-3	-1		
30 day Cum ABCD	-28	-26	-20	-16	-14	-10	3	-7	-5	-5	-3	-5	-6	-4		
# needed to +/-9														9/27		

213

TABLE A.3 Commodity number line sheets—for 12/12/01 use (Continued)

Crude Oil

	10/29	10/30	11/26	11/27	11/28	11/29	11/30	12/3	12/4	12/5	12/6	12/7	12/10	12/11	30	29
10:00 - 2:30	Z	Z	1869	1948	1915	1860	1944	2009	1965	1949	1854	1904	1837	1808		
net	0	0	-27	79	-33	-55	84	65	-44	-16	-95	50	-67	-29		
BIAS	s	N	n	n	n	n	n	n	n	n	n	n	n	n		
Sentiment	61	57	22	66	62	57	64	71	63	58	22	45	24	21		
plus-	0	0	0	0	0	0	0	0	-1	-1	0	1	0	0	0	0
ABCD	-2	-2	1	1	1	-2	4	2	-3	0	-2	4	-3	2	-8	
12 day Cum +/-	0	0	1	1	-3	1	2	2	4	4	-1	-1	-1	0		
12 day Cum ABCD	-17	-15	-2	0	0	-5	3	3	4	0	-1	-1	-2	2		
30 day Cum +/-	0	0	0	0	0	0	1	1	0	-1	-1	0	-2	0		
30 day Cum ABCD	-12	-14	-25	-19	-17	-19	-13	-11	-14	-20	-18	-11	-10	-8		
# needed to +/-9															10/29	

Natural Gas

	10/29	10/30	11/26	11/27	11/28	11/29	11/30	12/3	12/4	12/5	12/6	12/7	12/10	12/11	30	29
10:00 - 2:30	Z	Z	2696	2606	2720	2550	2701	2630	2563	2491	2565	2568	2747	2803		
net	0	0	-117	-90	114	-170	151	-71	-67	-72	74	3	179	56		
BIAS	s	N	n	n	s	n	s	n	n	n	n	s	s	s		
Sentiment	61	57	46	49	21	60	23	20	17	14	23	25	44	47		
plus-	0	0	0	0	0	0	1	0	0	0	0	0	1	0	5	6
ABCD	0	0	4	3	2	3	2	3	3	3	2	2	2	2		
12 day Cum +/-	12	12	3	7	0	-1	3	3	3	1	2	1	-1	2		
12 day Cum ABCD	0	0	3	7	0	-1	3	1	3	3	1	-3	-1	-1		
30 day Cum +/-	0	0	3	7	0	3	4	4	4	1	4	4	5	5		
30 day Cum ABCD	16	14	21	23	19	14	18	14	12	6	10	4	8	6		
# needed to +/-9															10/22	

Heating Oil

	10/29	10/30	11/26	11/27	11/28	11/29	11/30	12/3	12/4	12/5	12/6	12/7	12/10	12/11	30	29
10:00 - 2:30	Z	Z	5217	5394	5300	5180	5459	5565	5418	5314	5066	5168	5066	4999		
net	0	0	-125	177	-94	-120	279	106	-147	-104	-248	102	-102	-67		
BIAS	s	N	s	s	s	s	s	s	s	s	s	s	s	s		
Sentiment	61	57	21	62	60	55	66	75	70	62	25	36	27	23		
plus-	0	0	0	0	0	0	1	1	-1	0	0	0	0	0	-2	-11
ABCD	-2	0	0	2	2	-3	2	2	-2	-2	-2	-1	-1	2		
12 day Cum +/-	-7	-3	0	0	0	-1	3	1	0	0	0	-5	-5	0		
12 day Cum ABCD	0	0	-2	-2	-2	-2	-1	5	5	0	-2	-2	-5	-1		
30 day Cum +/-	-7	0	-2	-2	0	-2	3	-1	-2	0	1	-2	-2	-1		
30 day Cum ABCD	-3	-3	-15	-9	-5	-10	-8	-7	-11	-11	-10	-12	-12	-11		
# needed to +/-9															11/14	

214

Unleaded Gas

	10/29	10/30	11/26	11/27	11/28	11/29	11/30	12/3	12/4	12/5	12/6	12/7	12/10	12/11	30	29
10:00 - 2:30			5217	5381	5260	5190	5387	5580	5503	5420	5175	5250	5109	5061		
net		0	-56	164	-121	-70	197	193	-77	-83	-245	75	-141	-48	0	0
BIAS	Z	Z	Z	Z	Z	Z	F2	F2	F2	F2	F2	F2	F2	F2		
Sentiment	s 61	N 57	n 25	n 64	n 57	n 57	s 68	N 77	B 65	N 61	n 22	n 53	n 21	n 20		
plus	-2	-4	0	0	0	-2	1	2	0	0	0	1	-2	0		
ABCD	0	0	2	2	1	1	3	2	-4	-2	-4	4	1	2		
12 day Cum +/-	-16	-16	1	1	1	1	2	2	2	2	-1	-1	-3	2		
12 day Cum ABCD	0	0	5	7	5	3	8	10	6	6	2	3	3	1		
30 day Cum +/-			1	1	1	1	2	2	2	2	2	3	3	3		
30 day Cum ABCD	-15	-19	-20	-14	-12	-14	-9	-8	-14	-16	-18	-11	-9	-7		
# needed to +/-9															10/15	

London Brent Crude

	10/31	11/1	11/26	11/27	11/28	11/29	11/30	12/3	12/4	12/5	12/6	12/7	12/10	12/11	30	29
5:02 - 3:12	2037	1963	1836	1902	1869	1841	1914	1971	1921	1922	1839	1903	1817	1791		
net	2037	-74	-92	66	-33	-28	73	57	-50	1	-83	64	-86	-26	0	0
BIAS	Z	Z	F2	F2	F2	F2	F2	F2	F2	F2	F2	F2	F2	F2		
Sentiment	0	0	0	0	0	0	1	0	-1	-1	0	1	-1	0		
plus	-2	-3	-2	2	2	-2	2	2	-3	-4	2	4	-2	0		
ABCD	0	0	1	1	4	1	2	6	1	-5	-1	3	-1	-1		
12 day Cum +/-	-20	-23	2	2	1	1	2	2	3	0	-5	1	0	0		
12 day Cum ABCD	0	0	1	1	1	1	2	2	3	0	0	1	-1	-1		
30 day Cum +/-															0	0
30 day Cum ABCD	-30	-31	-23	-21	-19	-19	-17	-13	-12	-16	-12	-8	-6	-4	-4	
# needed to +/-9															9/27	

HO Crack

	10/29	10/30	11/26	11/27	11/28	11/29	11/30	12/3	12/4	12/5	12/6	12/7	12/10	12/11	30	29
10:05 - 2:30			364	359	348	365	348	333	310	282	273	266	291	291		
net	0	0	-36	-5	-11	17	-17	-15	-23	-28	-9	-7	25	0	0	0
BIAS	Z	Z	F2	F2	F2	F2	F2	F2	F2	F2	F2	F2	F2	F2		
Sentiment	0	0	0	0	0	0	0	0	0	0	0	0	0	0		
plus	0	0	-2	0	0	-2	0	0	-2	-2	-2	0	0	0		
ABCD	4	0	1	-7	-9	0	-7	-7	0	0	0	-10	-10	-10		
12 day Cum +/-	0	4	-5	2	2	9	2	2	-9	-8	-10	2	2	2		
12 day Cum ABCD	0	0	2	-1	-1	2	-5	-5	2	2	2	-15	-15	-13		
30 day Cum +/-						-3	-5	-5	-7	-11	-15	-15	-10	-2	-2	0
30 day Cum ABCD	-6	-6	-1	-1	-1	-4	-4	-4	0			-15	-15	-13	-13	
# needed to +/-9															12/5	

Continued

215

TABLE A.3 Commodity number line sheets—for 12/12/01 use (Continued)

HU Crack

	10/29	10/30	10/31	11/26	11/27	11/28	11/29	11/30	12/3	12/4	12/5	12/6	12/7	12/10	12/11	30	29
HU Crack 10:05 - 2:30				344	339	329	347	318	343	346	327	319	301	309	317		
net	Z	Z		F2	F2	F2	F2	F2	F2	F2	F2	F2	F2	F2	F2		
BIAS	0	0		-17	-5	-10	18	-29	25	3	-19	-8	-18	8	8		
Sentiment																	
plus-	0	0		0	0	0	0	0	0	0	0	0	0	0	0		
ABCD	-3	0		0	-1	-1	-1	0	2	2	0	0	0	0	0		
12 day Cum +/-	0	0		7	5	3	3	2	4	6	6	4	4	4	4		
12 day Cum ABCD	-9	-9		1	1	1	1	1	1	1	1	1	1	4	4		
30 day Cum +/-	0	0		4	4	4	4	4	6	8	6	8	10	12	14	0	0
30 day Cum ABCD	-13	-13							3	3	1	-1			1		
# needed to +/-9	-13														14		12/7

Live Cattle

	10/30	10/31	11/26	11/27	11/28	11/29	11/30	12/3	12/4	12/5	12/6	12/7	12/10	12/11	30	29
Live Cattle 10:05 - 2:00	6807	6807	6963	7020	7040	7058	7018	7000	6985	6988	6930	6860	6820	6850		
net	Z	Z	G2	G2	G2	G2	G2	G2	G2	G2	G2	G2	G2	G2		
BIAS	0		-47	57	20	18	-40	-18	-15	3	-58	-70	-40	30		
Sentiment	N	n	n	B	b	b	b	b	b	b	b	N	n	S		
plus-	57	59	83	85	77	75	71	68	66	62	61	55	55	59		
ABCD	-2	-2	0	1	0	0	0	-3	0	1	-2	-2	0	-1		
12 day Cum +/-	1	1	3	3	3	3	3	10	8	7	3	2	1	2		
12 day Cum ABCD	6	10	11	13	17	17	17	10	8	3	3	-1	-4	-6		
30 day Cum +/-	0	1	3	3	3	3	3	3	3	3	3	3	3	4	0	+
30 day Cum ABCD	-15	-11	13	15	17	17	14	14	13	11	5	5	5	1	4	1
# needed to +/-9															11/21	

Live Hogs

	10/30	10/31	11/26	11/27	11/28	11/29	11/30	12/3	12/4	12/5	12/6	12/7	12/10	12/11	30	29
Live Hogs 10:05 - 2:00	5165	5165	5415	5433	5485	5443	5525	5403	5320	5265	5305	5290	5160	5205		
net	Z	N	G2	G2	G2	G2	G2	G2	G2	G2	G2	G2	G2	G2		
BIAS	0		-7	18	52	-42	82	-122	-83	-55	40	-15	-130	45		
Sentiment	N	N	n	n	n	n	n	n	n	s	s	s	s	s		
plus-	57	85	69	70	73	66	73	22	18	15	23	22	18	25		
ABCD	0	2	0	1	0	0	2	-2	2	-4	2	0	-2	1		
12 day Cum +/-	2	0	-2	0	0	0	0	0	-2	1	1	1	1	2		
12 day Cum ABCD	0	2	-1	0	12	12	14	8	4	0	-1	2	-2	2		
30 day Cum +/-	-2	0	-1	10	0	0	0	0	0	0	2	2	0	-1	1	0
30 day Cum ABCD	0	0	4	10	0	6	8	10	8	8	3	8	6	6	6	
# needed to +/-9	-16	-12	3												11/27	

Pork Bellies

	10/30	10/31	11/26	11/27	11/28	11/29	11/30	12/3	12/4	12/5	12/6	12/7	12/10	12/11	30	29
Pork Bellies 10:05 - 2:00	7010	7010	7505	7612	7877	7865	7910	7685	7475	7408	7518	7485	7308	7400		
	G2	G2	C2	C2	G2	G2	G2	G2	G2	G2	N	n	n	G2		
net		7010	105	107	265	-12	45	-225	-210	-67	110	-33	-177	92		
BIAS	N	s	n	n	n	B	b	b	b	[15]	N	n	n	s		
Sentiment	57	83	74	77	82	75	76	25	14	0	44	37	25	28	0	0
plus-	0	0	0	0	0	0	0	0	0	0	1	0	0	1		
ABCD	-2	2	0	-2	2	-1	2	-2	-1	-2	4	1	-2	2	2	12
12 day Cum +/-	0	0	-2	-2	-1	-7	0	-1	-1	0	-8	-1	-6	-6		
12 day Cum ABCD	-8	-4	5	5	9	7	13	7	3	4	8	3	3	3		
30 day Cum +/-	0	0	0	0	0	0	0	0	0	0	-1	-1	-1	-1		
30 day Cum ABCD	-26	-22	3	7	7	9	11	11	11	9	13	12	10	12	11/29	
# needed to +/-9			4	4	0											

Soy Beans

	10/30	10/31	11/26	11/27	11/28	11/29	11/30	12/3	12/4	12/5	12/6	12/7	12/10	12/11	30	29
Soy Beans 10:30 - 2:15	4284		4430	4446	4362	4380	4482	4512	4472	4450	4442	4482	4462	4410		
	F2		H2	H2	H2	H2	H2	H2	H2	H2	H2	H2	H2	H2		
net	428 1/2	428 1/2	-11 3/4	1 3/4	-8 1/2	1 3/4	10 1/4	3	-4	-2 1/4	-3/4	4	-2	-5 1/4		
BIAS	n	[37]	N	n	n	s	s	N	n	s	s	n	N	n		
Sentiment	57	37	17	18	10	13	30	34	33	30	29	35	33	18	0	0
plus-	0	0	-2	0	-4	0	0	0	-1	0	-1	1	0	-2		
ABCD	2	-4	-2	4	2	-1	2	0	-2	0	-2	-1	-2	-1	-3	-7
12 day Cum +/-	0	0	-2	3	-5	-7	1	1	0	-1	-8	-4	-6	-6		
12 day Cum ABCD	1	-1	-3	3	4	4	-2	-1	-4	-6	-2	-3	-3	-7		
30 day Cum +/-	0	0	-4	4	4	-5	4	4	-4	-3	-5	-5	-5	-7		
30 day Cum ABCD	-11	-13	-4	2	-4	-4	-3	-1	-3	-3	-2	-5	-4	0		
# needed to +/-9																

Corn

	10/30	10/31	11/26	11/27	11/28	11/29	11/30	12/3	12/4	12/5	12/6	12/7	12/10	12/11	30	29
Corn 10:30 - 2:15	2054		2152	2160	2102	2114	2210	2210	2216	2190	2162	2190	2194	2200		
	Z		H2	H2	H2	H2	H2	H2	H2	H2	H2	H2	H2	H2		
net	205 1/2	205 1/2	-4 3/4	3/4	-5 3/4	1 1/4	9 1/2	0	3/4	-2 3/4	-2 3/4	2 3/4	1/2	1/2		
BIAS	N	[19]	N	n	s	s	N	n	n	n	n	n	[43]	n		
Sentiment	57	19	13	15	8	13	55	59	63	60	36	44	43	45	0	+
plus-	0	0	0	0	0	0	0	0	0	0	0	0	0	0		
ABCD	2	1	-2	1	-2	0	2	-1	0	-1	-2	0	0	1	1	2
12 day Cum +/-	0	0	0	1	0	0	0	0	0	-2	-1	1	0	-1		
12 day Cum ABCD	5	7	1	1	-3	-3	-1	-2	0	-1	-4	-1	-1	-1		
30 day Cum +/-	0	0	0	0	0	0	0	0	0	0	0	-1	-1	-1		
30 day Cum ABCD	-1	1	4	6	4	1	5	4	4	4	0	0	2	2		
# needed to +/-9																

Continued

TABLE A.3 Commodity number line sheets—for 12/12/01 use (Continued)

Wheat 10:30 - 2:15	10/30	10/31	11/26	11/27	11/28	11/29	11/30	12/3	12/4	12/5	12/6	12/7	12/10	12/11	30	29
	Z	2932	2850	2854	2822	2820	2800	2872	2840	2852	2814	2840	2834	2864		
net	O	293 1/4	-11 3/4	1/2	-3 1/4	-1/4	-2	7 1/4	-3 1/4	-1 1/4	-3 3/4	2 1/2	-1/2	3		
BIAS	N	b	H2	H2	H2	H2	H2	H2	H2	H2	H2	s	s	H2		
Sentiment	57	73	14	22	14	13	47	44	39	45	29	32	31	31		–
plus-																
ABCD	2	-1	0	1	0	0	0	-1	0	1	-1	1	0	1	0	0
12 day Cum +/-	2	0	-2	0	-2	0	0	-2	-2	-1	-2	2	0	2		-3
12 day Cum ABCD	0	-1	0	0	-3	-1	-1	-2	-5	-7	-9	-5	-5	-3		
30 day Cum +/-	2	4	-2	-1	-1	-7	-5	-5	-2	-7	-2	-2	-1	0		
30 day Cum ABCD	0	-1	-1	-1	-3	-4	-2	-9	-9	-9	-9	-9	-7	-3	12/3	

(In the Wheat Sentiment row the values 47 (11/30) and 44 (12/3) are boxed.)

British Bonds 3:00AM-12:30PM	10/31	11/1	11/26	11/27	11/28	11/29	11/30	12/3	12/4	12/5	12/6	12/7	12/10	12/11	30	29
	11801	11864	11650	11557	11601	11602	11625	11649	11658	11543	11465	11371	11400	11428		
net	Z	63	18	-93	44	1	23	24	9	-115	-78	-94	29	28		
BIAS	11801	Z	H2	H2	H2	H2	H2	H2	H2	H2	H2	H2	H2	H2		
Sentiment		86	29	-97	38	24	24	22	35	-170	-78	-94	29	28		
plus-	0	0	0	0	0	1	2	0	0	0	2	2	0	0		
ABCD	0	2	3	-2	0	2	2	0	3	2	1	-2	1	1	0	0
12 day Cum +/-	0	0	1	1	-5	1	1	5	6	2	2	1	2	2	1	1
12 day Cum ABCD	0	13	1	1	1	-1	3	2	2	2	2	2	2	2		
30 day Cum +/-	0	0	1	1	5	2	2	2	2	2	4	2	0	2	-2	-2
30 day Cum ABCD	13	17	10	8		7	9	9	12	8	4		0	-2		

German Bunds 2:00AM - 1:00PM	10/31	11/1	11/26	11/27	11/28	11/29	11/30	12/3	12/4	12/5	12/6	12/7	12/10	12/11	30	29
	11200	11286	11029	10932	10970	10994	11018	11040	11075	10905	10860	10774	10802	10827		
net	Z	86	29	-97	38	24	24	22	35	-170	-45	-86	28	25		
BIAS	11200	Z	H2	H2	H2	H2	H2	H2	H2	H2	H2	H2	H2	H2		
Sentiment																
plus-	0	0	0	0	0	0	0	1	0	1	0	0	0	0		
ABCD	4	2	4	-2	4	4	2	2	4	2	4	4	4	4	0	0
12 day Cum +/-	0	0	-6	-8	-9	-7	-3	-1	3	-1	-2	-2	-2	-4	4	4
12 day Cum ABCD	14	16	-1	-1	-1	-1	-1	0	0	-1	1	-1	-1	-1		
30 day Cum +/-	0	0	5	3	3	1	7	7	11	7	1	-5	-7	-9	-1	-1
30 day Cum ABCD	14	18	5	3	3	1	7	7	11	7	1	-2	0	-9	12/11	-9

218

DAX-DAX

	10/31	11/1	11/26	11/27	11/28	11/29	11/30	12/3	12/4	12/5	12/6	12/7	12/10	12/11	30	29
DAX-DAX 3:00AM-1:30PM			515150	506050	494100	493500	498400	500850	503200	527900	527900	522700	521101	514300		
net	0	0	-1750	-9100	-11950	-600	4900	2450	2350	24700	0	-5200	-1599	-6801		
BIAS	Z	Z	Z	Z	Z	Z	Z	Z	Z	Z	Z	Z	Z	Z		
Sentiment																
plus-	0	0	0	0	0	0	0	0	0	0	0	-1	0	0	0	0
ABCD	0	0	-2	-2	-2	0	0	4	2	2	0	-3	-2	2	3	
12 day Cum +/-	0	0	1	1	2	1	1	-1	1	0	0	1	-1	-1		
12 day Cum ABCD		-2	2	0	0	-2	-2	-2	-2	2	2	-1	-3	-1		
30 day Cum +/-			1	1	-1	-1	-1	1	-1	1	1	0	0	0	-3	+
30 day Cum ABCD	-4	-2	2	0	-2	-2	-2	2	4	6	6	3	1	3	4	
# needed to +/-9										3	3					

FT100

	10/31	11/1	11/26	11/27	11/28	11/29	11/30	12/3	12/4	12/5	12/6	12/7	12/10	12/11	30	29
FT100 3:00AM-12:30PM	50350	50800	53130	52730	52005	52000	51990	51890	52140	53370	53800	52770	51940	51680		
net	50350	450	105	-400	-725	-5	-10	-100	250	1230	430	-1030	-830	-260		
BIAS	Z	Z	Z	Z	Z	Z	Z	Z	Z	Z	Z	Z	Z	Z		
Sentiment																
plus-	1	1	-1	0	0	0	0	0	0	0	0	-1	0	0	-3	+
ABCD	2	2	-2	-4	-2	2	-2	-2	2	2	4	-2	-3	-2	4	
12 day Cum +/-	1	2	-4	-4	-3	4	-3	-2	-2	-2	-1	-3	-4	-2		
12 day Cum ABCD	4	6	-4	-8	-8	-8	-6	-2	-2	-2	-2	-3	-4	-3		
30 day Cum +/-	1	2	-2	-2	-1	-2	-2	-2	-2	-2	8	4	4	4		
30 day Cum ABCD	22	26	6	2	-2	0	0	0	0	2	3	3	4	4		
# needed to +/-9																

Nikkei

	10/30	10/31	11/26	11/27	11/28	11/29	11/30	12/3	12/4	12/5	12/6	12/7	12/10	12/11	30	29
Nikkei 7:45PM-1:30AM		10515	11055	10905	10675	10665	10675	10415	10450	10960	10835	10818	10605	10545		
net	0	10515	375	-150	-230	-10	10	-260	35	510	-125	-17	-213	-60		
BIAS	N	S	b	b	b	b	b	Z	n	n	n	n	n	S		
Sentiment	57	45	87	76	55	62	63	39	41	69	63	60	35	33		
plus-	-2	0	0	0	0	-2	0	0	0	0	0	0	-1	0	-1	0
ABCD	0	0	2	2	-2	-2	2	-2	-2	2	-2	-2	-2	-2	-14	
12 day Cum +/-	0	-2	1	2	2	2	3	2	1	1	1	1	0	-1		
12 day Cum ABCD	0	0	1	5	5	5	9	5	3	-3	1	1	-1	-6		
30 day Cum +/-	0	0	0	0	0	0	0	0	0	0	0	0	-1	-1		
30 day Cum ABCD	-10	-8	-4	-6	-10	-10	-10	-12	-12	-12	-12	-12	-14	-14		
# needed to +/-9														9/28		

219

TABLE A.4

Commodity pivot sheet—for 12/12/01 use

Symbol	High	Low	Close	Pivot High	Pivot Low	30dAvg	14dAvg	Mom#	Close8	Close7
SPZ1	115200	113650	113650	114275	113858	113231	114701+	−350	114000 *	112950
RSPZ1	115200	113650	113650	114275	113858	112971	114669−	−350	114000 *	112950
CRY	18893	18800	18891	18876	18847	18856	19008−	−375	19266	19251
NQZ1	169700	165550	165550	167025	166042	156979	162405+	5750	159800	156700
RNQZ1	169700	165550	165550	167500	166200	156363	162410+	5750	159800	156700
USH2	101 5/32	100 5/32	100 13/32	100 21/32	100 16/32	105 15/32	102 17/32−	−3 9/32	103 22/32	104 3/32
USDH2	101 4/32	100 6/32	100 13/32	100 21/32	100 16/32	105 12/32	102 17/32−	−3 9/32	103 22/32	104 3/32
EDH2	98100	97995	98065	98059	98048	97869	97833+	115	97950	97965
EDZ2	96330	96140	96260	96252	96235	96428	96112+	−55	96315	96350
COH2	1295	1241	1290	1283	1268	1189	1285−	−49	1339	1307
KCH2	4790	4615	4780	4754	4703	4798	4718−	160	4620	4610
CTH2	3720	3635	3711	3700	3678	3519	3724+	−216	3927	3774
OJF2	9080	8990	8990	9035	9005	9361	9355−	−520	9510	9490
SBH2	756	731	735	744	738	731	760+	−33	768	764
DXY	11637	11598	11605	11618	11609	11597	11640−	59	11546	11603
DXH2	11690	11655	11664	11673	11667	11664	11697−	59	11605	11659
FXEUUS.CSV	8925	8881	8916	8912	8903	8893	8871+	−46	8962	8917
RECH2	88870	88490	88810	88767	88880	88629	88367+	−430	89240	88840
RSFH2	6047	6011	6044	6039	6029	6061	6036−	−47	6091	6045
FXUSSF.CSV	16637	16537	16553	16587	16564	16511	16570+	143	16410	16545
RBPH2	14316	14268	14294	14293	14292	14269	14146+	138	14156	14172
FXBPUS.CSV	14393	14308	14374	14366	14351	14345	14220+	128	14246	14254
RJYH2	7973	7955	7962	7964	7963	8191	8091−	−179	8141	8105
FXUSJY.CSV	12633	12569	12621	12614	12601	12294	12432+	272	12349	12399
CDH2	6360	6329	6357	6353	6345	6294	6316+	4	6353	6346
GCG2	2734	2721	2729	2729	2728	2772	2747−	−20	2749	2779
RGCG2	2734	2721	2729	2729	2728	2771	2747−	−20	2749	2779
SIH2	4295	4230	4275	4271	4263	4168	4162+	118	4157	4227
RSIH2	4295	4245	4275	4273	4270	4168	4162+	118	4157	4227
PLF2	4730	4560	4607	4645	4642	4362	4514+	147	4493	4577
RPLF2	4645	4560	4607	4606	4603	4360	4512+	114	4493	4577
HGH2	6945	6840	6890	6893	6891	6736	7019−	−430	7320	7140
RHGH2	6945	6850	6890	6898	6893	6739	7025−	−430	7320	7140
CLF2	1845	1792	1808	1819	1812	1991	1910+	−136	1944	2009
RCLF2	1840	1792	1808	1816	1811	1987	1907+	−136	1944	2009
CLG2	1883	1832	1846	1858	1850	2012	1940+	−118	1964	2039
RCLG2	1875	1832	1846	1854	1849	2009	1937+	−118	1964	2039
NGF2	2854	2670	2803	2789	2762	2938	2733−	102	2701	2634
RNGF2	2820	2670	2803	2784	2745	2932	2733−	102	2701	2634
NGG2	2925	2750	2868	2858	2838	2987	2820−	82	2786	2746
RNGG2	2875	2750	2868	2850	2813	2983	2819−	82	2786	2746
HOF2	5085	4960	4999	5023	5007	5658	5342−	−460	5459	5577
RHOF2	5070	4960	4999	5015	5004	5650	5336−	−460	5459	5577
HUF2	5140	4990	5061	5065	5062	5475	5325−	−326	5387	5602
RHUF2	5140	4990	5061	5065	5062	5471	5325−	−326	5387	5602
LBCF2	1821	1780	1791	1801	1794	1919	1888−	−123	1914	1971
SCF2	1797	1791	1791	1794	1792	1929	1879+	−124	1915	1970
LGOF2	15450	15225	15275	15338	15296	17078	16449−	−1100	16375	17125
LCG2	6870	6815	6850	6848	6843	6922	6960−	−167	7017	7000
LHG2	5240	5105	5205	5194	5173	5357	5355−	−320	5525	5402
PBG2	7420	7230	7400	7375	7325	7366	7549−	−510	7910	7685
SH2	447	439	440 6/8	443	441 4/8	447 1/8	446 2/8−	−6 4/8	447 2/8	451
CH2	220 4/8	218	219 4/8	219 3/8	219 2/8	217 6/8	218 1/8−	−1	220 4/8	221
WH2	287	281	286 6/8	285 7/8	284	290 6/8	286 5/8−	−2 6/8	289 4/8	287 2/8
LGLH2	11457	11412	11428	11435	11430	11658	11553−	−197	11625	11649
DGBH2	10856	10818	10827	10837	10830	11054	10942−	−191	11018	11040
AXBH2	94105	94080	94105	94101	94093	94453	94195−	−220	94325	94365
DAXY	516915	507543	514645	513840	512229	497420	509156+	17543	497102	499386
MCAY	458017	451032	455194	454971	454525	449908	454615−	6612	448582	444550
LFTZ1	52000	51470	51680	51735	51698	52474	52620−	−310	51990	51890
SNIZ1	10615	10460	10545	10543	10538	10545	10699−	−130	10675 *	10415

TABLE A.4

Commodity pivot sheet—for 12/12/01 use *(Continued)*

Symbol	Close6	H/L Close	$Risk	High9	High20	High45	Low9	Low20	Low45	1.3XRng
SPZ1	114770		4155	116870	116870	116870	112950	112930	105920	2716
RSPZ1	114770		3745	116870	116870	116870	112950	112930	105920	2413
CRY	19048		678	19266	19266	19266	18858	18637	18352	198
NQZ1	164100		5176	172400	172400	172400	156700	155300	130850	8038
RNQZ1	164100		4602	172400	172400	172400	156700	155300	125450	7293
USH2	105		1296	105	108 24/32	110 14/32	99 15/32	99 15/32	99 15/32	1 17/32
USDH2	105		1199	105	108 24/32	110 14/32	99 15/32	99 15/32	99 15/32	1 14/32
EDH2	97965	High_20	275	98065	98065	98125	97780	97600	97505	144
EDZ2	96400		450	96400	96585	97095	95910	95865	95865	205
COH2	1271		306	1349	1349	1349	1221	1166	986	36
KCH2	4540	High_9	490	4780	5280	5280	4540	4540	4515	195
CTH2	3706		450	3927	3927	3927	3634	3460	3022	113
OJF2	9480	Low_20	161	9510	9600	9605	8990	8990	8175	165
SBH2	770	Low_9	146	784	784	784	735	714	615	20
DXY	11605		658	11627	11733	11733	11546	11546	11360	100
DXH2	11665		497	11705	11797	11797	11605	11605	11460	48
FXEUUS.CSV	8902		75	8962	8962	9106	8867	8777	8777	94
RECH2	88670		561	89240	89240	90900	88350	87470	87470	509
RSFH2	6047		392	6091	6091	6165	6011	5990	5990	30
FXUSSF.CSV	16537		665	16641	16673	16700	16410	16410	16236	184
RBPH2	14134	High_9	361	14294	14332	14516	14076	14018	14018	61
FXBPUS.CSV	14217	High_9	496	14374	14415	14623	14152	14104	14104	129
RJYH2	8097	Low_45	393	8141	8282	8400	7962	7962	7962	25
FXUSJY.CSV	12414	High_45	528	12621	12621	12621	12349	12155	12007	113
CDH2	6360		261	6360	6360	6405	6321	6240	6233	35
GCG2	2763	Low_45	190	2779	2793	2938	2729	2729	2729	31
RGCG2	2763	Low_45	159	2779	2793	2938	2729	2729	2729	27
SIH2	4153	High_20	330	4275	4275	4693	4097	4057	4057	85
RSIH2	4153	High_20	272	4275	4275	4693	4097	4057	4057	73
PLF2	4542		418	4744	4744	4744	4442	4197	4101	119
RPLF2	4542		316	4744	4744	4744	4442	4197	4101	97
HGH2	7090		334	7320	7320	7320	6850	6645	6130	159
RHGH2	7090		307	7320	7320	7320	6850	6645	6130	139
CLF2	1965	Low_9	955	2009	2190	2378	1808	1784	1784	127
RCLF2	1965	Low_9	765	2009	2190	2378	1808	1784	1784	100
CLG2	2001	Low_9	894	2039	2197	2382	1846	1806	1806	115
RCLG2	2001	Low_9	739	2039	2197	2382	1846	1806	1806	91
NGF2	2563	High_9	1747	2803	3041	3464	2491	2491	2491	232
RNGF2	2563	High_9	1451	2803	3041	3464	2491	2491	2491	188
NGG2	2703	High_9	1392	2868	3081	3452	2624	2624	2624	205
RNGG2	2703	High_9	1202	2868	3081	3452	2624	2624	2624	169
HOF2	5418	Low_45	945	5577	6183	6813	4999	4999	4999	295
RHOF2	5418	Low_45	800	5577	6183	6813	4999	4999	4999	240
HUF2	5503	Low_9	898	5602	5888	6426	5061	4975	4975	285
RHUF2	5503	Low_9	806	5602	5888	6426	5061	4975	4975	247
LBCF2	1929	Low_9	884	1971	1990	2275	1791	1733	1733	119
SCF2	1932	Low_9	171	1970	2096	2284	1791	1732	1732	17
LGOF2	16800	Low_45	530	17125	17500	20350	15275	15275	15275	729
LCG2	6985		273	7057	7057	7275	6820	6662	6515	124
LHG2	5320		390	5525	5525	5525	5160	5160	5037	146
PBG2	7475		708	7910	7910	7910	7307	6967	6607	274
SH2	447 6/8		250	451	454 6/8	465	438 2/8	436 4/8	432 4/8	7 3/8
CH2	221 2/8		140	221 2/8	221 2/8	226 2/8	211 6/8	210 4/8	210 4/8	3 3/8
WH2	283 6/8		217	289 4/8	297 2/8	302 2/8	281 6/8	281 6/8	281 6/8	6 4/8
LGLH2	11658		898	11658	11710	11866	11371	11371	11371	34
DGBH2	11075		632	11075	11075	11284	10774	10774	10774	64
AXBH2	94320		80	94380	94740	95000	94090	94060	94060	8
DAXY	503332		2884	527653	527653	527653	492466	491887	448055	17722
MCAY	444587		832	467755	467755	467755	444550	437658	416476	13034
LFTZ1	52140	Low_20	1297	53800	53800	53800	51680	51680	50180	1376
SNIZI	10450		781	10835	11055	11055	10415	10140	9935	287

Appendix

TABLE A.5

Commodity number line values—for 12/12/01 use

SYMBOL	Month	OPENING RANGE MINUTES	TRADING HOURS	A' VALUE	C' VALUE
C - Corn	H-March	5	10:30–2:15	1.6	1.2
CO - Cocoa	H-March	5	8:30–1:30	10	15
CT - Cotton	H-March	5	10:30–2:40	15	40
ED - Euro Dollar	H-March	5	8:20–3:00	5	5
GC - Gold	G-February	5	8:20–2:30	1.2	4
LC - Live Cattle	G-February	5	10:05–2:00	20	20
LH - Live Hogs	G-February	5	10:05–2:00	20	20
OJ - Orange Juice	F-January	5	10:15–2:15	150	150
PB - Pork Bellies	G-February	5	10:05–2:00	40	50
PL - Platinum	F-January	5	8:20–2:30	25	100
S - Beans	H-March	5	10:30–2:15	5	1
SI - Silver	H-March	5	8:25–2:25	3.14	4.64
W - Wheat	H-March	5	10:30–2:15	24	12
AXB-Aus Bonds	H-March	15	6:30pm–2:30am	3.5	5
HG - Copper	H-March	15	8:10–2:00	26	155
NQ - Nasdaq	H-March	15	9:30–4:15	17.5	20.5
SP- S&P 500	H-March	15	9:30–4:15	2	1.5
US - Bonds	H-March	15	8:20–3:00	7	10
LBC - Brent	F-January	20	5:02–3:12	7	12
Bpound/US	Cash	30	2:30am–3:00pm	28	56
Canadian $/US	Cash	30	8:00am–3:00pm	7	7
Euro/US	Cash	30	2:30am–3:00pm	12	23
JapYen/US	Cash	30	9:00pm–3:00pm	8	15
DGB-German Bund	H-March	30	2:00am–1:00pm	7	11
LFT-Footsie	H-March	30	3:00am–12:30pm	70	90
SB - Sugar	H-March	30	9:30–1:20	4	21
CL - Crude	F-January	5	9:45–3:10	8	13
HO - Heat	F-January	5	9:50–3:10	35	135
HU - Unleaded	F-January	5	9:50–3:10	25	85
KC - Coffee	H-March	5	9:15–1:32	115	150
NG - Natural	F-January	5	9:30–3:10	1.6	5.6

TABLE A.6

Commodity change in trend—December 2001

Sunday	Monday	Tuesday	Wednesday	Thursday	Friday	Saturday
2	3 Lumber US Bonds Corn Unleaded Gas Heat Crack	4 Gold Natural Gas	5 Sugar Live Cattle	6 S&P Cotton Silver	7 Swiss Franc Japanese Yen Orange Juice	8
9	10 Australian Dollar Heating Oil London Gas Oil Heat to Unl. Gas	11 British Pound Canadian Dollar London Brent Oil Unleaded Gas Crack	12 Beans Copper Unleaded Gas	13 Live Hogs Crude Oil Natural Gas	14 Sugar US Dollar Heat Crack	15
16	17 Cocoa Cotton Wheat Orange Juice	18 S&P US Bonds Gold	19 Japanese Yen Corn	20 Silver Pork Bellies Heating Oil	21 Canadian Dollar London Gas Oil Unleaded Gas Crack	22
23	24 Live Hogs Beans Heat to Unl. Gas	25 Australian Dollar	26 Wheat Orange Juice Live Cattle US Dollar	27 Sugar London Brent Oil	28 Heat Crack Natural Gas Silver Swiss Franc	29
30	31 Heating Oil Crude Oil Japanese Yen British Pound Unleaded Gas Crack S&P					

TABLE A.7

Energy equities change in trend—December 2001

Sunday	Monday	Tuesday	Wednesday	Thursday	Friday	Saturday
2	3 —	4 EPN	5 EE	6 BP	7 TOT DUK	8
9	10 XOM	11 ENE	12 ETR	13 RD EPN	14 SRE	15
16	17 —	18 —	19 DUK EE	20 —	21 —	22
23	24 —	25 XOM	26 RD EPG BP	27 TOT ETR	28 ENE EPN SRE	29
30	31 —					

TABLE A.8

Equity (reversal system) change in trend—December 2001

Sunday	Monday	Tuesday	Wednesday	Thursday	Friday	Saturday
2	3 ADBE, CBS, QLGC QQQ, SUNQ	4 AFFX, AOL, BGEN JPM, KLAC, MO NOK, SBC, TMX	5 AET, AMGN, BAC GM, GMST, GTW IMNX, LSI, SEBL, T UTX	6 AKAM, BEAS, CA CCU, DELL, HD HWP, IDPH, INKT ORCL, PG, QCOM	7 AES, AGN, CSCO FDX, IBM, JNJ, LEH	8
9	10 AMZN, CC, CRA HGSI	11 C, CCL, ENE SBUX, SNE	12 CAT, SCH, SUNW	13 ADRX, GLW, KLAC NT	14 AFFX, AIG, CLX MU, TLAB	15
16	17 AAPL, CB, CBS CPQ, CSCO, DELL GS, KO, LSI, PVN TXN	18 ADBE, CDO, DISH EMC, FDX, INTC PFE, T, TMX	19 AXP, DUK, GE, PG	20 AET, AGN, GMST LEH	21 HD, LU, USW	22
23	24 BGEN, IBM, MOT UN, UTX ADBE,CDO,DISH,T	25 —	26 AES, BAC, CCL COST, LLY, UAL TMX,PFE,FDX,EMC INTC	27 ADRX, BEAS, SGP TLAB	28 C, CA, DD, HWP JPM, QLGC, TXT	29
30	31 AMGN, ORCL QCOM					

TABLE A.9

Logical trader daily energy market commentary—for 12/12/01 use

Comm.	Month	High	Low	Close	Pivot	+/−	Pivot Range	
CRUDE	F	1840	1792	1808	1813	3	1810	1816
CRUDE	G	1875	1832	1846	1851	3	1848	1854
NAT GAS	F	2820	2670	2803	2764	19	2745	2783
NAT GAS	G	2875	2750	2868	2831	19	2812	2850
UNL GAS	F	5140	4990	5061	5064	1	5063	5065
UNL GAS	G	5280	5150	5220	5217	2	5215	5219
HEAT	F	5070	4960	4999	5010	5	5005	5015
HEAT	G	5200	5090	5145	5145	0	5145	5145
S&P	Z	115200	113350	113650	114067	208	113859	114275
NASDAQ	Z	169700	165300	165550	166850	650	166200	167500

Today's Logical Approach to Natural Gas F

Yesterday the logical trader for Natural Gas wrote about the moving average formation and a potential false breakout. With the higher call yesterday and the subsequent selloff, the ACD system indications of a confused market were confirmed.

For today, ahead of the AGA release prudence dictates keeping positions light. After the release, the bottom of the three day rolling pivot range @ 2.655–2.675 provides today's key support.

Two weeks ago on Wednesday, November 28, the market experienced a very volatile session. On that day the market posted a 3.200 in F and subsequently sold off toward 2.700 by the end of that day. The top of daily pivot range from that day at *2.93–2.95 provides today's key resistance.*

Today's Logical Approach to Crude Oil F

The past few days the daily pivot range has provided insight and a point of reference to get short intraday as the market heads lower.

For today, the daily pivot range is 18.10–16. Look to see if the market can confirm an ACD sell signal that sustains below 18.10 for a decline toward *today's key support at 17.45–50.* Be alert; the window of opportunity for price to challenge the 17.12 spike low will close by the end of tomorrow's trading as historical data suggests a change in trend by the end of this week.

A recovery from the open will work through the remnants of this week's decline toward *today's key resistance at 18.80–86.* This pivot level remains from Monday's trading during which price was unable to break above this daily pivot range and subsequently sent price lower.

TABLE A.10
Stock pivot sheet—for 12/12/01 use

Symbol	High	Low	Close	Pvthigh	Pvtlow	30dAvg	14dAvg	Mom#	Close8
A	30.21	29.26	29.29	29.74	29.44	25.744	27.608+	2.16	27.13
AA	38.77	37.75	38.53	38.44	38.26	36.644	38.464+	−0.07	38.6*
AAPL	22.85	21.65	21.78	22.25	21.94	20.087	21.397+	0.48	21.3
ABGX	33.29	31.1	32.04	32.19	32.09	32.59	34.979−	−3.96	36
ABI	34.37	33.25	33.25	33.81	33.44	30.652	33.616−	0.15	33.1
ABK	56.15	55.16	55.32	55.65	55.43	53.306	55.546+	−0.76	56.08
ABS	33.21	31.7	32.06	32.46	32.19	33.179	33.695−	−1.5	33.56
ABT	55.97	53.8	54.14	54.89	54.39	53.883	54.563+	−0.86	55
ABX	15.18	14.88	15.18	15.13	15.03	15.171	14.929+	0.05	15.13*
ACF	29.25	27.5	27.95	28.38	28.09	22.035	24.743+	4.85	23.1
ACS	99.8	96.55	96.98	98.18	97.38	93.662	95.696+	3.6	93.38
ADBE	35.8	33.65	33.98	34.72	34.23	31.68	34.072+	1.9	32.08
ADI	46.6	44.44	44.57	45.52	44.89	43.404	43.751+	2.07	42.5
ADLAC	27.83	26.7	27.17	27.26	27.2	23.373	25.075+	2.06	25.11
ADP	59.12	58.48	58.78	58.8	58.79	55.439	56.849+	3.32	55.46
ADRX	70.68	67.44	67.71	69.06	68.16	68.221	72.126+	−6.11	73.82
ADSK	42.19	39.95	40.73	41.07	40.84	36.196	37.758+	3.53	37.2
ADVP	27.88	26.02	27.15	27.08	26.95	28.254	27.226−	−0.54	27.69
AEIS	27.98	27.13	27.55	27.56	27.55	23.341	24.917+	3.89	23.66
AEOS	25.65	24.88	25.06	25.26	25.13	26.996	25.021−	0.62	24.44
AEP	42.32	41.44	41.7	41.88	41.76	42.584	41.883−	0.45	41.25
AES	14.7	13.53	13.93	14.11	13.99	15.388	16.34−	−2.59	16.52
AET	30.7	29.93	30.64	30.53	30.32	30.098	30.823+	−0.53	31.17
AFCI	20.34	19.45	19.67	19.9	19.74	19.776	19.997−	0.19	19.48
AFFX	36.89	34.5	35.75	35.73	35.69	34.174	36.534+	−0.47	36.22*
AFL	25.39	24.87	24.92	25.13	24.99	25.957	26.422−	−2.48	27.4
AGE	44.71	43.66	44.22	44.21	44.18	42.686	43.524+	1.62	42.6
AGN	77.07	75.45	75.78	76.26	75.94	73.418	76.144+	0.29	75.49
AHAA	25.55	23.126	23.55	24.34	23.81	26.345	25.611−	−0.45	24
AHC	58.2	57.5	57.53	57.85	57.64	58.028	57.629+	−0.57	58.1
AHP	60.45	58.44	58.75	59.44	58.98	58.179	59.613+	−1.35	60.1
AIG	80	79.16	79.7	79.66	79.58	81.134	81.592−	−2.7	82.4
AL	37.26	35.88	36.74	36.68	36.57	34.381	36.042+	0.74	36
ALA	19.73	19.28	19.34	19.51	19.4	17.665	18.571+	1.33	18.01
ALKS	24.65	21.29	23.01	23	22.97	25.544	24.667−	−1.37	24.38
ALL	32.4	31.5	31.5	31.95	31.65	32.567	33.121−	−2.74	34.24
ALO	24.2	23.3	24.01	23.92	23.75	24.08	23.94+	0.03	23.98
ALTR	25.55	24.42	24.56	24.99	24.7	23.785	24.074+	1.8	22.76
AMAT	45.35	43.5	43.94	44.42	44.1	39.806	41.653+	4.2	39.74
AMGN	65.88	63.88	64.3	64.88	64.49	61.464	65.675+	−2.13	66.43
AMKR	17.8	16.92	17	17.36	17.12	15.2	16.056+	1.43	15.57
AMR	23.22	22.1	22.75	22.72	22.66	19.993	21.575+	1.39	21.36
AMT	7.4	7	7.3	7.27	7.2	8.285	8.272−	−1.5	8.8
ANDW	22.35	21.68	21.91	22.01	21.94	21.385	21.931+	0.9	21.01
ANEN	19	18.14	18.26	18.57	18.36	16.488	17.538+	1.89	16.37
ANF	25.4	24.64	24.86	25.02	24.91	22.335	24.41+	0.86	24
ANN	30.25	28.05	28.62	29.15	28.8	26.669	28.627+	1.35	27.27
AOC	35.23	34.89	34.96	35.06	34.99	36.11	35.635−	−0.87	35.83
AOL	32.78	31.37	32	32.08	32.02	35.152	34.958−	−2.9	34.9
APA	48.69	47.16	47.43	47.92	47.59	48.309	47.047+	1.44	45.99
APC	54.3	53.3	53.7	53.8	53.73	54.737	53.378−	1.8	51.9
APCC	15.31	14.84	15	15.08	15.02	14.143	14.331+	1.24	13.76
APD	46.82	45.6	46.31	46.28	46.21	44.206	46.027+	0.59	45.72
APOL	47.75	45.74	45.74	46.75	46.08	42.722	44.115+	0.86	44.88
ARW	30.02	29.5	29.82	29.8	29.76	26.889	28.057+	2.3	27.52
ASMI	19.3	18.562	18.87	18.93	18.89	16.381	16.289+	4.06	14.81
ASML	19.23	18.64	18.64	18.93	18.74	17.496	18.168+	1.23	17.41
ASO	18.87	18.52	18.67	18.69	18.68	18.302	18.501+	0.35	18.32
AT	62.32	61.7	62.02	62.02	62.01	62.019	63.479−	−3.06	65.08
AVCT	26.3	25.64	25.64	25.97	25.75	21.474	24.666+	1.77	23.87
AVIR	47.1	45.08	46.03	46.09	46.05	37.108	41.02+	8.98	37.05
AVP	49.17	47.9	48.9	48.78	48.53	47.816	48.236+	1.16	47.74
AVT	25.95	25.3	25.34	25.63	25.44	23.218	24.33+	1.59	23.75
AW	12.75	12.46	12.74	12.69	12.6	11.259	11.7+	0.9	11.84
AXP	35.25	34.05	34.25	34.65	34.38	32.735	33.83+	1.34	32.91
AYE	35.79	34.96	34.98	35.38	35.11	36.113	35.066−	0.13	34.85
AZN	45.09	44.26	44.27	44.67	44.41	45.901	45.342−	−1.18	45.45
BA	37.65	36.65	37.07	37.15	37.1	34.89	35.698+	1.97	35.1
BAC	63.05	61.1	62.45	62.32	62.07	62.415	62.83−	1.07	61.38
BAX	51.75	51	51.33	51.38	51.35	49.319	50.587+	−0.67	52
BBBY	32.689	31.8	32.08	32.24	32.13	30.841	32.908+	−0.39	32.47
BBT	35.22	34.66	34.81	34.94	34.85	34.081	34.528+	0.66	34.15
BBY	70.47	68.67	69.2	69.57	69.32	65.436	70.268+	−2.19	71.39
BDK	38	37.74	37.97	37.94	37.87	35.591	36.871+	0.93	37.04
BDX	33.14	32.1	32.59	32.62	32.6	33.868	33.058+	−1.28	33.87
BEAS	17.15	16.53	16.78	16.84	16.8	15.887	17.057+	−0.01	16.79*
BEN	36.55	35.8	36.3	36.26	36.17	35.61	36.404−	0.55	35.75
BGEN	56.66	55.38	55.89	56.02	55.93	56.644	57.832−	−3.02	58.91
BHI	33.8	32.9	33.57	33.5	33.35	34.232	33.655+	0.6	32.97*
BJ	43.09	41.1	41.11	42.1	41.44	47.117	44.284−	−3.89	45

TABLE A.10
Stock pivot sheet—for 12/12/01 use *(Continued)*

Symbol	Close7	Close6	H/L Close	$Risk	High9	High20	High45	Low9	Low20	Low45
A	27.51	28.15		95	30.15	30.15	30.15	27.13	23.78	20.79
AA	37.85	38.1		92	39.95	39.95	39.95	37.85	36.3	31.51
AAPL	21.05	22.4		89	23.76	23.76	23.76	20.42	18.97	16.01
ABGX	35.26	35.79	Low_9	156	37.46	37.46	37.46	32.04	31.11	24.69
ABI	30.98	31.84		123	35.18	35.25	35.25	30.98	30.98	25.67
ABK	55.75	55.9	Low_9	128	56.35	56.35	56.35	55.32	51.56	48
ABS	33.54	33.8	Low_20	73	35.44	35.44	35.44	32.06	32.06	31.43
ABT	55.46	55.09	Low_9	87	55.5	55.5	55.5	54.14	52.03	50.98
ABX	15.29	15.25		32	15.49	15.49	16.93	14.96	14.06	14.06
ACF	22.15	22.91		172	28.61	28.61	36.25	22.15	22.15	14.98
ACS	93.61	95.4		195	97.57	97.57	97.57	93.38	91.29	87.3
ADBE	31.96	34.33		155	37.27	37.27	37.27	31.96	30.67	26.4
ADI	41.96	44.65		205	47.73	47.73	47.73	41.96	40.8	35.7
ADLAC	25.46	26.53		99	27.75	27.75	27.75	24.6	20.91	20.91
ADP	55.27	56.09		104	59.85	59.85	59.85	55.27	55.18	48.17
ADRX	72.57	72.89	Low_9	216	75.59	75.59	75.59	67.71	62.88	62.88
ADSK	36.69	37.15	High_45	112	40.73	40.73	40.73	36.69	33.95	33.22
ADVP	27.38	26.8		133	27.69	31.42	39.91	25.97	25.97	25.6
AEIS	22.59	26.83		141	28.91	28.91	28.91	22.59	21.7	16.33
AEOS	22.57	23.26		117	25.63	30.55	30.55	22.57	22.57	22.57
AEP	41.5	42.01		92	42.86	44.48	44.85	40.58	40.44	40.44
AES	16.07	16.61	Low_20	72	16.98	17.64	17.64	13.93	13.93	12.95
AET	30.82	30.94		65	31.55	31.55	32.01	30.63	29.46	27.64
AFCI	18.41	19.01		113	21.71	21.71	22.47	18.41	18.41	17.36
AFFX	35.61	36.03		160	38.09	38.09	38.09	35.51	32.74	16.2
AFL	26.99	26.8	Low_9	57	27.4	27.4	27.4	24.92	24.89	24.46
AGE	41.73	42.55		92	44.81	44.81	44.81	41.73	41.73	36.17
AGN	75.25	74.74		145	76.4	78.1	78.1	74.74	68.8	64.26
AHAA	24.15	26.39	Low_20	186	28.52	28.52	30.05	23.55	23.55	18.9
AHC	58.4	58.75	Low_9	131	60.26	60.68	68.62	57.53	54.15	54.15
AHP	60.99	60.1	Low_9	104	60.99	60.99	60.99	58.75	56.41	55.83
AIG	81.75	82		138	83.15	83.15	86.12	79.6	79.6	77.35
AL	35.32	35.83		83	37.53	37.53	37.53	35.32	34.3	29.65
ALA	17.52	18.42		60	19.89	19.89	19.89	17.52	16.88	11.41
ALKS	23.55	23.5	Low_20	116	25.44	27.1	28.19	23.01	23.01	20.11
ALL	33.95	32.8	Low_20	72	34.24	34.24	36.54	31.5	31.5	31.38
ALO	23.86	23.96		51	24.27	24.51	30	23.86	21.8	20.9
ALTR	22.49	24.32		138	26.98	26.98	26.98	22.49	21.83	18.5
AMAT	39.27	42.43		187	45.91	45.91	45.91	39.27	36.65	31.15
AMGN	65.48	66.66	Low_9	169	68.49	68.49	68.49	64.3	56.52	56.27
AMKR	15.399	16.53		78	18.02	18.02	18.02	15.399	14.18	10.82
AMR	20.94	21.29		82	23.34	23.34	23.34	20.94	17.01	16.46
AMT	8.09	8.1		66	9.35	9.35	16.27	6.9	6.41	5.98
ANDW	21.05	22.64		95	23.82	23.82	23.82	21.01	20.9	17.38
ANEN	16.31	17.8		86	19	19	19	16.31	15.2	13.85
ANF	24.5	24.8		93	26.02	26.02	26.02	23.39	20.75	17.7
ANN	28.4	28.84		115	31.96	31.96	31.96	27.06	26.1	21.67
AOC	35	35.58	Low_9	63	35.9	36.1	43.13	34.96	34.72	34
AOL	33.58	34.75		128	35.83	38.25	38.25	31	31	29.9
APA	47.06	47.93		145	49.23	51.14	54.41	45.99	43.85	43.85
APC	52.8	54.21		149	55.23	58.88	60.44	51.9	50.75	50.75
APCC	13.71	14.36		54	15.26	15.26	15.26	13.71	13.63	12.77
APD	45.6	46.61		93	47.59	47.59	47.59	45.48	43.01	36.84
APOL	44.57	45		118	47.13	47.13	47.13	44.26	39.62	39.62
ARW	27.26	27.95		76	30.7	30.7	30.7	27.26	26.18	22.01
ASMI	14.82	16.79	High_45	73	18.87	18.87	18.87	14.81	14.35	12.2
ASML	17.05	17.85		64	20.12	20.12	20.12	17.05	16.85	13
ASO	18.17	18.49		31	18.81	18.81	18.81	18.17	18.1	16.5
AT	64.98	64.59	Low_9	89	65.08	65.08	65.08	62.02	61.27	57.14
AVCT	23.75	25.6		105	26.62	26.62	26.62	23.75	22.47	15.5
AVIR	41.42	45.15		168	48.77	48.77	48.77	35.59	34.01	26.693
AVP	47.95	47.94		81	49.05	49.05	49.05	47.74	47.3	43.62
AVT	23.85	24.1		70	26.46	26.46	26.46	23.74	22.71	19.31
AW	11.36	11.69	High_20	46	12.74	12.74	13.84	10.74	10.74	9.1
AXP	32.14	33.35		121	35.16	35.16	35.16	32.14	32.14	29
AYE	34.86	35.5		74	36.04	38.27	38.74	34.01	34.01	34.01
AZN	44.5	45.37	Low_45	68	45.77	46.94	48.14	44.27	44.27	44.27
BA	35	35.38		90	37.3	37.3	37.68	35	33.61	32.6
BAC	61.43	62.34		129	63.6	64.99	64.99	61.38	61.38	52.52
BAX	51.48	51.38		96	52	52	53.45	49.6	48	45.95
BBBY	32.4	32.98	Low_9	114	34.94	34.94	34.94	32.08	30.77	24.3
BBT	33.85	34.38		48	35.12	35.12	35.12	33.85	33.85	32.1
BBY	72.55	72.37		192	73.31	73.31	73.31	68.3	64.97	47.2
BDK	36.57	37.05		86	39.4	39.4	39.4	35.55	34.49	32.25
BDX	33.98	34.68		85	34.68	34.68	38.11	32.02	32.02	32.02
BEAS	16.09	17.2		95	18.38	18.38	18.38	16.09	15.75	11.7
BEN	35.2	35.25		81	36.91	37.55	37.55	35.2	35.2	31.64
BGEN	57.35	59.41	Low_9	143	59.41	59.41	59.41	55.89	54.96	53.05
BHI	34.05	35.34		130	36.75	37.38	37.7	32.97	30.65	30.65
BJ	44.24	43.65	Low_45	147	45.15	50.36	52.85	41.11	41.11	41.11

Appendix

TABLE A.11

Equities—first two weeks of July 2001

Symbol	High	Date	Low	Date	Close	Date	Pivot Low	Pivot High	A Value	Aup	Adown
ADBE	47.84	1010702	39.82	1010713	40.37	1010713	41.52	43.83	0.38	48.22	39.44
ADI	46.31	1010702	38.41	1010710	43.04	1010713	42.36	42.81	0.56	46.87	37.85
AIG	87.10	1010703	83.27	1010711	84.51	1010713	84.74	85.19	0.25	87.35	83.02
AMAT	51.13	1010703	42.16	1010711	46.36	1010713	46.46	46.65	0.43	51.56	41.73
AMR	37.94	1010713	35.01	1010706	37.94	1010713	36.48	37.45	0.24	38.18	34.77
AOL	53.30	1010702	47.63	1010711	49.81	1010713	50.03	50.47	0.29	53.59	47.34
AXP	40.06	1010703	36.60	1010711	39.36	1010713	38.33	39.02	0.22	40.28	36.38
BBY	69.22	1010712	64.09	1010711	68.17	1010713	66.66	67.67	0.50	69.72	63.59
CAT	52.69	1010713	48.77	1010710	52.48	1010713	50.73	51.90	0.32	53.01	48.45
CLS	50.50	1010702	39.90	1010711	45.45	1010713	45.20	45.37	0.56	51.06	39.34
CMVT	58.75	1010702	23.50	1010711	26.82	1010713	31.59	41.13	0.78	59.53	22.72
CPQ	15.50	1010705	13.73	1010711	15.22	1010713	14.62	15.02	0.15	15.65	13.58
DAL	45.89	1010712	42.57	1010706	45.70	1010713	44.23	45.21	0.28	46.17	42.29
DUK	42.30	1010711	38.83	1010703	41.36	1010713	40.57	41.10	0.20	42.50	38.63
ENE	51.50	1010706	47.50	1010702	48.78	1010713	49.02	49.50	0.37	51.87	47.13
ENZN	63.30	1010703	51.34	1010712	55.11	1010713	55.85	57.32	0.60	63.90	50.74
GE	50.20	1010702	44.30	1010711	47.45	1010713	47.25	47.38	0.31	50.51	43.99
HWP	29.16	1010702	25.01	1010711	27.98	1010713	27.09	27.68	0.26	29.42	24.75
IBM	115.40	1010702	101.56	1010711	108.53	1010713	108.48	108.51	0.62	116.02	100.94
IP	38.84	1010713	35.21	1010706	38.65	1010713	37.03	38.11	0.18	39.02	35.03
IR	44.70	1010713	40.63	1010702	44.42	1010713	42.67	43.84	0.28	44.98	40.35
JBL	30.15	1010702	23.08	1010711	27.13	1010713	26.62	26.96	0.40	30.55	22.68
JNPR	32.85	1010702	24.01	1010711	27.44	1010713	27.77	28.43	0.53	33.38	23.48
KLAC	59.11	1010703	45.45	1010711	50.70	1010713	51.23	52.28	0.60	59.71	44.85
KO	46.14	1010713	44.29	1010711	46.01	1010713	45.22	45.75	0.21	46.35	44.08
LEH	77.00	1010705	68.44	1010711	75.19	1010713	72.72	74.37	0.50	77.50	67.94
LSI	20.50	1010702	17.05	1010711	19.19	1010713	18.78	19.05	0.23	20.73	16.82
MEDI	48.08	1010702	40.78	1010711	43.19	1010713	43.60	44.43	0.58	48.66	40.20
MER	59.85	1010703	51.50	1010711	54.50	1010713	54.89	55.68	0.41	60.26	51.09
MMM	117.50	1010703	109.25	1010702	112.23	1010713	112.61	113.38	0.67	118.17	108.58
MO	49.76	1010702	44.00	1010712	44.99	1010713	45.62	46.88	0.30	50.06	43.70
MRK	65.28	1010705	60.35	1010712	61.50	1010713	61.94	62.82	0.25	65.53	60.10
MSFT	73.82	1010703	64.20	1010711	71.34	1010713	69.01	70.56	0.54	74.36	63.66
NKE	45.99	1010712	40.33	1010710	45.13	1010713	43.16	44.47	0.36	46.35	39.97
NTAP	14.22	1010702	10.25	1010710	11.67	1010713	11.86	12.24	0.22	14.44	10.03
NXTL	17.50	1010702	14.30	1010711	17.02	1010713	15.90	16.65	0.23	17.73	14.07
PMCS	31.99	1010702	23.56	1010710	30.05	1010713	27.77	29.29	0.54	32.53	23.02
PSFT	49.35	1010702	39.75	1010711	43.91	1010713	44.12	44.55	0.54	49.89	39.21
QCOM	67.95	1010713	55.22	1010711	65.58	1010713	61.58	64.25	0.82	68.77	54.40
QLGC	65.67	1010702	46.68	1010711	53.06	1010713	54.10	56.18	0.83	66.50	45.85
SANM	24.00	1010702	19.00	1010711	22.14	1010713	21.50	21.93	0.33	24.33	18.67
SGP	37.63	1010710	34.50	1010712	36.89	1010713	36.07	36.62	0.21	37.84	34.29
SLB	54.65	1010706	48.70	1010711	50.45	1010713	50.86	51.68	0.46	55.11	48.24
SWY	49.70	1010705	40.75	1010712	43.05	1010713	43.78	45.23	0.35	50.05	40.40
TER	37.45	1010703	29.76	1010711	33.76	1010713	33.61	33.71	0.41	37.86	29.35
TLAB	19.35	1010702	14.47	1010711	16.98	1010713	16.91	16.96	0.26	19.61	14.21
UNH	65.99	1010713	61.00	1010705	65.79	1010713	63.50	65.03	0.28	66.27	60.72
VRSN	63.22	1010702	48.65	1010711	54.48	1010713	54.97	55.94	0.84	64.06	47.81
XLNX	42.48	1010702	35.08	1010710	40.90	1010713	38.78	40.19	0.50	42.98	34.58
YHOO	20.87	1010705	15.31	1010711	18.25	1010713	18.09	18.20	0.29	21.16	15.03

TABLE A.12

ACD system—commodities—three-day rolling pivot range—for 12/12/01 use

Futures Price Summary				Three Day Rolling Pivot Summary				
	3 D HIGH	3 D LOW	3 D SETTLE					
Crude Oil	1909	1792	1808	CLF2	3 D PIV	+/−′	3 D PIVOT BOX	
January	7-Dec	11-Dec	11-Dec		1836	14	1822	1850
	3 D HIGH	3 D LOW	3 D SETTLE					
Natural Gas	2820	2490	2803	NGF2	3 D PIV	+/−′	3 D PIVOT BOX	
January	11-Dec	7-Dec	11-Dec		2704	49	2655	2753
	3 D HIGH	3 D LOW	3 D SETTLE					
Unleaded Gas	5275	4990	5061	HUF2	3 D PIV	+/−′	3 D PIVOT BOX	
January	7-Dec	11-Dec	11-Dec		5109	24	5085	5133
	3 D HIGH	3 D LOW	3 D SETTLE					
Heating Oil	5200	4930	4999	HOF2	3 D PIV	+/−′	3 D PIVOT BOX	
January	10-Dec	7-Dec	11-Dec		5043	22	5021	5065
	3 D HIGH	3 D LOW	3 D SETTLE					
S&P	116550	113350	113650	SPZ1	3 D PIV	+/−′	3 D PIVOT BOX	
December	7-Dec	11-Dec	11-Dec		114517	433	114084	114950
	3 D HIGH	3 D LOW	3 D SETTLE					
Nasdaq	171100	164300	165550	NDZ1	3 D PIV	+/−′	3 D PIVOT BOX	
December	7-Dec	10-Dec	11-Dec		166983	717	166266	167700
	3 D HIGH	3 D LOW	3 D SETTLE					
Gold	2755	2717	2729	GCG2	3 D PIV	+/−′	3 D PIVOT BOX	
February	7-Dec	10-Dec	11-Dec		2734	2	2732	2736
	3 D HIGH	3 D LOW	3 D SETTLE					
Silver	4295	4220	4275	SIH2	3 D PIV	+/−′	3 D PIVOT BOX	
March	11-Dec	10-Dec	11-Dec		4263	6	4257	4269
	3 D HIGH	3 D LOW	3 D SETTLE					
US Bonds	10206	9913	10013	USDH2	3 D PIV	+/−′	3 D PIVOT BOX	
March	7-Dec	7-Dec	11-Dec		10021	5	10016	10026
	3 D HIGH	3 D LOW	3 D SETTLE					
Sugar	784	731	735	SBH2	3 D PIV	+/−′	3 D PIVOT BOX	
March	7-Dec	11-Dec	11-Dec		750	8	742	758
	3 D HIGH	3 D LOW	3 D SETTLE					
Coffee	4790	4560	4780	KCH2	3 D PIV	+/−′	3 D PIVOT BOX	
March	11-Dec	7-Dec	11-Dec		4710	35	4675	4745

TABLE A.13 Stock number line sheets—for 12/12/01 use

Date	Tues.Oct.30	Wed.Oct.31	Mon.Nov.26	Tue.Nov.27	Wed.Nov.28	Thu.Nov.29	Fri.Nov.30	Mon.Dec.3	Tues.Dec.4	Wed.Dec.5	Thu.Dec.6	Fri.Dec.7	Mon.Dec.10	Tue.Dec.11	
AA	33.17	32.31	38.24	38.28	37.94	37.98	38.8	37.66	38.05	39.95	39.5	38.91	38.51	38.48	
Net	-0.88	-0.86	-0.1	0.04	-0.34	0.04	0.82	-1.14	0.39	1.9	-0.45	-0.59	-0.4	-0.03	
plus-															
ABCD	0	-2	-2	1	0	0	2	-2	0	2	0	1	-2	-1	
12 Day Cum +/-	0	0	0	0	0	0	0	0	0	0	0	0	0	0	
12 Day Cum ABCD	5	5	4	0	2	1	0	0	-1	-1	3	1	4	2	
30 Day Cum +/-	-2	-2	0	0	0	0	1	1	1	1	1	1	0	0	
30 Day Cum ABCD	8	9	11	9	10	8	10	12	12	10	10	11	8	4	Wed.Oct.31
AAPL	17.6	17.56	21.37	21	20.53	20.42	21.3	21.04	22.41	23.75	22.79	22.53	22.54	21.81	
Net	-0.02	-0.04	1.53	-0.37	-0.47	-0.11	0.88	-0.26	1.37	1.34	-0.96	-0.26	0.01	-0.73	
plus-															
ABCD	0	0	2	-2	-1	0	0	0	2	2	-2	0	0	0	
12 Day Cum +/-	2	0	0	0	0	0	2	1	0	0	0	0	0	0	
12 Day Cum ABCD	-1	-2	0	2	3	2	1	4	5	8	10	6	8	7	
30 Day Cum +/-	1	1	1	0	0	0	1	1	1	1	1	0	0	0	
30 Day Cum ABCD	-2	4	5	4	3	2	5	8	9	9	15	11	9	9	Thu.Nov.8
ABGX	28.61	29.76	34.85	36.12	34.24	35.6	36	35.27	35.84	37.47	37.12	35.66	32.74	32.03	
Net	-0.69	1.15	1.42	1.27	-1.88	1.36	0.4	-0.73	0.57	1.63	-0.35	-1.46	-2.92	-0.71	
plus-															
ABCD	1	0	2	0	0	1	0	0	0	0	0	-2	0	0	
12 Day Cum +/-	-2	-2	-1	2	-2	-1	0	0	2	2	-1	-1	-2	1	
12 Day Cum ABCD	5	8	-2	-1	6	4	5	3	0	3	6	3	3	3	
30 Day Cum +/-	-4	-4	-3	-3	-3	-3	-1	-1	-1	-1	0	0	0	0	
30 Day Cum ABCD	5	8	0	4	4	0	4	4	1	1	5	2	-2	-6	
ABI	28.72	29.2	34.7	35.15	33.36	33.66	32.96	30.95	31.79	32.89	35.36	34.74	33.68	33.26	
Net	-0.88	0.48	0.34	0.45	-1.79	0.3	-0.7	-2.01	0.84	1.1	2.47	-0.62	-1.06	-0.42	
plus-															
ABCD	0	0	0	0	-4	4	-1	0	4	3	2	0	-4	-3	
12 Day Cum +/-	-2	-1	4	3	0	0	-1	-1	-1	-1	-1	-1	-1	-1	
12 Day Cum ABCD	-1	-1	-1	4	7	5	9	5	5	9	13	13	13	10	
30 Day Cum +/-	1	-9	-3	-2	-2	5	9	-2	-3	-3	-2	-2	-2	-2	
30 Day Cum ABCD	3	1	-3	-3	1	0	6	6	6	8	15	15	11	5	Thu.Dec.6

Symbol / Measure													Fri.Oct.26	Mon.Oct.29
ABK	48.54	47.99	55.42	55.41	54.03	55.35	55.97	55.66	56.1	56.1	55.92	56.35	55.33	55.33
Net	-0.29	-0.55	0.05	-0.01	-1.38	1.32	0.62	-0.31	0.44	0	-0.18	0.43	-1.02	0
plus-														
ABCD	0	0	0	-1	0	1	0	0	0	0	0	0	0	0
12 Day Cum +/-	1	1	-1	1	-2	2	-2	-1	-1	-3	-1	-1	-2	-1
12 Day Cum ABCD	2	0	5	3	6	6	7	3	5	5	2	-2	-1	0
30 Day Cum +/-	2	2	1	1	0	0	1	1	1	5	2	0	0	-4
30 Day Cum ABCD	7	5	11	9	8	5	9	9	13	11	10	6	6	1
ABS	31.52	31.92	33.38	33	33.32	33.7	33.57	33.44	33.79	35.33	34.91	34.05	33.65	32.05
Net	-0.84	0.4	-0.33	-0.38	0.32	0.38	-0.13	-0.13	0.35	1.54	-0.42	-0.86	-0.4	-1.6
plus-														
ABCD	0	1	0	0	1	0	0	0	0	0	0	0	0	0
12 Day Cum +/-	-2	2	-2	-2	2	-1	-2	-1	0	2	1	2	1	-2
12 Day Cum ABCD	-1	0	0	0	0	-5	1	1	1	-4	2	4	1	1
30 Day Cum +/-	2	1	-1	0	-6	1	-3	-4	-2	0	2	2	0	2
30 Day Cum ABCD	3	3	1	-1	-4	-2	1	1	2	-1	3	6	3	2
ABT	53.78	53.07	54.04	53.83	54.1	54.5	54.88	55.38	55.09	55.16	54.93	55.14	55.45	54.11
Net	-0.29	-0.71	0.14	-0.21	0.27	0.4	0.38	0.5	-0.29	0.07	-0.23	-0.21	-0.31	-1.34
plus-		-2												
ABCD	0	1	0	0	1	2	0	2	-2	-1	1	1	2	0
12 Day Cum +/-	2	1	1	1	3	5	0	0	0	0	1	6	4	-2
12 Day Cum ABCD	7	5	3	3	1	1	0	5	9	5	6	6	1	4
30 Day Cum +/-	2	2	4	3	3	1	1	0	1	0	2	2	1	1
30 Day Cum ABCD	7	8	13	11	9	9	12	14	16	12	13	12	8	10
ABX	15.81	15.57	14.16	14.68	14.85	14.93	15.13	15.3	15.28	15.4	15.48	15.09	15.03	15.18
Net	0.01	-0.24	-0.02	0.52	0.17	0.08	0.2	0.17	-0.02	0.12	0.08	-0.39	-0.06	0.15
plus-	-1	0	0	0	-1	0	0	0	0	0	0	0	0	0
ABCD	1	0	0	2	0	-1	0	0	2	0	2	-2	0	2
12 Day Cum +/-	4	2	-4	-6	-2	-5	-6	-5	-3	-1	-1	3	-1	-1
12 Day Cum ABCD	2	1	0	0	0	-1	-1	-1	-1	-1	-1	-1	-1	-1
30 Day Cum +/-	6	2	4	2	4	1	-2	1	1	1	5	7	3	8
30 Day Cum ABCD	12	8	13	11	9	9	16	14	12	12	13	12	8	10
ACF	16.15	15.49	24.74	24.3	22.76	22.8	23.12	22.15	22.9	23.11	27.92	28.6	28.25	27.96
Net	-1.19	-0.66	0.74	-0.44	-1.54	0.04	0.32	-0.97	0.75	0.21	4.81	0.68	-0.35	-0.29
plus-	0	0	0	0	-2	0	0	0	0	0	0	0	0	0
ABCD	0	-2	0	0	0	2	2	0	0	0	2	2	0	1
12 Day Cum +/-	0	0	4	2	4	-1	-1	2	-3	-1	-1	-1	-1	2
12 Day Cum ABCD	-1	-1	-1	-1	-1	-1	-1	0	-1	-1	-1	1	-1	-1
30 Day Cum +/-	-2	-2	-1	-1	3	1	1	0	1	0	0	-1	-1	4
30 Day Cum ABCD	-1	-3	1	1	3	1	1	3	0	0	0	1	5	4

Continued

TABLE A.13 Stock number line sheets—for 12/12/01 use (Continued)

Date	Tues.Oct.30	Wed.Oct.31	Mon.Nov.26	Tue.Nov.27	Wed.Nov.28	Thu.Nov.29	Fri.Nov.30	Mon.Dec.3	Tues.Dec.4	Wed.Dec.5	Thu.Dec.6	Fri.Dec.7	Mon.Dec.10	Tue.Dec.11	
ACS	90.61	88.06	96.05	95.92	94.4	95.25	93.51	93.63	95.4	96.3	97.13	97.54	96.75	96.95	
Net	-1.29	-2.55	-0.11	-0.13	-1.52	0.85	-1.74	0.12	1.77	0.9	0.83	0.41	-0.79	0.2	
plus-	0	-1	0	1	0	0	0	0	0	0	0	0	0	0	
ABCD	0	-2	-2	0	-2	2	-3	0	2	2	2	2	-1	-1	
12 Day Cum +/m	0	0	0	0	0	0	-1	-1	-1	-1	-1	-1	-2	0	
12 Day Cum ABCD	6	7	-4	-4	0	0	-1	-3	-5	-5	-1	2	6	4	
30 Day Cum +/-	1	0	-1	-1	-1	-1	-1	0	0	0	0	-1	-1	-2	
30 Day Cum ABCD	21	19	8	7	8	4	6	5	3	6	8	8	8	5	Thu.Oct.18
ADBE	28.74	26.4	34.93	34.28	32.06	33.62	32.09	31.97	34.36	36.64	37.25	36.45	35.73	33.86	
Net	-1.57	-2.34	2	-0.65	-2.22	1.56	-1.53	-0.12	2.39	2.28	0.61	-0.8	-0.72	-1.87	
plus-	0	0	0	0	0	0	0	0	0	0	0	0	0	0	
ABCD	-2	2	2	0	-2	2	0	-1	2	2	2	1	0	-2	
12 Day Cum +/-	-1	-1	1	1	1	1	0	0	-2	0	0	0	0	0	
12 Day Cum ABCD	5	4	0	0	2	-1	0	0	-2	1	5	5	7	7	
30 Day Cum +/-	0	0	0	0	0	1	1	1	1	1	1	1	1	1	
30 Day Cum ABCD	15	14	8	11	11	8	12	12	9	9	11	11	9	9	Tue.Sep.4
ADI	35.5	37.99	44.27	42.8	40.75	42.55	42.11	41.97	44.62	47.32	47.73	46.38	44.95	44.57	
Net	-2.5	2.49	2.07	-1.47	-2.05	1.8	-0.44	-0.14	2.65	2.7	0.41	-1.35	-1.43	-0.38	
plus-	0	0	0	0	0	0	0	0	0	0	0	0	0	0	
ABCD	-2	0	2	-2	-2	3	0	1	2	2	-1	-2	0	-2	
12 Day Cum pl/-	0	0	-2	-2	-1	-1	-1	-1	-2	0	0	0	0	0	
12 Day ABCD	-2	-4	-2	-2	-2	-6	-5	-5	-2	-1	2	3	3	3	
30 Day Cum +/-	0	0	-2	-2	-2	-2	-1	-1	-1	-1	-1	-1	-2	-2	
30 Day Cum ABCD	4	2	-2	0	0	-4	1	4	5	5	7	7	3	1	
ADLAC	21.99	22.1	23.02	23.2	23.15	24.6	25.11	25.46	26.5	27.76	27.72	26.7	26.35	27.07	
Net	-1.05	0.11	0.36	0.18	-0.05	1.45	0.51	0.35	1.04	1.26	-0.04	-1.02	-0.35	0.72	
plus-	0	0	0	0	0	0	0	0	0	0	0	0	0	0	
ABCD	-2	-2	1	-1	1	2	2	2	2	2	1	-2	1	0	
12 Day Cum +/-	-1	-1	0	0	0	0	0	0	0	0	0	0	0	0	
12 Day Dum ABCD	-1	-3	3	6	3	6	8	12	14	16	16	15	11	11	
30 Day Cum +/-	-1	-1	-1	-1	-1	-1	0	0	0	0	0	-1	0	0	
30 Day Cum ABCD	-8	-10	-3	-1	-3	-2	2	2	4	4	6	7	4	7	0

232

TABLE A.14

Gartman's 20 ridiculously simple rules of trading

1. ***To trade successfully, think like a fundamentalist; trade like a technician.*** It is imperative that we understand the fundamentals driving a trade, but that we understand the market's technicals also. Then, and only then, can we, or should we, trade.

2. ***Trade like a mercenary guerrilla.*** Our duty is to fight on the winning side, to be willing to change sides immediately upon detecting that the other has gained the upper hand, and to deploy our capital (both mental and monetary) on that side. Of the two types of capital, the mental is the more important and expensive of the two.

3. ***The objective is not to buy low and sell high, but to buy high and to sell higher.*** We cannot know what price is low. Nor can we know what price is high. We can, however, have a modest, reasonable chance at knowing what the trend is and acting upon that trend.

4. ***In bull markets we can only be long or neutral,*** and in bear markets we can only be short or neutral. That may seem self–evident; it is not, however.

5. ***"Markets can remain illogical far longer than we can remain solvent,"*** according to our good friend, Dr. A. Gary Shilling. There is wisdom in knowing that illogic often reigns. Markets are often enormously inefficient despite what the academics have believed, and return to rationality immediately upon forcing us to exit a position!

6. ***Sell markets that show the greatest signs of weakness, and buy those markets that show the greatest strength.*** Metaphorically, when bearish we need to throw our rocks into the wettest paper sacks, for they break most readily. In bull markets, we need to ride upon the strongest winds . . . they shall carry us higher than lesser ones.

7. ***Resist the urge to trade against the consensus too early.*** The consensus may be wrong at major turning points, but it is right and can remain right for long periods of time in the midst of a great move. Patience, rather than impatience, is far better when considering any trade.

8. ***Try to trade the first day of a gap (either higher or lower), for gaps usually indicate violent new action.*** We have come to respect "gaps" in our twenty-five years of watching markets; however in the world of twenty-four hour trading, they are becoming less and less important, especially in forex dealing. Nonetheless, when they happen (especially in stocks) they are usually very important.

9. ***Trading runs in cycles: some good; most bad.*** Trade large and aggressively when trading well; trade small and modestly when trading poorly. In *good times,* even errors are profitable; in *bad times* even the most well researched trades go awry. This is the nature of trading; accept it.

10. ***Margin calls are the market's way of telling you that your analysis and position taking are wrong.*** Never meet a margin call . . . liquidate.

11. ***Never, ever under any circumstance add to a losing position*** . . . not ever, not ever! No more need be said; to do otherwise is illogical.

12. ***Respect outside reversals after extended bull or bear runs.*** Reversal days on the charts signal the final exhaustion of the bullish or bearish forces that drove the market previously. Respect them. We may not wish to reverse our position, but we must at minimum learn to avoid trading in the old trend's direction. And even more important shall be the respect paid to weekly and the even more rare, monthly, reversals. Pay heed!

13. ***Keep your technical systems simple.*** Complicated systems breed confusion; simplicity breeds elegance.

14. ***Respect and embrace the very normal 50–62% retracements that take prices back to major trends.*** If a trade is missed, wait patiently for the retracement. Draw a box on the chart between those levels and watch how often prices retrace into that box, then act.

Continued

TABLE A.14

Gartman's 20 ridiculously simple rules of trading *(Continued)*

15. *Know that in trading/investing, an understanding of mass psychology is often more important than an understanding of economics* . . . most, or at least much of the time.
16. *Establish initial positions on strength in bull markets and on weakness in bear markets.* The first addition should also be added on strength as the market shows the trend to be working. Henceforth, subsequent additions are to be added on retracements.
17. *Bear markets are more violent than are bull markets* and so also are their retracements.
18. *Be patient with winning trades; be enormously impatient with losing trades.*
19. *Understand that the market is the sum total of the knowledge and wisdom of all of those who deal in it; we dare not argue with the market's wisdom.* If we learn nothing more than that, we have learned very much indeed.
20. *Finally, all rules are meant to be broken.* The trick is knowing when . . . and how infrequently this rule may be invoked!

The Gartman Letter, Used by Permission.

TABLE A.15
ACD Methodology

Thursday, April 18, 2001

Commodity	Month	High	Low	Close	Pivot	+/-	Pivot Range	
Crude Oil	K	2599	2516	2594	2570	12	2558	2582

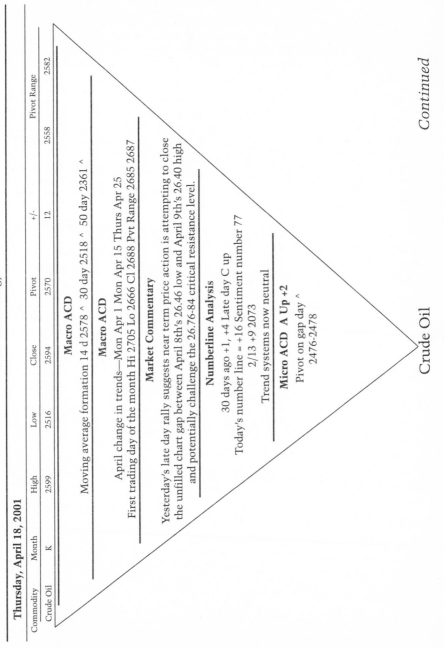

Macro ACD

Moving average formation 14 d 2578 ^ 30 day 2518 ^ 50 day 2361 ^

Macro ACD

April change in trends—Mon Apr 1 Mon Apr 15 Thurs Apr 25
First trading day of the month Hi 2705 Lo 2666 Cl 2688 Pvt Range 2685 2687

Market Commentary

Yesterday's late day rally suggests near term price action is attempting to close the unfilled chart gap between April 8th's 26.46 low and April 9th's 26.40 high and potentially challenge the 26.76-84 critical resistance level.

Numberline Analysis

30 days ago +1, +4 Late day C up
Today's number line = +16 Sentiment number 77
2/13 +9 2073
Trend systems now neutral

Micro ACD A Up +2
Pivot on gap day ^
2476-2478

Crude Oil

Continued

TABLE A.15
ACD Methodology (*Continued*)

Thursday, April 18, 2001

Commodity	Month	High	Low	Close	Pivot	+/-	Pivot Range	
Natural Gas	K	3480	3350	3477	3436	21	3415	3457

Macro ACD

Moving average formation 14 d 3334 N 30 day 3217 ^ 50 day 2894 ^

Macro ACD

April change in trends—Mon Apr 8 Thurs Apr 18
First trading day of the month Hi 3550 Lo 3325 Cl 3531 Pvt Range 3438 3500

Market Commentary

Recovery rebound from the 3.060 double low at the daily pivot range is positioning price to resume the prevailing bull trend toward 3.650 in the coming sessions. Use the 3-day rolling pivot range at 3.348-3.360 as a point of reference stop.

Numberline Analysis

30 days ago +1,+2
Today's number line = +6 Sentiment number 79
4/15 +9 3430
Trend systems still neutral

Micro ACD A Up +2

Pivot on gap day ^
331-334

Natural Gas

ACD Methodology

Thursday, April 18, 2001

Commodity	Month	High	Low	Close	Pivot	+/-	Pivot Range	
S&P's	M	113440	112400	112790	112877	43	112834	112920

Macro ACD

Moving average formation 14 d 112518 ^ 30 day 114247 N ^ 50 day 113010N possible outside up week above 113350 4/14-4/19

Macro ACD

April change in trends—Thurs Apr 4
First trading day of the month Hi 114990 Lo 113420 Cl 114450 Pvt Range 114205 114369

Market Commentary

Yesterday's failed trade above 113350 suggests possible failed outside up week. Begin to shed speculative longs and await ACD confirmation for a potential selloff to unfold back toward 1100.

Numberline Analysis

30 days ago +1, +2,
Today's number line = -1 Sentiment number 60
4/3 0 from +9
Trend systems still short

Micro ACD Point D 0

S & P's

Continued

TABLE A.15
ACD Methodology (*Continued*)

Thursday, April 18, 2001

Commodity	Month	High	Low	Close	Pivot	+/-	Pivot Range	
U.S. Bonds	M	10025	9927	10002	10007.5	43	10005	10010

Macro ACD

Moving average formation 14 d 10003 ^ 30 day 9911 N ^ 50 day 10019^

Macro ACD

April change in trends—Mon Apr 1–Thurs Apr 25
First trading day of the month Hi 9824 Lo 9731 Cl 9808 Pvt Range 9808 9812

Market Commentary

The inability to sustain the ACD sell signal under 9928 suggests a near term exhausted market. Expect recovery rally attempts in the coming sessions back toward 101+.

Numberline Analysis

30 days ago 0, -2,
Today's number line = -1 Sentiment number 55
4/12 0 from -9
Trend systems still long

Micro ACD A Down -2
Reversal A up ^10020 today

U.S. Bonds

GLOSSARY

ACD methodology   A logical approach to trading that provides traders with low-risk high-reward trading scenarios. This approach can be implemented both in micro and macro time frames.

ACD opening range   A consistent time frame based on an opening of a given market, which is essential to calculating the ACD points, and is used as an area of reference throughout the day.

ACD system   The ACD system is a trading system developed by the author, Mark B. Fisher, which can be applied to virtually any commodity, stock, or currency.

A down (A ∨)   A price level set at a specific number of ticks away from the opening range that is determined by the A values (see *A values*) for a particular stock or commodity below the bottom of the opening range. This is an entry level to establish a short position/bias.

A up (A ^)   A price level set at a specific number of ticks away from the opening range that is determined by the A values (see *A values*) for a particular stock or commodity above the top of the opening range. This is an entry level to establish a long position/bias.

A values   A specific number of ticks that is used to determine the distance to a Point A up (A ^) or a Point A down (A ∨). The A values will vary depending upon the commodity or stock traded.

Bearish phase of the market A bearish phase of the market (when prices are moving steadily lower) occurs when several pivot moving averages (see *pivot moving averages*) of varying time frames are all sloped downward.

Bullish phase of the market A bullish phase of the market (when prices are moving steadily higher) occurs when several pivot moving averages (see *pivot moving averages*) of varying time frames are all sloped upward.

Bus people The term *bus people* refers to the amateurs, the uninformed, or the uninitiated in the market who, when it comes to investing, are almost always 100 percent wrong.

C down (C ⌄) A price level set at a specific number of ticks away from the opening range for a particular stock or commodity below the bottom of the opening range. (see *C values*). This is an entry level to establish a short position/bias. A C down (C ⌄) can be made only if the market has previously had a confirmed A up (A ^) (see *A up*).

C up (C ^) A price level set at a specific number of ticks away from the opening range for a particular stock or commodity above the opening range (see *C values*). This is an entry level to establish a long position/bias. A C up (C ^) can be made only if the market has previously had a confirmed A down (A ⌄) (see *A down*).

C values A specific number of ticks that is used to determine the distance to a Point C up (C ^) or a Point C down (C ⌄). C values will vary depending upon the commodity or stock traded. In commodities, C values are different than A values (see *A values*). In stocks, A and C values are the same for each stock.

Change in trend This ACD tool utilizes proprietary computer-generated pattern recognition techniques to identify statistically, on average, how long minor or major trends should last in a given market. Based on various pattern recognition studies, the ACD change in trend indicator makes projections for possible turning points in various markets for the upcoming month. The statistical analysis is based upon over 15 years' worth of historical price data on all major commodities and equities.

Confused market A confused market occurs when the pivot moving averages (see *pivot moving average*) for varying time frames are diverging, with one sloped upward, one sloped downward, and one sideways.

Daily pivot range The daily pivot range is calculated based upon the high, low, and close of the previous trading day. The ACD system identifies this price range as the meat of the market from the previous trading day.

Daily pivot range formula This is the daily pivot range formula to be used when applying the ACD methodology:

$$\frac{\text{High} + \text{Low} + \text{Close}}{3} = \frac{\text{Daily}}{\text{Pivot Price}} \qquad \frac{\text{High} + \text{Low}}{2} = \frac{\text{2nd}}{\text{Calculation}}$$

$$\frac{\text{Difference between Daily Pivot Price}}{\text{and Second Calculation}} = \frac{\text{Daily Pivot}}{\text{Differential}}$$

$$\frac{\text{Daily Pivot Price}}{+/- \text{ Pivot Differential}} = \text{Daily Pivot Range}$$

Discipline The concept of discipline cannot be stressed enough. If you don't have the wherewithal to keep yourself in check, the concepts, ideas, and methodology of the ACD system will not help you. (See Chapter 7, "The ACD Version of 'Ripley's Believe It or Not'!")

Failed Point A A failed Point A set up can occur based on one of the two following scenarios: (1) The market may approach a Point A value and fail to trade at that value, subsequently reversing its direction and trading back into the opening range. Or, (2) the market may approach a Point A value, trade at that value and even potentially through it. However, it does not stay at the Point A value for at least half of the ACD opening range time frame before reversing its direction and trading back into the opening range.

Failed A against/within the pivot If the pivot range (see *pivot range*) proves to be strong enough support or good enough resistance to stop the market at or near a Point A value, the result is a failed A against the pivot. For example, a failed A up

$(A \wedge)$ within the pivot range confirms resistance in that area and increases the likelihood of success if a short position is established at that level. Conversely, a failed A down $(A \vee)$ within the pivot confirms support at that level and increases the likelihood of success if a long position is established at that level.

Failed C   A failed Point C setup can occur based on one of the following scenarios: (1) The market may approach a Point C value and fail to trade at that value, subsequently reversing its direction and trading back into the opening range. Or, (2) the market may approach a Point C value, and then trade at that value and even potentially through it. However, it does not stay at the Point C value for at least half of the ACD opening range time frame before reversing its direction and trading back into the opening range.

Failed C against the pivot   A failed C against the pivot, otherwise known as the *Treacherous Trade*, generally occurs under highly volatile market conditions. The market attempts to reverse its bias at Point C, but runs directly into the meat of the market from the previous trading session, otherwise known as the daily pivot range. The market snaps like a rubber band off this area and reverses back towards the opening range, providing the trader with a clear point of reference at the failed C level.

Fear and greed   Fear and greed are the two key ingredients that every trader needs to possess in the right combination in order to be successful. By fear, I mean a healthy amount of respect for the market that you are participating in. A trader must also be greedy and willing to press winning trades and maximize market opportunities.

"Gartman's 20 Ridiculously Simple Rules of Trading"   Published by Dennis Gartman, author of The Gartman Letter, "Gartman's 20 Ridiculously Simple Rules of Trading" offer advice and words of wisdom for any trader. (See Appendix.)

Good news/bad action   A classic trading scenario that allows the trader to combine the ACD system with market psychology. This setup requires an anticipated directional move by the market based on new fundamental developments. However, for reasons that bewilder most traders, the market fails to technically respond to that news in the anticipated direction.

Island Reversal Formation An Island Reversal Formation occurs when the market has a fake-out to the upside or the downside, gapping lower the day after previously gapping higher (or vice versa).

Late-day Point C pivot trade This is the Rolls Royce of all ACD system trading scenarios. This setup's high probability of success, coupled with its very low risk, make it extremely attractive. The trade works best if it occurs late in the day, trapping speculators who feel they must liquidate by the close.

Liquidity Liquidity refers to whether there is a tight enough bid/offer spread and sufficient volume on both sides of the market to allow a trader to enter or exit a position without a high degree of slippage. The ACD system requires sufficient liquidity to enable you to enter and exit at or near specific ACD levels. For example, a five-lot trader may find sufficient liquidity to trade a market like platinum futures, while a 500-lot scalper would find platinum "too small" to trade.

Maximize size, minimize risk The concept of maximizing size and minimizing risk is a vital ingredient to any successful trading strategy. The ACD methodology applies this concept in identifying trading scenarios that utilize low-risk reference areas such as the opening range, pivot range, and other ACD areas.

Macro ACD The ACD system can be applied to longer-term trading, not just micro day-trading or scalping. Traders utilize ACD indicators such as plus/minus days, number line values, change in trend, rolling pivots, first two weeks of the year, and pivot moving average slopes in adopting a macro bias for a given market.

Mad as hell (MAH) trade The I'm mad as hell (MAH) and can't take it anymore trade is a trading scenario identified by the ACD system in which traders who have been fighting the prevailing trend become utterly frustrated and eventually capitulate. This scenario usually occurs after there has been an extended holiday or break. During this time off, traders have had the time to stew over their losses and have decided to throw in the towel as soon as the market reopens.

Micro ACD   The ACD system can be effectively utilized on a very short-term basis by floor- and day-traders. Critical components to micro ACD include Point As, Point Cs, the opening range, the daily pivot range, pivot first hour highs and lows, Point Bs, and Point Ds.

Minus day   The ACD system defines a minus day according to the following formula: Opening Range > Pivot Range > Close = Minus Day.

Momentum   This macro ACD indicator can be utilized by longer-term traders to help them identify when to exit trades. In the ACD system, momentum is used to clearly show who the winners and losers are in a market over a specific period of time. This ACD tool compares the close of a market today in relation to its close eight days ago to determine whether the shorts or the longs have the upper hand.

Moving averages   Moving averages are traditionally based on closing prices. Rather than basing moving averages on closes, which are nothing more than arbitrary points in time, ACD uses pivot moving averages (see *pivot moving averages*).

Moving average divergence (MAD) trade   This ACD technique allows the trader to fade extreme moves in market direction. The moving average divergence (MAD) trade works best when the pivot moving averages are confused (with one sloping upward, one downward, and one flat), as there is less opportunity for a trend to reestablish itself quickly. It is also critical for a MAD scenario to have a well-defined point of reference. Furthermore, you should enter the trade with either a good or failed Point A, or a good or a failed point C, depending upon market conditions. The ideal MAD trade also incorporates the concept of an island reversal formation (*See Island Reversal Formation*).

Moving average fake-out (MAF) trade   The moving average fake-out (MAF) trade utilizes pivot moving averages (see *pivot moving averages*) defined by the ACD system. The slope of all the pivot moving averages must be clearly defined in one direction. After a significant move in the direction of the slope of the pivot moving averages, the market begins a retracement and breaks either above or below the shortest-term pivot moving average. However, the market does not retrace far enough to violate any of the other pivot moving averages, and eventually snaps back in the direction of the prevailing pivot moving average slope. This provides the trader with a clear point of reference to establish a position in the direction of the prevailing trend.

Neutral market A neutral market is evident when all the pivot moving averages (see *pivot moving averages*) for varying time frames are parallel to each other and flat. At this time, the ACD methodology dictates traders remain on the sidelines and wait for a breakout.

Next! The concept of *Next!* is based upon the premise of seeking immediate gratification once you enter a trade. The ACD system refutes the no pain, no gain notion that says in order to be successful one must endure all the emotional abuse and financial pain that the market can inflict upon you while waiting for losing positions to turn into winners. Under the concept of Next! if the market doesn't move your way within a short time of putting on a trade, just get out and move on to the next one.

Number line The main purpose of the number line is to identify a potentially developing trend. That generally occurs when the cumulative sum of the past 30 trading days based on macro ACD (see *macro ACD*) goes from 0 to a $+/-9$, a level it must maintain for two consecutive trading days in order to be considered significant.

Outside reversal week This ACD setup examines the relationship between the current trading week and the prior week of trading. As highlighted in the examples of Enron and the 1929 and 1933 Dow Jones Charts (see Chapter 6), this scenario provides the trader a low-risk point of reference to identify potential major market reversal areas.

Pivot first hour highs and lows In this setup, the trading activity over the first hour of the day is used to determine whether the daily pivot range engulfs the first-hour high or low. A subsequent A up or A down confirms an intraday bias and affords the trader an excellent low-risk trade entry point.

Pivot on gap   When the market gaps open, above or below the daily pivot range, and never trades into the daily pivot range from that day, a pivot on gap day has been established. That pivot on gap day level becomes critical support or resistance for future trading sessions.

Pivot moving averages   Pivot moving averages are moving averages that use the pivot rather than the close for calculation purposes. These pivot moving averages truly represent where most of the volume traded each day.

Plus day   The ACD system defines a plus day according to the following formula: Opening Range < Pivot Range < Close = Plus Day.

Point A through the pivot   If the market trades through both the Point A (up or down) and the daily pivot range (see *daily pivot range*), there is a low-risk trade to establish a position in the direction of the confirmed A. Instead of risking to Point B, a trader need only to risk to the opposite side of the daily pivot range.

Point B   Point B is the price at which your bias shifts to neutral. Once a Point A (up or down) has been established, your stop is now Point B. The B level is the bottom of the opening range for an A up, or the top of the opening range for an A down.

Point C through the pivot   If the market trades through both the Point C (up or down) and the daily pivot range (see *daily pivot range*), there is a low-risk trade to establish a position in the direction of the confirmed C. Instead of risking to Point D, a trader need only to risk to the opposite side of the daily pivot range.

Point D   Point D is the price at which your bias shifts to neutral and is your stop after the market has already established a C in one direction. Once Point D has been hit, the trader has been chopped up enough for the day and should walk away from that market for the rest of the trading day.

Points of reference   The cornerstone of ACD is the concept of where to get out if you are wrong. ACD provides traders with reference levels to lean against to minimize their trading risk.

Random walk theory The random walk theory states that the market's movements are random and totally unpredictable. It goes on to state that, over the long run, no one can outperform the general market. In my opinion, the ACD methodology directly refutes this theory (see *ACD methodology* and *statistically significant*).

Reversal trade Over the past two to three years, this has clearly been the best system to trade. Whether traded in open outcry pits or over a screen, it hasn't mattered. This trade is not the typical reversal scenario that you have read about in other books or trading publications. The ACD reversal trade identifies market failure patterns that enable the trader to enter positions before the crowd begins to panic and thus benefit from the ensuing market move.

Rolling pivot range The rolling pivot range, usually spanning three to six trading days, acts as a reference point for entering and exiting trades. ACD uses the rolling pivot range as a trailing stop for winning positions. It also provides traders a point of reference to quickly exit losing positions. One of its best functions is that it helps prevent a trader from turning winning positions into losing ones.

Sentiment divergence This ACD setup relies upon divergences occurring between market price action and human sentiment. This trade tries to catch traders who don't believe in recent market price behavior and who have faded the recent move. This setup alerts the trader if the market gaps away from these traders and tries to capitalize on the ensuing panic liquidation that inevitably takes place.

Significant time frames A short-term scalper should not pay attention to long-term indicators, or vice versa. In order to be successful, a trader must use indicators that best suit his trading style and be consistent in its application. For example, a longer-term trader may make significant use of the first two weeks of the year indicator (see Natural Gas example, Chapter 2, Figure 2.5), while the short-term trader may not use this indicator at all.

Slope When using pivot moving averages (see *pivot moving averages*), the critical element is the change in slope of those lines. A change in slope measures the rate of change in market perception.

Small pivot ranges   A trading day that has a normal trading range but produces a very narrow daily pivot range for the following day usually is an indication that there will be a more volatile trading session the following day.

Statistically significant   The ACD methodology is based upon the premise that the opening range of each day's trading session is statistically significant. In layman's terms, this means that the opening range is not like all the other 5- or 10-minute intervals of the trading day. Rather, the opening range is the statistically significant part of the trading day, marking the high or low for the day (in volatile markets) about 20 percent of the time. This concept directly refutes the random walk theory (see *random walk theory*).

Sushi roll   In the ACD system, sushi roll is the name given to a particular early-warning indicator of a change in market direction. The sushi roll utilizes five rolling trading days (or for a shorter–term perspective, five 10-minute bars). The sushi roll compares the latest five increments of time to the prior five increments of time to determine if the market is changing direction.

System-failure trades   This trade should be made when markets are choppy and directionless. Under these conditions, Point As and Point Cs have very little follow-through. In fact, under these conditions the markets often reverse and stop you out. System-failure trades try to identify when the market fails at these levels and fades those moves. System-failure trades tend to work best when the slope of the pivot moving average lines are in a confused state (see *confused market*).

Three-day rolling pivot   The three-day rolling pivot may be used by those who take intermediate-term positions, spanning several days or even in the case of some profitable trades, weeks. As the name suggests, this pivot is made up of the high, low, and close of the past three trading days (see *pivot range*).

Time factor   In trading, time is actually a much more important variable than price. When determining whether you have made a good A up (A ^) or good A down (A ∨), it is much more important how much time the market spends at that level than at what price it trades. Unsuccessful traders tend to rely too much on price and not enough on time when entering or exiting the market.

Trend reversal trade (TRT)   In this ACD setup, the market must gap to a new high or low, make a good A up (A ^) or A down (A ∨) in the opposite direction of the gap, and must be followed by a failed C up /down later in the trading session. If the market then retraces back to the opening range, the trader should fade the failed C and look to capture a significant market reversal.

Two-way swing area   A two-way swing area is a price level that acts as a critical support/resistance level for the market. A two-way swing area is established after the market gaps below prior significant support or gaps above prior significant resistance (see Nasdaq Composite scenario, Chapter 6.)

Volatility   Volatility measures how much movement the market has over a certain period of time. A market may have good volume, but if it doesn't move intraday, it would not make sense to apply the ACD methodology to trading that market.

INDEX

('i' indicates an illustration; 't' indicates a table)

A down
    combined strategy, 58-59, 59i
    description of, 239
    macro values, 84i-93i, 96i
    pivot first hour, 72
    reference point trades, 30
    rubber band trade, 28
    time factor, 21i, 21-22, 23
A level, determination of, 15
A up
    calculating, 16, 20i, 20
    combined strategy, 57-58, 58i
    description of, 239
    macro values, 84i-93i, 96i
    pivot first hour, 72
    reference point trades, 30
    rubber band trade, 28
    time factor, 21, 22-23
A values, description of, 239
ACD system, description of, 239
ACD trading methodology
    description of, 239
    five rules of, 31
    internship, 1-2, 173-174, 189
    opening range, 10-15, 13i, 14i
    origins of, 5-6
    pivot-moving averages, 116
    statistical significance, 248
    symmetry of, 21, 41, 55, 72, 127, 158

table, 235t-238t
    use of, 3-4, 9-10, 190, 191-202
    website, 3-4
American Depository Receipts
    (ADRs), 11

B level, calculation of, 15-16
Bearish bias, 38, 98-99
Bearish market phase, description of, 240
Bearish moving average, slope, 122i
Bias, ACD determination, 200-201
Black Monday (1987), 176-177
Black-box system traders, risk management, 184
Bullish bias, 38, 98-99
Bullish market phase, description of, 240
Bullish moving average, slope, 120i
Bus people, 33, 99, 147, 240
Buying dips trades, 29-30

C down
    description of, 240
    market values, 87i-90i
    time factor, 22i, 23
C up
    description of, 240
    market values, 87i-90i
    time factor, 23, 23i, 24

C values, description of, 240
Casey, ACD trader, 191-194, 204
Cashier math, 7
Change in trend (December 2001)
    commodities, 223t
    energy equities, 223t
    equity (reversal system), 224t
    general description of, 240
Commodities
    first day of the month table, 205t
    first two weeks of January 2001
        table, 206t
    opening range, 10
    three-day rolling pivot range
        (12/12/01) table, 229t
    trading, pit experience, 192
Commodity change in trend
    (December 2001), 223t
Commodity number line sheets
    (12/12/01) table, 207t, 219t
Commodity number line values,
    222t
Commodity pivot sheet (12/12/01),
    220t-221t
Comp, casino rewards, 183
Confused market, 117-118, 241
Confused moving average
    MAD trade, 125i, 126i
    slopes, 119i, 121i
Crack trades, 186-187
Crash of 1929, ACD analysis, 156-
    160, 157i, 159i
Crash of 1987, 176-177
Crossover point, 17
Crude Oil F, market commentary
    (12/12/01), 225t

Daily pivot differential, 37-38
Daily pivot number, calculation of,
    37-38
Daily pivot price, calculation of, 37-
    38
Daily pivot range. *See also* Pivot
    range
    calculation of, 37-38
    description of, 241
    market direction, 36, 38

small, 44-46, 45i, 247-248
    use of, 38-39, 134
Daily pivot range formula, 37-38, 47,
    241
Daily pivot sheets (12/12/01)
    commodities, 220t-221t
    $ risk, 185
    stocks, 226t-227t
Daily Sentiment Index (DSI), 175-176
Discipline
    ACD method, 4, 27-28, 241
    ACD traders, 198-200, 202, 204
    necessity of, 172
Discretionary traders, 184, 185
Domicile market, 11
Dove, ACD trader, 201-202
Dow Jones Industrial Average (1929),
    156-158, 157i, 160
Dow Jones Industrial Average (1932),
    159i, 160

Ego involvement
    ACD method, 4, 6, 7-8
    trading practices, 167-168
Energy equities change in trend
    (December 2001), 223t
Equities, first two weeks of July 2001
    table, 228t
Equity (reversal system) change in
    trend (December 2001), 224t
Exits
    Casey, 193
    and momentum, 137-138
    and RPR, 135-137, 136i
    reversal trades, 141
    trading strategy, 133

F&G Commodities, 181
Fade the market, 124
Failed point, 26-27
Failed Point A
    against the pivot, 62-65, 63i, 64i,
        65, 241-242
    macro values, 92i-95i
    occurrences of, 241
    pivot range, 62-65, 63i, 64i, 65

Failed Point C
against the pivot, 74-75, 242
macro values, 91i, 96i
occurrences of, 242
TRT, 147-149, 150
Fake out, 48, 127
Fear, ACD traders, 181, 242
50-day pivot-moving average
kindergarten trader, 129i-131i
line slope types, 119i-122i
market trends, 116-117
moving average fake-out (MAF),
123i
14-day pivot-moving average,
kindergarten trader, 129i-131i
line slope types, 119i-122i
market trends, 116-117
moving average fake-out (MAF),
123i

Gambling theory, ACD method, 4, 194
Gap days, pivot ranges, 44-46, 45i,
245-246
Gartman, Dennis, 180-181, 242
"Gartman's 20 Ridiculously Simple
Rules of Trading," 180-181, 233t-
234t, 242
Good A through pivot, 56i, 56-57, 65,
246
Good news/ bad action, 4, 164-165,
242
Granite, ACD trader, 202-203
Grease, crude oil trader, 76-79
Greed, ACD traders, 181, 242
Gulf War, crude oil trading, 181-183,
193

Harry the Hoof, 190
"House, the," 183-184

Indicators, multiple, 60, 61
Information, analysis/collection, 6-7
Instant gratification rule, 99, 100,
101, 188
Intraday volatility, 34
Island Reversal Formation, 127-128,
128i, 243

Jones, Paul Tudor, 3

Kindergarten trader, 129, 129i-132i

Late-day Point C pivot, 69-71, 76-79,
243
Liquidity, market, 3, 34, 243
LIZA, trading ability, 163, 164
Logical trader daily energy market
commentary (12/12/01), 225t
Long position
A point, 16
establishment of, 200, 201
failed A, 64

Macro ACD, use of, 243
Macro strategy
number line, 98-101
trading plan, 1
trend identification, 101-102
valid signal, 100
value assignment, 83, 84i-96i
Mad as hell (MAH) trade, 150-151,
243
Crash of 1929, 158
Market efficiencies theory, 5-6
Market not meeting the call, trading
practices, 166-167
Market trends
change program, 151-152
macro strategy, 97-100, 101-102
and momentum, 137
no clue, 167
pivot moving averages, 116, 117
Sushi Roll, 152-153, 153i-154i,
248
Maximize size, minimize risk
strategy, 243
Maximum trades, time factor, 19
MBF Clearing Corp.
proprietary traders, 184-186
summer internship, 1-2, 173-
174, 189
trade scenarios, 185
website, 2
Metallgesellschaft, energy trades, 187-
188

Micro ACD, 243-244
Micro strategy, 1, 83
Micro trades, 197
Midterm
    answer key, 111-112
    exam questions, 109-111
Minimum trades, time factor, 19
Minus day, description of, 244
Minus days, pivot range, 49, 50, 51i, 60
Momentum, 244, 137-138
Money, personal value system, 189-190
Moving average divergence (MAD) trade, description of, 244
Moving average divergence (MAD) trades, 124-125, 125i-126i, 127-128, 128i
Moving average fake-out (MAF) trade, description of, 244-245
Moving average fake-out (MAF) trades, 122-124, 123i
Moving averages, 113, 244
MVP, personnel management, 167-168

Nasdaq crash (2000), 193-194
Natural Gas F, market commentary (12/12/01), 225t
Neutral bias, macro values, 98-99
Neutral market, 118, 245
Neutral moving average
    MAD trade, 125i, 126i
    slopes, 119i, 121i
Next!, ACD method, 4, 188-189, 245
No pain/no gain, 4, 188
NOT-I, personnel management, 168-169
Number line
    calculation of, 97-98
    coffee trade, 103, 104t-105t, 105-107
    description of, 245
    market values, 97
    purposes of, 100-101
    trade size, 103
Number line sheets (12/12/01)
    commodities, 207t-219t
    stocks, 230t-232t

Number line values, commodities, 222t

OHNO, heating oil broker, 80-81
Once-in-a-blue-moon trades, 102
Opening range
    A down, 21i, 21-22, 23, 28, 30
    A up, 16, 20i, 20-21, 22-23, 28 23, 23i, 28, 30, 31-32, 32i
    ACD concept, 10, 12, 239
    ACD traders, 195-196, 200-204
    B level, 15-16
    C down, 22i, 23
    C up, 23, 23i, 24
    failed C down, 31-32, 32i
    Point A, 13i, 13-15, 14i, 19
    Point C, 16-17, 17i
    Point D, 17, 18i
    statistical significance of, 12-13
Outside reversal week
    Crash of 1929, 158, 160
    description of, 155-156, 156i, 245

Pivot first hour highs and lows, description of, 71-74, 245
Pivot moving average lines, 128
Pivot moving averages
    calculation of, 113-114
    combined strategy, 118-119
    description of, 246
    kindergarten trader, 129, 129i-131i
    line slope, 114-116, 115i, 116i
    line slope types, 119i-122i
    MAF, 122-124, 123i
Pivot on gap, 245-246
Pivot range
    with A down, 58-59, 59i
    with A point, 55-65, 56i, 58i, 59i, 63i, 64i
    with A up, 57-58, 58i
    ACD traders, 195-196, 200-203
    assigned value, 49-51
    calculation of, 36-38
    concept of, 35-36
    failed A, 62-65, 63i, 64i, 65
    failed C, 74-75
    long term, 52-54, 53i

Index

natural gas trades, 44, 44i
Point C, 66, 67i, 67-71, 69i, 79-81
small, 247-248
Pivot range formula, 37-38, 47, 241
Pivot range strategies, 40-43, 40i, 41i, 42i, 43i
Pivot sheet (12/12/01)
commodities, 220t-221t
stocks, 226t-227t
Plus day, description of, 246
Plus days, pivot range, 49, 50, 51i, 60
Point A
calculation of, 13i, 13-15, 14i, 55
combined strategy, 55-65, 56i, 58i, 59i, 63i, 64i
reversal trade, 139-141
scalping tool, 196
time factor, 19
Point A through pivot, 56i, 56-57, 65, 246
Point B, 15-16, 246
Point C
calculation of, 16-17, 17i, 65-66
combined strategy, 66, 67i, 67-71, 69i, 74, 79-81
failed down, 31-32, 32i
late-day trade, 69-71, 76-79
normal trade, 66-67
risk management, 198
time factor, 20
Point C through the pivot, 67, 68, 69, 246
Point D
calculation of, 17, 18i
description of, 246
normal trade, 67
Points of reference
ACD method, 4, 11, 28-30, 29i
description of, 246
MAD trades, 124-125, 125i-126i
RPR, 133
Price, and trading, 193
Price reference points, 28-29

Random walk theory, 5, 11-12, 246-247
Reference points. *See* Points of reference

Retail bus people, 33, 99, 147, 240
Reversal day, description of, 152
Reversal trade, description of, 247
Reversal trades, 139-141, 142i-144i
RIBI, ACD trader, 198-200
Risk
combined strategy, 57, 59-60, 67, 68, 69
limited exposure, 27-28
Risk management
ACD system, 4, 198
getting lost, 179-180
market losses, 186-188
trader performance, 167-170
trading practices, 164-167
RN, ACD trader, 174, 194-196
Rolling pivot range (RPR)
description of, 247
position management, 133-137, 136i
Rubber band trade, 24-26, 25i, 27, 28
pivot strategy, 40, 41-42

"Scalp trade," 185, 195-196, 202-203
Selling rallies, 29-30
Sentiment daily index, 175-176
Sentiment divergence, 247
Short position
A point, 14-15
C point, 17
failed A, 27, 63
Slippage, 16
Slope
description of, 247
moving averages, 114-115, 117
Speedy, ACD trader, 197-198
Spread trade, 192, 199
Stock number line sheets (12/12/01)
table, 230t-232t
Stock pivot sheet (12/12/01), 226t-227t
Sugar market, ACD indicators, 177-179
Sushi Roll
description of, 248
market change, 152-153, 153i-154i
System-failure trades, 75, 99, 100, 101, 248

30-day pivot-moving average
    kindergarten trader, 129i-131i
    line slope types, 119i-122i
    market trends, 116-117
    moving average fake-out (MAF),
        123i
30 day trading cycle
    coffee trade, 103, 104t-105t,
        105-107
    cumulative tally, 97
    as indicator, 50-51, 60-61, 65, 76
    market trends, 99, 101-102
Three-day rolling pivot, 47-49, 49i,
    136i, 248
Three day rolling pivot range
    (12/12/01), commodities, 229t
Time factor
    casino betting, 183-184
    importance of, 18-19, 32-33, 99-
        100, 147, 188, 248
    key price reference, 62
    and RPR, 135
Time frames
    and ACD traders, 195, 200-202
    opening range, 12
    pivot range, 38
    selection of, 160-161

    significant, 46i, 46-49, 52, 247
TOE, risk manager, 174
Trade size
    maximize strategy, 59-60, 61, 67,
        69, 103
    risk management, 184
Trader, abilities of, 1, 6
Trades, hard ones, best ones, 4, 148,
    150
Trading career, monetary value
    system, 189-190
Trailing stop, 47-48
Treacherous trade, 74-75, 242
Trend reversal trade (TRT), 146-150,
    249
    Crash of 1929, 158
Two-way swing area, 145i, 145-146, 249

Vernon, ACD trader, 200-201
Volatility
    ACD system, 3, 12, 34, 249
    number line, 98, 101

Walk around the block trade, 147-
    148
Wall Street Journal, market
    statistics, 6